KU-642-274

NEW HORIZONS IN CRIMINOLOGY

CLIMATE CHANGE CRIMINOLOGY

Rob White

First published in Great Britain in 2018 by

Bristol University Press
University of Bristol
1-9 Old Park Hill
Bristol
BS2 8BB
UK
t: +44 (0)117 954 5940
bup-info@bristol.ac.uk
www.bristoluniversitypress.co.uk

North America office:
Bristol University Press
c/o The University of Chicago Press
1427 East 60th Street
Chicago, IL 60637, USA
t: +1 773 702 7700
f: +1 773-702-9756
sales@press.uchicago.edu
www.press.uchicago.edu

British Library Cataloguing in Publication Data
A catalogue record for this book is available from the British Library

Library of Congress Cataloging-in-Publication Data
A catalog record for this book has been requested

ISBN 978-1-5292-0395-0 hardcover
ISBN 978-1-5292-0398-1 ePub
ISBN 978-1-5292-0399-8 Mobi
ISBN 978-1-5292-0396-7 ePdf

Cover design by Bristol University Press
Front cover image: istock
Printed and bound in Great Britain by CPI Group (UK) Ltd,
Croydon, CR0 4YY
Bristol University Press uses environmentally responsible print partners

Contents

List of tables		iv
Acknowledgements		v
Preface by Professor Andrew Millie		vi
one	Climate change and criminology	1
two	Global warming as ecocide	19
three	In the heat of the moment	41
four	Climate change catastrophes and social intersections	59
five	Climate change victims	79
six	Carbon criminals	97
seven	Criminal justice responses to climate change	117
eight	Criminological responses to climate change	139
References		155
Index		181

List of tables

2.1	Stifling dissent	38
3.1	Crime and climate change	45
4.1	Gender-based vulnerabilities in disaster responses	66
4.2	Climate change and social conflict	69
4.3	Pressures on basic essentials of life	75
6.1	Commodification of nature	102
6.2	Productive and unproductive labour and consumption	103
7.1	Trends in climate change litigation	118
7.2	Greening justice	125
7.3	An eco-justice action plan	137
8.1	The climate change–crime nexus	143
8.2	Five pillars of Climate Change Criminology	146

Acknowledgements

This book is the culmination of work undertaken over a number of years. It has benefited from comments, suggestions and criticisms from many colleagues and friends over this time, particularly from those involved in the international green criminology community. It represents a summation of what has been done up to this point as well as a forward projection to pathways that have yet to be trodden. My thanks are extended to all those who have assisted in this ongoing journey.

Special thanks are due to Ashleigh Barnes who helped out towards the end of the project, to Andrew Millie for his superb general editor work, to Ron Kramer for his passion and his ideas, and to the people at Bristol University Press who put the manuscript into final publication shape. To my wife Sharyn, extra special thanks for your support and encouragement.

This is for my children, and all children, everywhere. It is also for Matilda and other non-human animals, everywhere. Finally, it is for Planet Earth, our home.

NEW HORIZONS IN CRIMINOLOGY

Series editor: Professor Andrew Millie, Department of Law and Criminology, Edge Hill University, UK

Preface

Climate Change Criminology is the fifth title in the New Horizons in Criminology book series. The series is home for concise authoritative texts that are international in scope and reflect cutting-edge thought and theoretical developments in criminology. They are short, accessible books written so that the nonspecialist can understand them, by explaining principles and developments clearly before going deeper into the subject. The books are written by leading authors in their fields and I was delighted when Rob White agreed to contribute on the subject climate change criminology. Climate change is possibly the most important issue we face and warrants far greater prominence across the full breadth of criminology. It is certainly a topic that is not going to go away in a hurry. Rob is a prolific author and a leading authority on green criminology. For instance, his many publications include books on *Crimes Against Nature* (2008), *Transnational Environmental Crime* (2011), *Environmental Harm* (2014) and *Green Criminology* (2014, with Diane Heckenberg).

This book is significant as it is the first to suggest a distinct 'climate change criminology', yet it draws on a rich history of green and critical scholarship. Rob suggests this new book is not polemical, but hopes it provides 'an interesting, considered, thought-provoking and passionate account of Climate Change Criminology' and a call for criminology to 'join us in the fight for climate justice' by addressing some of the most pressing concerns facing the planet.

The book considers a wide range of topics, including global warming, ecocide, heat and criminality and environmental catastrophe. It looks at the victims of climate change in the global north and south, and both human and non-human. And in asking who is responsible for climate change, it examines the 'criminals' – with a special focus on carbon criminals. Here there is much to interest scholars of state and corporate harms and crimes. The book also explores both criminal justice and criminological responses to climate change.

For some, issues of climate change may seem a distant threat; yet crises of energy production, pollution, food production and distribution mean it is an issue of social justice and inequality for today. As Rob highlights, for those living on the islands of Tuvalu, the Maldives and Kiribati, rises in sea levels mean concerns are focused on survival. Furthermore, by considering non-humans alongside humans, Rob also highlights climate change as an issue of ecological justice.

In mapping the boundaries of a climate change criminology, Rob suggests five areas of concern, these being: 1) a focus on crimes and harms, 2) awareness of global connectedness and eco-justice, 3) examination of causes and consequences, 4) a focus on issues of power and interests, and 5) support for social action and agitation. Of course, others may produce a different list; but one of the chief aims for the book is to open up debate and further dialogue. Rob recognises that this is just the beginning for climate change criminology.

The book is both accessible and challenging. It will be essential reading for green and critical criminologists, yet it should also be important reading for the rest of criminology and beyond. I am delighted to see this important book in print. The challenge for criminology is how it responds to the book's call to 'join us in the fight for climate justice'.

References

White, R. (2014) *Environmental Harm: An Eco-justice Perspective*, Bristol: Policy Press.

White, R. and Heckenberg, D. (2014) *Green Criminology: An Introduction to the Study of Environmental Harm*, Abingdon: Routledge.

White, R. (2011) *Transnational Environmental Crime: Toward an Eco-global Criminology*, Abingdon: Routledge.

White, R. (2008) *Crimes against Nature: Environmental Criminology and Ecological Justice*, Abingdon: Routledge.

ONE

Climate change and criminology

Introduction

This book is the first to describe its subject matter as *Climate Change Criminology*. As part of this, it brings together existing research and scholarship on climate change from a criminological perspective, while forging a blueprint for further work in this area. In terms of overall orientation, the project reflects a critical criminology perspective since its approach places power and social interests at the centre of the analysis. Issues of social and ecological justice, and inequality, feature highly, as does the intent to 'study up' (that is, to examine the rich and powerful) as well as consider the consequences of global warming for the vulnerable and less powerful. The project is also firmly located within a green criminology framework, one that understands eco-justice (and, indeed, climate justice) as involving transgressions against humans, ecosystems, and animals and plants. The scope is global, the literature international.

While providing an overview of literature in this area, the book is more explicitly critical in both content and approach than some previous work undertaken in this area. However, it is not polemical. The intent is to provide an interesting, considered, thought-provoking and passionate account of Climate Change Criminology in a way that will invite others to follow suit. The overarching message is 'join us in the fight for climate justice'. The book provides some of the reasons why this is urgent and important.

This chapter explains key terms such as 'global warming', 'climate change' and 'weather', and provides a brief summary of the main characteristics and consequences of global warming. The chapter discusses the silences within criminology about climate change (itself, arguably, a form of denialism), and its rising importance within the field. It then outlines the main features of Climate Change Criminology as an emerging perspective.

Climate change, the Anthropocene and criminology

Global warming describes the rising of the earth's temperature over a relatively short time span. *Climate change* describes the inter-related effects of this rise in temperature: from changing sea levels and changing ocean currents, through to the impacts of temperature change on local environments that affect the endemic flora and fauna in varying ways (for instance, the death of coral due to temperature rises in sea water or the changed migration patterns of birds). *Weather* is the name given to the direct local experience of things such as sunshine, wind, rain, snow and the general disposition of the elements. It is about the short-term and personal, not the long-term patterns associated with climate in general. As the planet warms up, the climate will change in ways that disrupt previous weather patterns, and will in some places even bring colder weather although overall temperatures are on the rise (Lever-Tracy, 2011).

Climate disruption has also been used to describe the nature of these global changes. This term has been used in order to emphasise the fact that increases in global average temperature 'does not simply translate into modest, uniform warming but rather triggers surprisingly sharp changes in extreme weather and disrupts longer-term weather and climate patterns' (Steffen, 2018). Heavy snow in the United Kingdom and parts of Western Europe in 2018 is thus symptomatic of changes to what were considered to be the normal air circulation patterns, just as shifts in ocean circulation patterns have resulted in the bleaching of coral reefs off the eastern coast of Australia. Disruption of these normal patterns is one of the manifestations of climate change as a biophysical phenomenon.

Concern about global warming has been expressed for many years by many people, including scientists in different disciplines. Today, climate change is accepted by the majority as a serious and urgent issue. This is so, even though it has been denied and downplayed by contrarians, many of whom have friends in or who occupy high places (Brisman, 2012; Kramer, 2013a). Part of the reason for mass concern is that climate and weather events seem to now touch or affect every person living on the planet. It does this directly and indirectly, in ways that are understandable and threatening to ordinary people. Unseasonal weather (such as droughts), extreme weather events (such as cyclones/hurricanes) and natural disasters (such as tsunamis) are increasingly examined within the context of worldwide climatic changes. Such events materially bring home the concrete effects of global warming to many millions of people. The presumed longer-term effects, such as rising ocean levels, are also not so long term for many people living in the low-lying countries of the Pacific and Indian oceans. The citizens of Tuvalu, the Maldives and Kiribati do not have the luxury of debating climate change – the waters are already diminishing their living spaces; their present concerns are focused on survival, including where to move and how to make a different kind of future for themselves.

The divides between the global North and South, geographically and metaphorically, are already deepening as crises related to food production and distribution, energy sources and pollution, and changing climates re-order the old world order (IPCC, 2014; Oxfam, 2018). Social inequality and environmental injustice will undoubtedly be the drivers of continuous conflicts for many years to come, as the most dispossessed and marginalised of the world's population suffer the brunt of food shortages, undrinkable water, climate-induced migration and general hardship in their day-to-day lives. Women will suffer more than men, people of colour more than the non-Indigenous and the non-migrant, the young and the elderly more than the adult, and the infirm and disabled of all ages. The privileged will strive to protect their advantage, with exclusion and coercion key weapons of choice in doing so.

The urgency and reality of climate change issues was eloquently conveyed in a May 2010 letter signed by 284 members of the US National Academy of Sciences published in *Science* claiming that:

> There is compelling, comprehensive and consistent objective evidence that humans are changing the climate in ways that threaten our societies and the ecosystems on which we depend. Many recent assaults on climate science and, more disturbingly, on climate scientists by climate change deniers are typically driven by special interests or dogma, not by an honest effort to provide an alternative theory that credibly satisfies the evidence. (Quoted in Lever-Tracy, 2011: 10–11)

If anything, most disagreement surrounding climate change today is over how quickly global warming is proceeding rather than over whether it is happening. By October 2012, for instance, it was reported that (Boyer, 2012):

- the Arctic is warming twice as quickly as was initially projected in the 'worst case' scenarios for the major international climate science report in 2007;
- in 2012, the rate of ice loss from the Greenland land ice was an all-time record;
- the global food crisis, with climate change as a major driver, was in its fifth year in 2012, and is set to intensify as the effects of recent and continued drought and flooding in key exporting countries are felt down the food chain;
- half the corals of the Great Barrier Reef in Australia have disappeared since 1980;
- the water of the world's oceans now carries about double the heat energy it held in 1990;
- the current global emissions trajectory will see surface warming pass 2°C by 2040 and pass the catastrophic level of 5°C around 2100.

Even if human emissions were stopped in this exact moment, the atmosphere would continue warming for another 25 years. Moreover,

> the ocean will continue to store heat from the atmosphere for yet more years, preventing or inhibiting the cooling of the planet until long after we're dead and buried. The only question is, how far will the warming go? The more carbon dioxide we put into the atmosphere, the hotter it will get. (Boyer, 2012: 14–15)

The science of climate change demonstrates that global warming is not only 'real', and escalating, but is primarily due to anthropogenic or human causes (IPCC, 2013). Global warming is transforming the biophysical world in ways that are radically and rapidly re-shaping social and ecological futures. For example, the Intergovernmental Panel on Climate Change (IPCC) (2014) – comprising scientists from around the world who undertake work that is rigorously peer reviewed and who lean toward cautious or conservative estimates in regards trends and patterns of change – has reported that:

- warming of the climate system is unequivocal, and since the 1950s, many of the observed changes are unprecedented over decades to millennia. The atmosphere and ocean have warmed, the amounts of snow and ice have diminished, sea level has risen, and the concentrations of greenhouse gases have increased (p 3);

- each of the last three decades has been successively warmer at the Earth's surface than any preceding decade since 1850 (p 3);
- ocean warming dominates the increase in energy stored in the climate system, accounting for more than 90% of the energy accumulated between 1971 and 2010 (p 4);
- over the last two decades, the Greenland and Antarctic ice sheets have been losing mass, glaciers have continued to shrink almost worldwide, and Arctic sea ice and Northern Hemisphere spring snow cover have continued to decrease in extent (p 4);
- the rate of sea level rise since the mid-nineteenth century has been larger than the mean rate during the previous two millennia (p 4).

Scientific data continues to demonstrate the depth and scale of the problem. The damage caused by global warming will be felt in the form of extreme weather events, increased competition for dwindling natural resources, outbreaks of disease and viral infections, further extinctions of species, continued pressure to trade off food for fuel, intense social conflict and much criminality (Crank and Jacoby, 2015; White and Heckenberg, 2014). The IPCC (2014: 6) points out that:

> Evidence of observed climate change impacts is strongest and most comprehensive for natural systems. In many regions, changing precipitation or melting snow and ice are altering hydrological systems, affecting water resources in terms of quantity and quality...Many terrestrial, freshwater and marine species have shifted their geographic ranges, seasonal activities, migration patterns, abundances and species interactions in response to ongoing climate change... Some impacts on human systems have also been attributed to climate change, with a major or minor contribution of climate change distinguishable from other influences... Assessment of many studies covering a wide range of regions and crops shows that negative impacts of climate change on crop yields have been more common than positive impacts...Some impacts of ocean acidification on marine organisms have been attributed to human influence.

A series of regional key risks have been identified by the IPCC (2014). These include increased damage from wildfires, heat-related human mortality and increased damage from river and coastal urban floods. They include a distributional shift and reduced fisheries catch potential at low latitudes, compounded stress on water resources, increased mass coral bleaching and mortality, reduced crop productivity and livelihood and food security, and the loss of livelihoods, settlements, infrastructure, ecosystem services and economic stability. Other risks include significant change in composition and structure of coral reef systems, coastal inundation and habitat loss, spread of vector-borne diseases, and increased flood damage to infrastructure and settlements ecosystems.

Conceptually, the IPCC (2014: 13) has developed reasons for concern (RFCs) that aggregate climate change risks and illustrate the implications of warming and of adaptation limits for people, economies and ecosystems across sectors and regions. The five RFCs are associated with: (1) unique and threatened systems, (2) extreme weather events, (3) distribution of impacts, (4) global aggregate impacts, and (5) large-scale singular events. The RFCs provide a system of classification and measurement, one that demonstrates that the risks and threats to ecosystems, humans and flora and fauna are considerable, and growing.

In a similar vein, the *Lancet* Countdown tracks progress on the health impacts of climate hazards as well as other indicators for the purposes of a global overview of health and climate change (Watts et al, 2017). The initiative is an international, multidisciplinary research collaboration between academic institutions and practitioners around the world. The health and social consequences of events resulting from climate change – such as rising temperatures, heat waves, and increases in the frequency of complex extreme weather events such as windstorms, floods and droughts – are far reaching and include reduced labour productivity through to heat-related deaths and the spread of infectious diseases. This important initiative plans to monitor the association between health and climate change over time.

The last major IPCC Report was released in 2014. Since then, it has been reported that July 2016 was the hottest month in recorded history around the world (Colangelo, 2016); and temperatures continue to rise. This is part of a longer-term and rapidly accelerating trend toward even greater warming.

The key drivers of global warming are carbon dioxide emissions and deforestation (McGarrell and Gibbs, 2014), although it is carbon that is seen of crucial importance, maintaining the focus of public debate and government policy (see IPCC, 2013; 2014). What is important is that each of these drivers stems from human activity. It is thus humans who are generating rapid climate change on a global scale.

The Anthropocene

> Human influence on the climate system is clear, and recent anthropogenic emissions of green-house gases are the highest in history. Recent climate changes have had widespread impacts on human and natural systems. (IPCC, 2014: 2)

The global changes caused by human activity, especially over the last couple of centuries, has been described as delimiting a period called the Anthropocene (Shearing, 2015). The basis for this distinction rests upon the rapidity of the global warming and the human contributions to escalating temperatures. The most common reference point for the beginning of the Anthropocene epoch is the industrial revolution from the mid-1700s in Europe (Shiva, 2008). Over 200 years of industrial revolution has been driven and underpinned by powerful forces (nation-states, companies, armies) pursuing sectional interests. This has been achieved through global imperialism, colonialism and militarism that have served to entrench a dominant worldview and the material basis for producing and consuming natural resources in particular ways – what today is referred to as global capitalism (Greig and van der Velden, 2015).

The impacts of these trends historically have been dramatic. For example, people who for thousands of years had lived in harmony with nature (that is, through intrinsically adopting ecologically sustainable practices), including in some of the most humanly inhospitable places in the world (such as Arctic tundra and Australian deserts), were subjected to dispossession, displacement and destruction of their communities. These processes are mirrored in the contemporary exploitation of natural resources worldwide (Gedicks, 2005; Klare, 2012; Le Billon, 2012). Exploitation of natural resources in unsustainable ways has continued unabated and this includes activities that directly contribute to additional greenhouse gases. The overall impact of human activity on global warming is now clear and unequivocal (Hansen, 2009; Shearing, 2015; Watts et al, 2017), as are the specific contributions of so-called 'dirty industries' such as coal and gas (Heede, 2014). Biophysical changes have been and will continue to be accompanied by various threats to human security including crime. Yet, the perpetrators of global warming continue to do what they do and government responses remain muted and limited.

Part of the reason why the responses to climate change has been so little and so late has to do with the nature of 'slow crisis' (White,

2012a). Floods in Brazil, Australia and Sri Lanka in early 2011 were generally interpreted publicly as once-in-a-100-year phenomena. Much the same was said about 'Super Storm Sandy' along the East coast of the United States in 2012. Cyclones and hurricanes are considered 'normal' to certain regions of the world, even though the frequency and intensity might be changing, as illustrated by the ferocity of Hurricane Harvey that touched down in Texas in 2017. There is no one single earth-shattering event that demarcates the 'crisis' of climate change. Transformation is progressive and longitudinal. It is not abrupt, completed or singularly global in impact.

Over the past three or four decades, public debate on climate change has generally focused on two issues:

- Is climate change actually occurring?
- Is climate change caused by human activity or is it simply part of a natural process of change?

Today, most governments and most people worldwide at least acknowledge that there is a problem and that it must in some way be addressed.

There continues, however, to be political disagreement when it comes to the causes of climate change. This is because how this question is answered has important social and economic consequences. If climate change is 'natural', then what governments can do is to try to adapt to changed circumstances as best as they can, since change is inevitable (and blameless). In this scenario existing institutions are not perceived to be the cause of the problem, although they will nonetheless be implicated in the changes that must occur into the future (such as caps being put on carbon emissions).

If human activity is found to be at the genesis of climate change, then this implies that substantial change is needed to the dominant mode of production characteristic of much world activity. Global production and consumption patterns, for example, feature an insatiable energy appetite (which, in turn, justifies use of destructive energy sources such as coal-fired power stations) and are founded upon a growth model (that feeds polluting and waste industries). The attribution of global warming to human activity also assigns a certain responsibility to the most polluting and damaging industries and countries to make right the wrongs to which they have contributed through their actions. Mitigation and adaptation in this scenario demand redress as well as a major alteration to existing ways of doing things.

Specific understandings and responses to the heating up of the planet thus carry with them important expectations about potential courses of action. Consideration of this also leads to a third question of public importance:

- If global warming is intentional, preventable and caused by human acts and omissions, then should such harms be criminalised and how should the perpetrators be dealt with by criminal justice institutions?

This last question is of most relevance and fundamental concern to criminology. Or, at least it should be.

Climate change and criminology

Climate change is the most important international issue facing humanity today, yet until recently criminology has devoted very little attention to this particular issue. This is changing (Lynch and Stretesky, 2010; Agnew, 2011; 2012;2013; White, 2008; 2011; 2012a; 2012b; Kramer, 2013a; 2013b; Crank and Jacoby, 2015; Holley and Shearing, 2017). Nonetheless, the gap in interest between these few and mainstream criminologists is notable.

For example, recent international criminology conferences in the United States, Britain and mainland Europe, Australia and Asia have featured very few papers, if any, on climate change. The main game still appears to be street crime, gangs, cybercrime, domestic violence and the usual crime categorisations. As the reference list to this book demonstrates, there has been relatively little published on the topic of climate change within criminology forums as such. It is notable, as well, that few funded research projects pertaining to climate change and crime are apparent.

In its own way, this silence within criminology as a field of inquiry is itself a form of denialism – involving as it does passive denial of topicality and importance. There is thereby a systematic failure by this group of social scientists to grapple with and respond to the most important ecological, social and *criminological* issue of the day. The 'same old, same old' continues to predominate even in the face of overwhelming evidence that massive social and environmental upheavals are already here with much more on the way.

Climate change and global warming pose a number of important questions for criminology. Not the least of these are problems relating to personal and national security, and the management of social conflict. Moreover, as governments and communities search for solutions to the underlying issues of climate change, and adopt measures to mitigate and adapt to the consequences of global warming, other problems will also inevitably emerge. Indeed, certain responses to climate-related issues generate their own sort of negative feedback loop, resulting in further degradation of environments and further threats to basic human rights. The pressures associated with these emergent harms (stemming from climate change responses) will in their own way add to the social conflicts already associated with climate change.

At a descriptive level we can identify many different sorts of social conflict that stem from or are closely associated with climate change. In developing a climate change research agenda, we need to consider the kind of value-adding that criminology can provide to interpretation and action on these issues. To put it simply, what distinctive contribution can criminology make with respect to issues surrounding global warming?

For criminology there is no doubt that new typologies of harm have to be developed, new methodologies for global research instigated, and new modes of social control devised if we are to adequately address present issues. Tackling potential climate-related crimes has implications for law reform, policy development within criminal justice agencies, and contemporary environmental management practices.

One aim of this book is to elaborate on what criminology offers conceptually (for example, concepts such as ecocide, state-corporate crime) and practically (for example, situational crime prevention, environmental law enforcement) in relation to global warming and its consequences (that include old crimes such as trafficking and assaults, and new crimes such as water theft and carbon emission scheme fraud). The impacts of climate change imply a re-conceptualisation of environment-related criminality. Criminology can offer insight into the definitions and dynamics of this behaviour and outline potential areas of redress. However, if it is to do so then two key issues must first be acknowledged. The first relates to the sheer scale of the problem – global warming is a planetary issue. The second pertains to the vested interests embedded in the existing *status quo* – the contributors to and perpetrators of global warming are powerful and unlikely to be easily persuaded about the right course of action to prevent and respond to it.

Key themes of climate change criminology

Climate Change Criminology, as conceptualised and described in this book, is informed by four key thematic considerations. It is these themes that provide the theoretical lens by which a specifically criminological understanding and interpretation of climate change might best be conveyed. These themes are inextricably intertwined at the level of policy and practice.

Crime and harm

> Climate Change Criminology views criminality in terms of criminal and/or harmful behaviour that contributes to the problem of global warming and that prevents adequate responses to climate change related consequences.

At the heart of criminology is the notion that a wrong committed by someone warrants a social response, and that the nature of this response depends upon the seriousness of the wrong. The content and extent of the wrong determines whether or not it is considered criminal, and the kinds of penalties or sanctions that might be utilised to deter and punish offenders carrying out certain acts or omissions. Considerations of what is wrong, the consequences of the wrong, the intent of the wrong-doer and the circumstances within which wrongdoing occur all feature in deliberations of criminality.

At an institutional level, however, crime is what the law says it is; that is, certain acts (and omissions) are defined in the legal system as being criminal while others are not. Given that powerful interests (such as business lobby groups) frequently influence what is included within legal definitions of crime the term is sometimes used by criminologists to describe social harms that have not yet been legally defined as criminal. This includes harms related to and stemming from global warming, and so this wider definition of crime is fundamental to Climate Change Criminology.

Criminal law is normally reserved for the punishment of socially unacceptable behaviour. Harm to the environment is, in many situations, considered to be acceptable (for example in certain circumstances we are prepared to allow certain types of pollution under licence or authorisation) because it is an inherent consequence of many industrial activities that provide significant benefits (Bell et al, 2017: 271). Crime, in this context, de-values the harm in that some types of harm are seen as less damaging than others, and thus warrant different treatment than those perceived to be more serious. This is captured in the notion of *malum prohibitum*, which refers to crimes that are criminal not because they are inherently bad, but because the act is prohibited by the law of the state. These are seen to be wrong because they breach regulation and are thus less serious per se. From this perspective, environmental protection is less about crimes against the environment and more about balancing economic and environmental interests.

On the other hand there is *malum in se*, a phrase used to refer to conduct assessed as inherently wrong by nature, independent of regulations governing the conduct (for example, murder, rape). These acts are seen to be naturally evil as judged by the sense of a civilized community. They describe perceptions that certain acts or omissions are a real harm-in-itself. For Climate Change Criminology, many activities of industry and government are considered as such insofar as they directly and indirectly contribute to the larger harm of global warming. This is not a matter for regulation; it is an issue of prohibition, prosecution and prevention.

Climate Change Criminology wishes to theorise and critique both illegal climate-related environmental harms (that is, harms such as carbon emission fraud currently defined as unlawful and therefore punishable) and legal climate-related harms (that is, harms currently condoned as lawful, such as carbon emissions stemming from coal-fired power stations, but which are nevertheless socially and ecologically harmful).

Global connectedness and eco-justice

> Climate Change Criminology is informed by a global perspective that views the world as an interconnected whole in which acts and omissions in specific locales have social and ecological ramifications for what occurs elsewhere on the earth.

The concept of ecology refers to the complex interactions of non-human nature, including its abiotic components (air, water, soils) and its biotic components (plants, animals, fungi, bacteria). Humans are implicated in these interactions as the relationship between humans and the environment is crucial to understanding how environments change over time, for better or for worse (Merchant, 2005). Climate change, almost by definition, is a global phenomenon. This means that it will have an impact on eco-systems around the planet and that there will be major ecological and social consequences within and across territorial distances. What happens in one part of the world therefore will be of importance to another part, and vice-versa. Substantial movements in humans and non-human entities due to climate change are anticipated and will continue to re-shape the living patterns of each.

Eco-justice refers to the relationship of humans generally, to the rest of the natural world, and includes concerns relating to the health of the biosphere, and more specifically plants and animals that also inhabit the biosphere (Smith, 1998; Cullinan, 2003; White, 2013a). The main concern is with the quality of the planetary environment (that is seen to possess its own intrinsic value) and the rights of other species (particularly animals) to live free from torture, abuse and destruction of habitat. Specific practices, and choices, in how humans interact with particular environments present immediate and potential risks to everything within them. Eco-justice notions of justice and rights see humans as but one component of complex ecosystems that ought to be preserved for their own sake, as supported by the notion of the rights of the environment. In this framework, all living things are bound together and environmental matters are intrinsically global and trans-boundary in nature. Eco-justice demands that how humans interact with their environment be constantly evaluated in relation to potential harms and risks to specific creatures and specific locales as well as the biosphere generally.

The global perspective adopted by Climate Change Criminology is one that not only is cognisant of the state of being of the non-human and the abiotic – that is, of animals, plants, rivers and mountains – but of the particularities of the human condition. Specifically, different social formations reflect varying degrees of inequality, opportunity and resource allocation. A 'southern criminology' approach sensitises us to the ways in which the Global South and Global North are materially and geographically constructed, and of the importance of democratic conceptions of perception, knowledge and social interest (Carrington et al, 2015). This precludes reliance solely on views of global warming and climate change exclusively from the vantagepoint of privilege and dominance. Rather, it obliges one to consider not only the divides of class, race, ethnicity, age and gender, but the contributions to global knowledge (including adaptive and preventative responses to climate change) emanating from the vulnerable, the dispossessed, the disadvantaged and the ignored.

A fundamental admonition of Climate Change Criminology is 'get to know your planet'. This means gaining a strong sense of geography and knowledge of place. The impacts of climate change will be felt in specific locales and regions. They will manifest in shifts in populations of birds, fish, other non-human animals and humans. As global warming increases, its consequences will be felt worldwide. This, too, has implications for a criminological imagination informed by the pursuit of social and ecological justice.

For criminology, a global perspective has to be seen today as part of core business. Globalisation as a concept alerts us to the heightened ties across the planet in regards economics, politics, culture, information, science and technology. Global warming as a phenomenon means that no one will be immune from the effects of climate change, and no strategy of mitigation and adaptation will be fully successful unless undertaken in conjunction with others around the planet.

Causes and consequences

> Climate Change Criminology examines the causes of global warming, which continue to be in play even with scientific evidence and foreknowledge of its impacts, and explores the diverse consequences of climate change.

Climate change research and strategic planning is typically framed around the concepts of 'mitigation' and 'adaptation'. Mitigation refers to efforts to diminish the contributing factors that produce global warming, such as reducing the amount of carbon emissions and other greenhouse gases flowing into the atmosphere. Adaptation refers to measures designed to cope with the changes wrought by climate change, such as efforts to prevent coastal erosion by erecting cement ocean barriers.

For criminology, the focus on causes and consequences has a slightly different meaning and orientation to the usual mitigation and adaptation literature. The criminological project centres on the perpetrators and victims of crime and harm. Accordingly, analysis of the causes of climate change, from a criminological perspective, focuses on who is doing what in causing the problem and/or making it worse. Criminological attention on the consequences of climate change examines the issues from the point of view of victimology, which encompasses who is victimised by the biophysical consequences of global warming, to what extent, how, and why.

The pursuit of climate justice involves examination of the perpetrators of harm associated with global warming. Hence, the concern is to identify the causes of climate change and the specific institutions, agencies and individuals implicated in activities and omissions that contribute to global warming. Issues of culpability, accountability and responsibility are pertinent to such analyses. If global warming is indeed due to anthropogenic causes, then Climate Change Criminology wants to know who is doing what to prevent it, stop it, encourage it and/or expand it. Attention is given to systemic or system-wide underpinnings of the Anthropocene, and the particular actors (human and non-human, that is, corporations) involved in making decisions regarding production and consumption globally.

Climate Change Criminology also examines wider victims of climate change. This includes consideration of transgressions against humans, specific biospheres or environments, and non-human animals. This can be conceptualised in terms of the three key aspects of eco-justice:

1. *environmental justice* – the main focus is on differences within human populations: social justice demands access to healthy and safe environments for all, and for future generations;
2. *ecological justice* – the main focus is on 'the environment' as such, and to conserve and protect ecological wellbeing, for example forests, is seen as intrinsically worthwhile;
3. *species justice* – the main focus is on ensuring the wellbeing of both species as a whole such as whales or polar bears, and individual animals, which should be shielded from abuse, degradation and torture. (White, 2013a)

Within this broad framework, issues of differential and universal victimisation are discussed.

Power and interests

> Climate Change Criminology focuses on the role of contemporary political economic systems and of the powerful in creating the conditions for further global warming while abrogating their responsibilities to deal with the substantive changes and suffering arising from climate change.

It is a criminological truism that crime and crime control are socially and historically constructed. That is, the definition of crime is variable, depending upon time, place and cultural setting. So too, crime control varies across social contexts, from highly repressive forms of intervention through to restorative justice conflict resolution methods. Law and order is fundamentally shaped by those groups and classes that wield the greatest social, economic and political power, generally reflecting their own sectoral interests. This occurs within the context of the particular balance of social forces within any given society (for example, the nature and degree of class struggles, gender inequalities, ethnic and racial divisions).

Climate justice is fundamentally concerned with the intersection of environmental destruction and degradation, and the social injustices arising from this (that take the form of disparities in how communities experience nature and utilise its natural resources). It has two dimensions. On the one hand, powerful interest groups exploit the planet for their own profit while simultaneously having the resources to distance themselves from the worst effects of this exploitation. On the other hand, it is the most vulnerable groups and communities around the world which experience the most negative effects of this environmental exploitation, including climate change, and who thereby suffer the most damage.

Ecocide is the term used to describe environmental harm that critics argue should be subject to criminalisation if and when caused by human action (Higgins, 2012). In this book the concept is also applied to the global scale in that the consequences of climate change are planet-wide, transformative and catastrophic. This is considered in greater depth in the next chapter. For now, the crucial observation is that ecocide is the result of the systematic destruction and diminishment of environments stemming from pollution and the exploitation of natural resources.

For Climate Change Criminology, it is important to expose the power and interests that underpin both the representation of climate change issues (for example, depictions of the root causes of the problem and ideal solutions to it) and the material aspects of climate change (for example, who is causing and benefiting from harmful activities, and who is suffering from their consequences). As indicated above, sophisticated accounts of climate justice also acknowledge that it is the non-human as well as the human that are affected by contemporary social structural arrangements and exploitive relations. Climate Change Criminology views the greatest threat to environmental rights, ecological justice and non-human animal wellbeing as stemming from system-level structures and pressures that commodify most aspects of social existence, that are based upon the exploitation of humans, non-human animals and natural resources, and that privilege the powerful over the interests of the vast majority (human and non-human, biotic and abiotic).

A key defining feature of crimes of the powerful is that such crimes involve actions (or omissions and failures to act) that are socially harmful and carried out by elites and/or those who wield significant political and social authority in the particular sectors or domains of their influence. Such harms are inseparable from who has power, how they exercise this power, and who ultimately benefits from the actions of the powerful. Powerful social interests not only perpetuate great harms, they also obscure and mask the nature of harm production. They are also best placed to resist the criminalisation process generally. Given these realities, criminological understandings of crimes of the powerful generally refer to harm-based criteria (in addition to existing legal definitions) in describing certain activities as crimes. As well as expressing moral condemnation, the use of such language is to some degree aspirational – describing acts that *ought* to be criminalised because of the nature and extent of the harms they incur. This applies to Climate Change Criminology just as it does to other types of critical criminology.

Conclusion

Climate Change Criminology rests upon the four pillars of crime and harm, global connectedness and ecological justice, causes and consequences, and power and interests. These are separate but inextricably linked domains of analysis, interpretation and critique. Each area demands novel ways of thinking about the problem, employing methods and approaches that necessarily push the boundaries of contemporary criminological theory and the purview of modern criminal justice institutions.

In several important respects Climate Change Criminology parallels work which focuses on 'social harm' as a constitutive concept (Hillyard and Tombs, 2007; Hillyard et al, 2004; 2005). For example, as outlined by Pemberton (2016), the analytical focus on social harm has tended to highlight three important issues. First, social harms are ubiquitous precisely because they stem from and are ingrained in the structures of contemporary societies. Much the same can be said about global warming. Second, social harms are generally not caused by intentional acts as such, but result from the omission to act or societal indifference to suffering and exploitation. Again, contributions to greenhouse gases produced in the pursuit of profit and economic growth should not be conflated with direct intent to do harm (the intention is to make profits, harm is a by-product of this). Third, such harms are entirely preventable in that the consequences of certain social actions or inactions are generally foreseeable. Such is the case, as well, with climate change.

What makes a social harm 'social' is the fact that it does not stem from natural causes (for instance, a cyclone or earthquake causes harm). It is intrinsically caused by humans. It is humans, in concert, who are responsible for the harm. How they do so, however, is a social process embodying relations of power, domination and resistance. Analysis and response to this is central to the project of Climate Change Criminology.

TWO

Global warming as ecocide

Introduction

Global warming continues to radically transform the world as we presently know it. These changes encompass multiple social and ecological dimensions; among these are species extinctions, major shifts in wind and water currents, reductions in the pool of fresh water reserves worldwide, and the migration of human and non-human populations around the globe (IPCC, 2014). Specific ecosystems are being fundamentally altered and the Earth as a whole is entering a new period of unbalance and rebalance. In this process, there are many casualties.

This chapter defines and describes the concept 'ecocide' (which refers to destruction of ecological systems and habitats). This includes the everyday activities that contribute to climate change and thus to ecocide on a larger and small scale. As part of this discussion it introduces the notion of state–corporate nexus by examining how industries (such as the energy, food and tourism industries), supported and abetted by governments, contribute to global warming.

The chapter also discusses denial and the use of techniques of neutralisation in regard of public debates over climate change, and the specific nature of 'contrarianism' as a conscious self-interested resistance to needed mitigation and adaptation strategies. It concludes by exploring the concept of 'paradoxical harm' – those harms that emerge because of the adoption of measures that from the very beginning, were never designed to address the essential causes of global warming.

Ecocide as a crime

Anthropocentrically driven changes in climate that negatively affect humans, eco-systems and non-human species (plants and animals) can be conceptualised criminologically as a specific sort of crime. Justice in this case is defined not so much by how we respond to harm, but by how we broadly define it to begin with. In this instance, the harm manifests in ways that differentially, unequally and universally affect the non-living but sustaining systems of Planet Earth and its inhabitants.

The term ecocide is used to conceptualise this harm-defining process. Ecocide has been defined as 'the extensive damage, destruction to or loss of ecosystems of a given territory, whether by human agency or by other causes, to such an extent that peaceful enjoyment by the inhabitants of that territory has been severely diminished' (Higgins, 2012: 3). Where this occurs as a result of human agency, then it is purported that a crime of ecocide has occurred.

Ecocide as an ecological concept has been used to describe natural processes of ecosystem decline and transformation, as well as human-created destruction of ecosystems (Higgins, 2010). The former includes instances where, for example, kangaroos consume a paddock of its grasses and shrubs to the extent that both the specific environment and its inhabitants are negatively affected. There is no grass left and as a result the kangaroo mob may starve due to lack of resources or are forced to migrate. In another instance, the migration and/or transportation of 'invasive' species, such as the crown of thorns starfish off the east coast of Australia or the introduction of trout into the central highland lakes of Tasmania, can lead to diminishment or death of endemic species of fish and coral – again a form of ecocide.

The term ecocide has also been applied to extensive environmental damage during war (Freeland, 2015), as in the case of the use of defoliants (for example, Agent Orange) in the Vietnam War, and the blowing up of oil wells and subsequent pollution during the first Gulf War in Iraq and Kuwait. These actions involved intent to actually produce environmental destruction in pursuit of military and other goals.

Ecocide is defined first and foremost by the destruction, degradation and demolishment of ecosystems and specific environments. When this occurs due to particular types of human activity, then ecocide also becomes terminology that describes a new form of criminality. For example, specific acts of environmental destruction, within particular war-time contexts, are officially considered crimes against humanity (Freeland, 2015). For some, this particular legal definition is too restrictive, and especially given present environmental trends including global warming, does not address those activities that may have even greater impact than those associated with military action (Higgins et al, 2013; White, 2017a).

The notion of ecocide in a more general criminal sense – one that includes destruction and degradation of environments outside of a war or military context – has been actively canvassed at the international level for a number of years, from at least the 1960s (Gray, 1996; Higgins et al, 2013). For example, there were major efforts to include it among the crimes associated with the establishment of the International Criminal Court, although the final document refers only to war and damage to the natural environment. It has been pointed out that 'For over a decade, in work undertaken by the United Nations, debates and drafting exercises *included* Ecocide until it was finally removed from the text that became known as the Rome Statute, which codifies the four Crimes against Peace' (Higgins et al, 2013: 258).

Nonetheless, environmental activists and international lawyers have continued to call for the establishment of either a specific crime of 'ecocide' and/or the incorporation of ecocide into existing criminal laws and international instruments (Higgins, 2012). Recent efforts, for example, have sought to make 'ecocide' the fifth International Crime Against Peace (Higgins, 2010; 2012). It has been argued that criminalisation in this instance is significant in that it can be used as 'both a normative strategy, centred on its social and symbolic properties, and also as an authoritative legal strategy, expressed most strongly through the call for the creation of a crime of ecocide, which would apply to states and businesses at the international and national levels' (Haines and Parker, 2017: 100). The urgency and impetus for this has been heightened by the woefully inadequate response by governments, individually and collectively, to global warming. Climate change is rapidly and radically altering the basis of world ecology; yet very little substantive action has been taken by states or corporations to reign in the worst contributors to the problem. Carbon emissions are not decreasing and 'dirty industries', such as coal and oil, continue to flourish.

Ecocide as a criminal offence can be conceptualised in several ways. One can distinguish between perspectives that privilege humans and human wellbeing in its definitions of harm, with those that include the non-human in its conceptualisations. Doing wrong and harming others is anthropocentrically framed and its basic considerations stem from and reflect the human rights paradigm. Ecocide in this sense accords well with the existing approach of the Rome Statute. Protection of human rights is paramount and this includes protections pertaining to one's living environment. Thus, the demise of environmental amenity and security is considered a derogation of the duty to protect and enhance human rights. For example, the major consideration of the Council of Europe (2012) *Manual on Human Rights and the Environment*, which reflects legislation and case law across Europe, is with the impact of environmental changes on individuals, rather than human impacts on the environment *per se*. In other words, the central concern is with human interests and human rights.

Other conceptions of the crime of ecocide, however, see it as being premised on the idea of Earth stewardship. Paradigms of trusteeship and stewardship are very different to those based upon private property conceptions of ownership. As Brian Walters (2011: 266) points out, 'Ownership implies that you can use land but don't have responsibility to others to care for it.' The Earth is seen to be 'held in trust', and it is humans who have the responsibility to provide the requisite stewardship. Threats to Nature itself can be conceptualised as, in essence, a crime of ecocide, and thus punishable by law. Ecocide in this instance is closely aligned to the concept of ecocentrism.

Ecocentrism refers to viewing the environment as having value for its own sake apart from any instrumental or utilitarian value to humans (Berry, 1999; Williams, 2013). Fundamentally, it is based upon several key principles that relate to the intrinsic value of nature (including flora and fauna), the precautionary principle, the primacy of environmental wellbeing and remediation (Williams, 2013). Protection of the environment may be based on either one, or a combination of conceptions of the *rights of* nature (both as subject with rights, or object worthy of protection) and *duties to* nature (its intrinsic worth which therefore imposes a moral obligation and duty of care) (Fisher, 2010). A fundamental aspect of ecocentrism is to see entities such as animals, plants and rivers as potential rights-holders and/or as objects warranting a duty of care on the part of humans, since their interests are seen to be philosophically significant (that is, deserving greater respect and formal recognition) (Schlosberg, 2007).

The notion of ecocide also invites comparison with other crimes that, at least superficially, bear similarities. For instance, ecocide is not the same as homicide (even though foreknowledge of consequences combined with anthropocentric causation implies preventable death); it is not the same as suicide (even though the agents of harm are themselves included as victims of harm); and it is not the same as genocide (even though there are clear similarities in terms of disregard by perpetrators of the magnitude of the harm and disrespect of specific collectivities/victims) (White, 2014; 2015b; 2015c). On the other hand, climate change might well be described as a form of genocide through 'geocide', that is, the killing of people through the killing of the Earth (Brook, 1998). Ecocide conceptualised in criminal terms has elements in common with several terms that deal fundamentally with concepts of death.

In its criminological formulation, ecocide describes an attempt to criminalise human activities that destroy and diminish the wellbeing and health of ecosystems and the species within these, including humans. Climate change and the gross exploitation of natural resources are leading to our general demise – hence increasing the need for just such a crime. From an eco-justice perspective, ecocide involves transgressions that violate the principles and central constituent elements of environmental justice, ecological justice and species justice (White, 2013a). The transgressions are not only apparent in relation to environmental victims (human and non-human), but have temporal dimensions that traverse the past, present and future.

Claims of ecocide levelled against individuals, corporations and governments have an important rhetorical value regardless of whether or not new laws are passed or relevant international tribunals set up. With respect to this, ecocide as a concept should be read primarily as a political intervention, one that attempts to allocate blame and assign the label of wrongdoing to particular actors and specific kinds of acts and omissions. In this sense, it is a framing device that provides a useful short-hand conceptual tool to describe gross harms stemming from real-world activities. Those who contribute the most to global warming are among those perpetrators firmly in the sights of those who view ecocide as the most important crime of the twenty-first century.

Business as usual and state–corporate crime

Ecocide associated with global warming does not occur in a social and political vacuum. Rather it stems directly from the nexus between business and government. It is substantially driven by systemic imperatives within which the state has a central role.

Put simply, at a structural level the 'everyday practices' that sustain environmental degradation and global warming are ingrained in western advantage and lifestyle. Moreover, these are justified on the basis that ameliorative action could jeopardise corporate profits or even survival, as well as the economic prosperity and/or economic development of particular nation-states. Agnew (2013: 58) has observed how commonplace activities in affluent western countries such as the United States contribute to ecocide: 'These ordinary acts have several characteristics: they are widely and regularly performed by individuals as part of their routine activities; they are generally viewed as acceptable, even desirable; and they collectively have a substantial impact on environmental problems.' For example, the livestock grazing that supports meat consumption is a major source of deforestation, water pollution and climate change – accounting for 18 per cent of greenhouse gas emissions (Agnew, 2013). For many in the west, the contribution to ecocide takes the form of living in large climate-controlled homes, using cars reliant upon diesel or petrol (or 'gas'), having high meat consumption, and continually purchasing consumer products.

Wealthy countries have the resources and opportunity to engage in such harms on a mass scale. Conversely, according to Agnew (2013) there is a corresponding lack of (enough) resources to undertake responsible use of natural resources (the costs associated with purchase of a hybrid or fully electric car, for instance). Second, the risk of sanction for engaging in ordinary harms is low, while, alternatively, the risk of sanction for engaging in environmentally responsible behaviours is quite different (witness the social response to 'hippie lifestyles', veganism and so on). Third, the disposition for engaging in ordinary harms is strong, while that for engaging in environmentally responsible behaviours is low. The bottom line is that 'The harms increase one's stake in conformity, since they provide a range of possessions and a lifestyle that most are reluctant to relinquish' (Agnew, 2013: 69).

Some have interpreted these forms of consumerism as reflecting a strong anthropocentric worldview. Anthropocentrism involves a range of philosophies and practices that include disregard through to stewardship models of care for the environment (De Lucia, 2015). Nonetheless, the defining characteristic of anthropocentrism is that humans are ends-in-themselves, while other entities are only means to attain the goals of humans. This is the case even when ecologically benign measures or 'ecosystem approaches' to natural resource management are adopted insofar as these methods are employed primarily for anthropocentric (or human-centred) purposes (De Lucia, 2015). From an anthropocentric perspective, harm to the environment is thus only of consequence when it is measured with reference to human values (for example, economic, aesthetic, cultural) (Lin, 2006).

By de-centring human interests and human perspectives, it is nonetheless possible to view humans as part of a larger web of life and as relatively unimportant in ecological and geological terms (Pelizzon and Ricketts, 2015). To go beyond anthropocentrism, from this point of view, is not to ignore the concrete realities of ontology (our essential being) but rather to acknowledge the choices and values ingrained in how humans regulate their moral behaviour. Fundamentally, what humans do in relation to the non-human is a moral decision.

Yet such decisions are made in particular political economic contexts. The 'choices' ingrained in environmental exploitation (of human beings and of the non-human world) stem from systemic imperatives to exploit the environment for the production of commodities for human use (discussed further in Chapter Six). In other words, how humans produce, consume and reproduce their life situations is socially patterned in ways that are dominated by global corporate interests. The power of consumerist ideology and practice manifests itself in the manner in which certain forms of production and consumption become part of a taken-for-granted common sense – the experiences and habits of everyday life.

There is thus a close link between capitalism as a global system of production and consumption, and environmental degradation and transformation generally. The key aspects of contemporary political economy include accumulation as the economic engine, one that is based upon the exploitation of natural resources, non-human animals and people (Foster, 2002; O'Connor, 1994).

The state–corporate nexus

The political economic relations of global capitalism are crucial in any discussion of environmental harm insofar as how, or whether, human activity is regulated is still primarily a matter of state intervention. The ways in which nation-states (and varying other levels of government) attempt to deal with environmental concerns is contingent upon the class interests associated with political power. In most cases today the power of transnational corporations find purchase at the interface between the interests and preferred activities of the transnational corporation and the specific protections and supports offered by the nation-state. The latter can be reliant upon or intimidated by particular industries and companies. Tax revenue and job creation, as well as media support and political donations, may depend upon particular state–corporate synergies. This of course can undermine the basic tenets of democracy and collective deliberation over how best to interpret the public or national interest.

The structure and allocation of societal resources via the nation-state also has an impact upon how environmental issues are socially constructed. Spending on welfare, health, energy, transportation, education and other forms of social infrastructure makes a big difference in people's lives. Recent fiscal crises (especially noticeable in European countries such as Greece, Ireland and Spain) and the far-reaching impact of the global economic crisis in 2008 have had the global impact of making ordinary workers extremely vulnerable economically. Under such conditions, there is even greater possibility to either reduce environmental protection, or to increase environmentally destructive activity, to the extent that existing state legislation and company practices are seen to put fetters on the profit-making enterprise. This is so whether the activity is in the metropole countries (such as Germany, United Kingdom, France and the US) or in the periphery (such as Indonesia, Nicaragua, Zimbabwe and Venezuela).

The question of climate justice and how to foster more sustainable forms of living inevitably leads one to consider the nature and dynamics of *state–corporate crime*. This is because the perpetrators and the responders to global warming tend to be one and the same: namely, nation-states and transnational corporations.

State–corporate crime has been defined as 'illegal or socially injurious actions that result from a mutually reinforcing interaction between (1) policies and/or practices in pursuit of the goals of one or more institutions of political governance and (2) policies and/or practices in pursuit of the goals of one or more institutions of economic production and distribution' (Michalowski and Kramer, 2006: 15). Four categories of state–corporate crime have been identified (Tombs and Whyte, 2015: 64–65): state-initiated crime (for example, government agencies play the leading role and are assisted by corporations); state-facilitated crime (for example, failure to regulate or wilful blindness to corporate wrongdoing); corporate-initiated state crime (for example, corporations wield their economic power to coerce states into taking deviant actions); and corporate-facilitated state crime (for example, when corporations provide the means for a state's criminality).

It has been argued that climate change provides a classic example of state–corporate crime. Specifically, corporate and state actors interact with each other in ways that create harms in four ways (Kramer and Michalowski, 2012):

1. by denying that global warming is caused by human activity;
2. by blocking efforts to mitigate greenhouse gas emissions;
3. by excluding progressive, ecologically just adaptations to climate change from the political arena;
4. by responding to the social conflicts that arise from climate change by transforming themselves into fortress societies that exclude the rest of the world.

State–corporate crime relates to both *acts* (for example, support for the Alberta Tar Sands, see below) and *omissions* (for example, failure to regulate carbon emissions and bolstering reliance upon dirty energy sources). Failure to act, now, to prevent global warming can and should be considered criminal, especially given the evidence-base and foreknowledge of consequence. Yet, things continue much as they have, the status quo is maintained, and the harms mount up. This is the essence of criminal ecocide. Further elaboration of specific instances of state–corporate crime, across its different categories, is therefore of primary concern to Climate Change Criminology.

Business as usual is protected under the guise of arguments about the 'national interest' and the importance of 'free trade', which usually reflect specific sectoral business interests. Humanity has certain common interests – universal human interests – such as the survival of the human race in the face of things such as global warming and the threat of nuclear Armageddon. These common human interests need to take priority over any other kind of interests if humans are, as a species, to survive. Yet, this is clearly not happening. In part, this is due to resistance and contrarianism perpetrated by powerful lobby groups and particular industries. This is most evident in state support for risky businesses in countries such as the United States, Canada and Australia:

- oil and coal industries and other 'dirty' industries;
- coal-seam fracking and other threats to prime agricultural land;
- deep-drill oil exploration and exploitation;
- mega-mines and open-cut mining.

Accompanying support for these industries, there is resistance to global agreements on carbon emissions and use of carbon taxes.
Simultaneously, there is state and business agreement about desired (and profitable) changes in land use, such as deforestation associated with cash crops, biofuels, mining and intensive pastoral industries. Indeed, tropical deforestation is now responsible for some 20 per cent of global greenhouse emissions (Boekhout van Solinge, 2010). Indonesia and Brazil have become respectively the third and fourth CO_2-emitting countries of the world, mainly as a result of the clearing of rainforest. States have given permission and financial backing to those companies engaged in precisely what will radically alter the world's climate the most in the coming years – greenhouse gas emissions.

The exploitation of Canada's Alberta tar sands provides another case in point. This massive industrial project involves the active collusion of provincial and federal governments with big oil companies (Smandych and Kueneman, 2010). The project is based upon efforts to extract and refine naturally created tar-bearing sand into exportable and consumable oil. One result of the project is a wide range of different types of harm to the ecosystem, animals and humans. For example, the tar sands oil production is the single largest contributor to the increase of global warming pollution in Canada. It is destroying vast swathes of boreal forest, it contributes greatly to air pollution, and it is having negative health impacts on aquatic life, animals and humans who live nearby (Smandych and Kueneman, 2010; Klare, 2012).

For those who study this type of environmental degradation, one that is associated with considerable social and ecological harm, the concept of state–corporate environmental crime is considered entirely appropriate as a descriptor (Smandych and Kueneman, 2010). Placed within the larger global context of climate change, the scale and impact of this project also fits neatly with the concept of ecocide. The role of the federal and provincial governments is crucial to the project, and in propelling it forward regardless of manifest negative environmental consequences.

The normal operations of capitalist enterprise, singularly and collectively based upon production of carbon emissions, in turn, contribute to global warming, as indicated by the Intergovernmental Panel on Climate Change (IPCC, 2013):

- the atmospheric concentrations of carbon dioxide, methane and nitrous oxide have increased to levels unprecedented in at least the last 800,000 years;
- carbon dioxide concentrations have increased by 40 per cent since pre-industrial times, primarily from fossil fuel emissions and secondarily from net land use change emissions;
- continued emissions of greenhouse gases will cause further warming and changes in all components of the climate system. Limiting climate change will require substantial and sustained reductions of greenhouse gas emissions.

These trends stem from the active collusion of government with industry. Snapshots of particular industries also help to illustrate how ingrained the ordinary destructive practices of businesses are, and the naturalness of their occurrence.

Farming and climate change

Farming practices are implicated in both mitigation (fostering and accelerating or stopping and curbing the drivers of climate change) and adaptation (adjusting or not adjusting to the impacts of climate change) with regard to global warming. Indeed, farming of various kinds (that include non-food purposes) and food production specifically (including its transportation and consumption) are inextricably intertwined with climate change issues.

Many farming processes directly contribute to the causes of global warming. For instance, profit-oriented systems of food production – frequently reliant upon mass production techniques and genetically modified organisms (GMOs) – increase carbon emissions (for example, via animal flatulence and deforestation) while simultaneously undermining the resilience of natural systems to withstand the effects of climate-related changes (for example, through reduction in biodiversity). This is an accelerating phenomenon. Changes in climatic conditions, for example, are putting new and additional pressures on existing global food stocks. One response by governments and agribusiness has been to foster ever greater reliance upon large-scale agricultural techniques and methods, and on new technologies such as the use of GMOs (Robin, 2010; R. Walters, 2011). This has involved converting land to industrial forms of agricultural production, and the application of practical restrictions on what is being grown and how. These, in turn, have implications for both climate change and human wellbeing.

The rise of transnational agro-industrial food systems is manifest at the ground level in the form of large-scale commercial agriculture and intensive farming practices, frequently based upon monocultures and specialisation (Larkins et al, 2013). Globally, both the scale and content of farm practices have been radically altered in the last century. The specific dollar value of certain types of farming is also driving intensification of farming practices, as is population density in rural areas which contributes to pressures to produce more on less land (Jayne et al, 2014).

It has been estimated that livestock production contributes to around 14.5 per cent of global anthropogenic greenhouse gas emissions (Kim et al, 2015). It has been observed that enteric fermentation (that is, cow and other ruminant animal farts) is the single largest livestock contribution to climate change (29%), followed by manure (26%), feed crop production (24%) and deforestation for feed crops and pastures (9%) (Kim et al, 2015). Expanding meat and dairy production therefore increases contributions to global warming. The overarching consequences are thus known, but, business continues as usual even in the face of the factual certainties provided by the agricultural and climate sciences about its negative impacts.

The rise of 'flex crops' is having a major impact on biodiversity (Borras et al, 2013) and this, too, has implications for climate change. Flex crops refer to a single crop or commodity that is highly valuable precisely because of its multiple characteristics and uses. Typically, a flex crop straddles multiple commodity sectors (food, feed, fuel, and other industrial commodities), geographical spaces, and international political economy categories. The four key flex crops are maize, oil palm, soybean and sugarcane. Important producers and exporters of flex crops and commodities include, for example, Argentina for soya, Malaysia and Indonesia for palm oil, and Vietnam for fast-growing trees (Borras et al, 2013). One type of crop, such as fast-growing trees, can be sold as a commodity in respect to diverse markets, including in this case timber products, biofuel and/or carbon offsets.

The economic incentive behind flex crops is linked to fires started in order to cheaply clear land for palm oil and pulp and paper plantations (ABC, 2015a). The subsequent smoke haze now regularly negatively affects people living in Malaysia, Singapore, Brunei, Cambodia, the Philippines, Vietnam and Thailand (Varkkey, 2013). According to some estimates, Indonesian forest and agricultural fires that regularly cloak South-East Asia in acrid haze spew more greenhouse gases into the atmosphere each day than all United States economic activity (ABC, 2015b). For example, according to the World Resources Institute, over several months in 2015 carbon emissions from the fires had exceeded average US daily output on 26 out of 44 days (ABC, 2015b). A major reason for this is the fires involve the burning of tropical peatlands that store some of the highest quantities of carbon on the planet.

Climate change, in turn, has certain consequences for current farming practices. The increasing scarcity of fresh water, for example, is of particular concern. The amount of fresh water on earth (from both surface and groundwater sources) is limited. Drought, high temperatures leading to increased rates of evaporation, and the world's exponential population growth have all contributed to its increasing scarcity. It was estimated that around 85 per cent of the world's population live in the world's driest regions and that by 2015, 3.5 billion of the earth's inhabitants would be living in water stressed conditions. In Africa alone, over 300 million people live in arid areas, which cover approximately 66 per cent of the continent (Global Initiative, 2014). Only 2.5 per cent of the planet's water is fresh water and of use to human and animal life on earth (Panjabi, 2014). Restricted quantities of clean water make it a particularly valuable property for those who own and control it. The securitisation and theft of water (Global Initiative, 2014), water-related corruption and violence, and water market price fixing (Kenya Water for Health Organisation, 2009) are emerging as important issues. Global warming will only make the existing situation worse.

Sudden changes in temperature as well as longer-term shifts in climatic conditions have enormous implications for animals and plants at the heart of the farming enterprise (Sundström et al, 2014). Heat stress increases mortality in animals raised for food, and can make them less able to withstand disease. Temperature changes will simultaneously change the composition of grass species, thereby affecting food sources for grazing animals. The dearth of adequate supplies of fresh water also has ramifications for the spread of disease and general health and wellbeing.

Reductions in biodiversity in the field and the paddock also threaten crops and livestock populations alike. Food production is increasingly influenced by localised changes in biodiversity, and by the overarching effect of global warming. Climate change is altering the physical and biological world in many ways. For instance, two-thirds of the North Sea's fish species have shifted in both latitude and depth, and worldwide movements are occurring in respect to mobile species (Macaulay, 2016). Simultaneously, local species may be placed under threat due to changes in temperature, moisture, wind and carbon dioxide that may diminish their ability to withstand familiar pathogens, much less competing species newly invading their spaces.

The threats to biodiversity are many and profound, including reliance upon GMOs and monocultures, a situation likely to be made worse by the consequences of climate change (SCBD, 2010). These trends also affect resilience. For instance, 'over the ages farmers have relied upon diverse crop varieties as protection from pests, blights and other forms of crop failure' (French, 2000: 61). Reducing this diversity affects the inbuilt mechanisms that helped to protect the soil and the vitality of the overall agricultural process.

Tourism and climate change

Worldwide, people are going to the wilderness and to ecologically biodiverse regions in great numbers for the purpose of holidays and getaways. They are doing so with the encouragement of, and frequently subsidies provided by, governments (local, regional and national). Tourism is generally viewed as being good for employment and for business. It is the supposed economic saviour of poor and local elite alike. More often than not, the local attraction is the natural resource, the plants and animals and landscapes of a particular place.

Tourism involves the (mass) movement of people around the planet for the purposes of leisure and relaxation, including sport, viewing of and engagement with local environments, visits to heritage sites and museums, and interaction with those not-from-home. It covers diverse activities and involves millions of participants. The industry includes the tourist as well as the tourism operator, governments, non-government organisations, transportation companies, restaurants and cafes, local residents and many other stakeholders and observers.

While generally applied to specific geographical and ecological domains (such as for example, the Great Barrier Reef in Australia), ecocidal tendencies of many kinds also have purchase as criminal harms at the global level (South, 2010). At this level, tourism certainly warrants critical scrutiny.

The sheer number of people tramping into the outbacks and deserts and mountains and rainforests of the world is increasing every year. The population size of the planet is translating into huge numbers of people on the move – and this is just not the refugee and asylum seeker, it is the adventurer-with-passport. They are travelling longer distances and taking even more trips than ever. The travellers include the privileged and financially advantaged classes of the North, South, East and West, as well as those who scrimp and save in the hope of gaining last glimpses and first encounters of the unique wonders of the world. Natural beauty and low-cost travel and accommodation are proving combinations too tantalising to resist. For others, expense is not the issue – here, the concerns are luxury, access and exclusiveness.

All this comes at a cost, however. The explosion of tourist travel has been accompanied by rapid expansion of air travel worldwide. Aviation accounts for the bulk of transportation CO_2 emissions stemming from tourism, and carbon emissions are the main cause (along with deforestation) of global warming (Peeters and Dubois, 2010). When booking a trip, people also have the choice of pushing the 'carbon neutral', but additional cost, button – although who does this, and where the money actually goes is perhaps still something of a mystery.

Meanwhile, everywhere that people go there is generally also the establishment of a 'universal menu'. This features items such as steak and chips, hamburgers, Asian noodles, Mexican tacos, fish, vegetarian and even vegan offerings. There are variations to this menu, but the substantive intent is more or less the same. The food is intended to accommodate diverse food tastes and to resonate with those who come from afar. Accordingly, food is trucked in from everywhere to suit the needs of the hotel, cruise ship, train and airplane traveller – strawberries from the USA, bananas from Guatemala, olive oil from Spain, salmon from Scotland, kiwi fruit from New Zealand, steak from Argentina – the world is the tourists' pantry (as it is for many other consumers in the west). The cost of transport is factored in as simply another cost of doing business, regardless of its contributions to global carbon emissions.

Accompanying the growth in tourism are other climate-related issues as well. Among these is the problem of waste and what to do with what the tourists leave behind. This, too, generates its own paradoxes and contradictions. For instance, the low-lying Maldives, in becoming reliant upon tourism, simultaneously grapples with the waste generated by tourism in ways that contribute to the undermining of its very existence (Smith and Raymen, 2016). Fire (from burning wastes) and water (from rising sea-levels) thus are combined in a perceived moment of self-preservation, in which tourism is both hero and villain. From this, the demise of the island chain thereby becomes inevitable.

Energy and climate change

Measures to deal with climate change through development of new energy sources and restriction or regulation of carbon emissions need to be understood in the context of unequal trading relations between countries. From a world systems perspective, there is an energy rift between regions resulting from unequal energy flows between the producers and users of resources. Such analysis is based upon significant social, economic and military differences between metropole (for example, US, Japan, Germany, UK, France), semi-periphery (for example, Russia, Brazil, Mexico, China) and periphery (for example, Bolivia, Haiti, Zimbabwe, India) countries (see Baer and Singer, 2009).

For example, in the period 1860 to the Second World War, research has found that both developed and less developed countries were almost self-sufficient in energy – this changes in the 1950s as the less developing countries began exporting energy to the developed core countries that were beginning to consume more than they produced (Lawrence, 2009). Not surprisingly, less developed countries (dependent upon foreign investment in manufacturing) have been found to emit higher levels of noxious gases per capita, and the total carbon dioxide emissions and emissions per unit of production are higher than in the core countries. Nonetheless, the core's usage remains disproportionate to its population. According to Lawrence (2009: 348), 'In 2005, [the core's] percentage of total world energy use was 61.2 percent and in 2004 CO_2 emissions were 60.4 percent, yet its population was only 21.5 percent of the world total.'

Stretesky and Lynch (2009) argue that on the basis of analysis of carbon emissions and consumer imports to the United States, it is US consumer demand that is fuelling harmful production practices in other importing countries. They examined the relationship between per capita carbon dioxide emissions and exports for 169 countries.

The data suggest that consumption practices in the United States are partially responsible for elevated per capita carbon dioxide emission in other nations, and that carbon dioxide trends in other nations are in part driven by US demands for goods. US consumers, however, are unaware of how their consumption fuels rising global carbon emissions, because of the disconnection or dissociation between the two phenomena.

Much public debate has occurred over the regulation and reduction of carbon emissions. At the heart of the matter is the fact that carbon emissions are directly contributing to global warming, and that without adequate mitigation and adaptation strategies the problems associated with climate change will get worse before they get better. The urgency surrounding the reigning in of carbon emissions has been matched by the audacity of businesses in lobbying to defend their specific economic interests (Bulkeley and Newell, 2010). Given the vested interests involved in protecting and maintaining existing interstate inequalities, as well as those associated with particular industries (such as oil and coal), the stifling of carbon emissions has been slow and well below what is needed to counter present global warming trends (IPCC, 2013). Private profits continue to dominate public interests, usually with government collusion.

The push toward biofuel production also reflects the interests of large agricultural businesses, who patent the monocultural crops designed as 'energy crops'. Powerful interests, including car manufacturers and grain farmers, have benefited from the search for energy alternatives to fossil fuels. The shift to biofuel is seen as a key source of green fuel supply for the world's car manufacturers. Greater demand for biofuel crops such as corn, palm oil or soya also means that farmers are finding the growing of such crops very lucrative economically.

As discussed above, the profitability of biofuel production is leading to the establishment of large-scale plantations in places such as Indonesia and Brazil. This process has seen the clearing of rainforests and in some instances the forcing of Indigenous people off their lands. This deforestation process has been going on for a number of years, and has been supported by organisations such as the International Monetary Fund (French, 2000). Cutting down trees also has a direct bearing on global warming. It has been estimated that by 2022, biofuel plantations could destroy 98 per cent of Indonesia's rainforests and that 'Every ton of palm oil used as biofuel releases 30 tons of CO_2 into the atmosphere, ten times as much as petroleum does' (Shiva, 2008: 79).

Nonetheless, biofuel production in places such as the United States and the European Union is encouraged through strong incentives (for example, tax credits) and mandates such as energy legislation (for example, mandatory blending requirements that dictate fuel sources be mixed together). Biofuel production activities are not carbon neutral (for example, the energy consumed by, and emissions from, intensive farming practices). In fact, this led to a European Union directive in 2009 that biofuels be subject to the meeting of agreed sustainability criteria, including achieving minimum levels of greenhouse gas savings and that they should not be obtained from land with high biodiversity value (Redgwell, 2012: 39).

Paradoxical harms

Responses to climate change pressures can lead to paradoxical phenomena that create new harms or reinforce particular harms as a result of intending to reduce particular existing harms. This *paradoxical harm* is harm that arises out of an apparent contradiction (for instance, we have to pollute certain parts of the planet in order to save it from other types of pollution). Specific examples of paradoxical harm include the adoption of compact fluorescent light globes to save energy (but which contain toxic mercury), promotion of nuclear energy (but which involves disposal of nuclear waste), and carbon emission storage (that penetrates and despoils the subterranean depths of land and sea) (White, 2012b).

It is important not to equate paradoxical harm with the notion of unintended consequences. This is because in many instances the harms are actually well known, and the acts leading to the generation of the harms are intentional. The harm is paradoxical in the sense that while seemingly contradictory (we generate harms as a means to forestall other harms), it is perfectly logical from the point of view of the imperatives of the system as a whole. Economic and social interventions that sustain the status quo (and that include maintaining the viability of 'dirty' industries) are favoured over those that might tackle the key drivers of climate change and that could diminish the burgeoning threats to ecological sustainability worldwide. For example, climate-related energy issues can be analysed in terms of the use of alternative energy sources, and efforts aimed at dealing with carbon emissions. In each case the answer to the energy crisis involves measures that in some way contribute to other types of environmental harm.

Developments relating to both food and energy production reveal a series of paradoxical harms that are generated in the context of strategic decisions regarding how production (and consumption) are to take place. When it comes to food the key issues are shortages, unequal distribution globally and emerging social conflict. In responding to these, however, measures involving further industrialisation of agricultural and pastoral production and the adoption of bio-technologies are contributing to greenhouse gases, pollution and loss of habitat and biodiversity. When it comes to energy, again there are problems relating to shortages, global unequal distribution and expanding demand. However, poor regulation of carbon emissions, and reliance upon biofuels and other new technologies is likewise contributing to global warming, as well as transferring problems to poorer countries and adding additional forms of toxic pollution into the equation.

Contrarianism and techniques of neutralisation

> Then there's the evidence that higher concentrations of carbon dioxide (which is a plant food after all) are actually greening the planet and helping to lift agricultural yields. In most countries, far more people die in cold snaps than in heat waves, so a gradual lift in global temperatures, especially if it's accompanied by more prosperity and more capability to adapt to change, might even be beneficial.
>
> In what might be described as Ridley's paradox, after the distinguished British commentator: at least so far, it's climate change policy that's doing harm; climate change itself is probably doing good; or at least, more good than harm.
>
> (Former Australian Prime Minister Tony Abbott in a speech to the Global Warming Policy Foundation, Westminster, London, 10 October 2017)

Investigation of state–corporate collusion frequently draws upon the criminological notion of techniques of neutralisation (Sykes and Matza, 1957; Cohen, 2001). This refers to the ways in which business and state leaders join up in attempts to prevent action being taken, in this case on climate change. The politics of denial at both the level of ideology and policy are propped up by various techniques of neutralisation, with the net result being inaction in addressing the key factors contributing to climate change, such as carbon emissions.

These types of denial should not be conflated with scepticism as such, but rather as a form of contrarianism. As Brisman (2012: 43) notes: 'while scepticism can be both a healthy part of the scientific process and an excuse to present political or value-laden perspectives (that are masked behind a scientific façade), contrarianism suggests an ideological, rather than scientific, impetus for disagreement'.

Criminological work on the politics of climate change in the United States has demonstrated close connections between business and the government culminating in a form of state–corporate contrarianism (Brisman, 2013a; Kramer, 2013a; Kramer and Michalowski, 2012; Lynch et al, 2010). One social consequence of this type of response to climate change and global warming is that it tends toward inaction on climate change issues at precisely the time when action is what is needed (Brisman, 2012). This is particularly evident at the time of writing under the Trump regime in Washington.

Typically, techniques of neutralisation involve the following kinds of denials:

- *denial of responsibility* (against anthropocentric or human causes as source of problem);
- *denial of injury* ('natural' disasters are 'normal');
- *denial of the victim* (failure to acknowledge differential victimisation especially among poor and Third World);
- *condemnation of the condemners* (attacks on climate scientists);
- *appeal to higher loyalties* (American or Chinese or Australian economic interests ought to predominate).

The net result is inaction on addressing the key factors contributing to climate change, such as carbon emissions. More than just this, however, in a perverse twist of the 'greed is good' credo of Wall Street, techniques such as denial of injury even includes the proposition that 'climate change is good' as illustrated at the beginning of this section in the statement made by a recent Australian Prime Minister. These words were uttered in October 2017. They are contemporary, not historical.

There are many avenues by which nation-states and transnational corporations escape or minimise negative media coverage for acts or omissions that cause harm, proactively use green washing techniques to make them seem environmentally responsible or good corporate citizens, threaten critics and environmental activists with law suits, and generally make life difficult for those trying to expose their wrongdoing (see Table 2.1). The powerful have many ways in which to protect and project their interests (Athanasiou, 1996; Beder, 1997; White and Heckenberg, 2014).

The phenomenon of greenwashing is well known to environmental activists and commentators and this, too, can be seen as a strategy of denial and obfuscation. It refers to companies and governments putting a green 'spin' on their activities in ways that make them look as if it is a protector of the environment and concerned about environmental issues. It is big business for all concerned, as seen by the fact that most of the top public relations firms today include environmental PR as one of their specialties. Earth Day, for example, has massive sponsorship by the largest corporations (Pearse, 2012). Being seen to be green is good for business.

Table 2.1: Stifling dissent

Method	Example
Strategic lawsuits against public participation	Use of law suits to preoccupy and cool out activists
Use of freedom of information laws	Seeking information to undermine the work situation and professional credibility of activists
Libel suits	Use of libel laws to dispute statements and gag criticism
Accusations of political correctness	Ideological challenges that belittle the message of progressive politics and climate change activism
Changes in electoral law	Using electoral rules to marginalise smaller parties and/or make it difficult for alternative voices to be elected
Propaganda campaigns	Misrepresentation of democratic protests as illegitimate and illegal
Skewed state intervention	Allocating resources and political priorities to the policing of climate change protests rather than into law enforcement directed at environmental crime
Funding restrictions	Restricting or stopping funding for free legal services and community legal centres that attempt to intervene on environmental matters

Source: Drawing from White, 2008.

There is a close intersection, therefore, of global warming, government action or inaction and corporate behaviour (Lynch and Stretesky, 2010) and how these contribute to the overall problem of climate change. In this instance the state is itself implicated as a perpetrator of harm. Government subsidies for coal-fired power stations and government approval of dams that destroy large swathes of rainforest constitute substantial crimes against nature. In the light of the existing scientific evidence on global warming, continued encouragement of such activities represents intentional harm that is immoral and destructive of collective public interest in the same moment that particular industries and companies benefit.

Many of the activities of destruction and transformation of nature could not occur without close collusion between private companies and particular nation-states (Michalowski and Kramer, 2006). Government policies set the context within which contemporary neoliberal practices and ideologies flourish. The emphasis here is on 'the market' as determiner of who gets what, and on the individual taking responsibility for their opportunities and life chances. The environment is viewed as part of the national economic calculus, rather than as having intrinsic importance. Resource extraction companies, such as big oil, coal and gas companies, tend to receive privileged support from governments regardless of the damage they cause to specific environments or the contributions they make to global warming (Kramer and Michalowski, 2012; Kramer, 2013a; 2013b; Ruggiero and South, 2013). Public policy is framed in terms of supporting big business (through tax breaks and via policies that allow continued carbon emissions to occur), and corporations in turn are generous contributors to the coffers of mainstream political parties. Both states and companies regularly engage in techniques of neutralisation whereby they decry their critics, deny the extent and nature of environmental harm, and excuse themselves from accountability for environmental destruction accompanying economic enterprise (Brisman, 2012).

In Australia, for example, former Environment Minister Greg Hunt once proclaimed that he takes climate change seriously. Nonetheless, in 2014 he approved a Queensland coal mining project, Australia's largest ever, subject, of course, to 'the absolute strictest of conditions'. Left out of these 'conditions' was any mention of the mine's impact on atmospheric carbon levels, as one commentator pointed out:

> When Carmichael coal is exported to India and burned, it will release 100 million tonnes of carbon dioxide each year for the mine's lifetime of more than half a century. This is about one-fifth of Australia's annual total from all sources, way beyond any single enterprise in our history. (Boyer, 2014: 13)

As this incident further illustrates, not only is there state–corporate collusion in perpetrating harm, but responsibility for such harm is frequently externalised as well. This externalisation occurs both directly ('we are selling the coal to India') and indirectly ('no one country can do it alone'). Economy yet again trumps ecology and is defended by those whose ostensible task is precisely to protect the environment.

Conclusion

At a systems level, the treadmill of production embodies a tension or 'metabolic rift' between economy and ecology (Foster, 2002; 2007; Stretesky et al, 2014; Lynch and Stretesky, 2014). Pro-capitalist ideologies and practices ensure continued economic growth at the expense of ecological limits. Effective responses to climate change need to address the deep-seated inequalities and trends within the treadmill of production that go to the heart of the ownership, control and exploitation of resources.

The crime of ecocide is rarely embedded, however, in state legislation. This is, in part, because the state is directly implicated in perpetuating activities that contribute to global warming. The state therefore has little interest in passing laws that will bring it and its private sector partners to book. Hence, it is environmental activists and critical green criminologists who have tended to use the term to morally condemn practices which by act or omission make things worse rather than better when it comes to climate change mitigation and adaption. This condemnation is vitally important, not least because 'denouncing the crime of ecocide is a political and moral statement that seeks to shift the onus onto states and businesses to know and govern and do business within ecological limits, before breaching planetary boundaries, rather than just prosecute after the fact' (Haines and Parker, 2017: 90). We need to prevent the harm (issues of mitigation) as well as respond to it (issues of adaptation and compensation).

THREE

In the heat of the moment

Introduction

Studies of the nexus between climate change and crime tend to focus on either the *consequences* of climate change for crime (that is, climate change leads to certain sorts of crime), or the *causes* of global warming (that is, certain sorts of behaviour lead to climate change).

Across a range of studies, different levels of analysis are apparent. Those focusing on individual-level explanations (such as psycho-biological responses to temperature change) appear to have most relevance for adaptation strategies (that is, how to respond to climate change). Approaches that focus on structural level causes tend to be more concerned with issues of mitigation (that is, how to prevent climate change) and are more critical of entrenched policies and power structures. This chapter discusses studies that deal with the consequences of climate change, including but not exclusively from criminological perspectives.

The chapter begins by providing several initial typologies of climate change offences. It then examines mainstream criminological accounts that focus attention on the relationship between temperature changes and human behaviour. It describes literature that argues that crime rates change as temperatures increase. It also looks at the impact of climate change on human (and non-human) migrations, and more generally the social strains likely to accompany climate change – and how these translate into particular kinds of crimes and violations of human rights. The final section examines crimes linked to responses to climate change, in particular crimes stemming from and associated with the market in carbon emission credits.

Heat matters

The realities of climate change are acknowledged, to some degree, by the fact that the countries of the world are united in their stated attempts to prevent temperatures rising beyond certain limits. The sole exception to this (as of November 2017) is the United States of America. Member states of the United Nations have, in the Paris Agreement (United

Nations, 2015), agreed to strengthen the global response to climate change by among other means holding the increase in the global average temperature to well below 2 degrees Celsius above pre-industrial levels and to pursue efforts to limit the temperature increase to 1.5 degree Celsius above pre-industrial levels (United Nations, 2015: Article 2.1 (a)). It is recognised that this would significantly reduce the risks and impacts of climate change. It is a good plan, perhaps, but is it enough? And is it in time?

Global warming basically means that the planet is heating up. Scientists now speak of the transition from the Holocene (which included about 12,000 years of relatively stable climate) to the Anthropocene (in which there are absurdly rapid rises in temperature due to human causes) as originating with the Industrial Revolution in England (see Holley and Shearing, 2017). The real damage is much more recent than this, however. For example, it has been reported that the biggest change in climate has come since 1970 (Edwards, 2017). This is not surprising given that more than half of the carbon that humans have put into the atmosphere has been put there in just the past three decades (Wallace-Wells, 2017). Meanwhile, 2016 was the hottest year on record globally (Hamilton-Smith, 2017) and the last decade has been the warmest of the last three, which together have been warmer than all preceding decades since 1850 (Australian Academy of Science, 2015). There are no signs that this trend is going to diminish.

Extreme weather events are projected to worsen as global warming continues apace. In fact, things are going to get a lot worse, fast. Consider the following.

> Until recently, permafrost was not a major concern of climate scientists, because, as the name suggests, it was soil that stayed permanently frozen. But Arctic permafrost contains 1.8 trillion tons of carbon, more than twice as much as is currently suspended in the Earth's atmosphere. When it thaws and is released, that carbon may evaporate as methane, which is 34 times more powerful as a greenhouse-gas warming blanket as carbon dioxide when judged on the timescale of a century; when judged on the timescale of two decades, it is 86 times as powerful. In other words, we have, trapped in Arctic permafrost, twice as much carbon as is currently wrecking the atmosphere of the planet, all of it scheduled to be released at a date that keeps getting moved up, partially in the form of a gas that multiplies its warming power 86 times over. (Wallace-Wells, 2017: 1)

There are a series of feedback loops that ensure that global warming will increasingly accelerate. These include the melting of permafrost through to the *albedo effect* in which the presence of less ice globally (especially in the Arctic circle and contained in the ice sheets of Antarctica) means less sunlight being reflected, and therefore more absorbed and hence greater warming. Bush fires in Australia and forest fires in Portugal in 2016–2017, not to mention the fires in the United States, further added to the global release of carbon dioxide emissions while simultaneously reflecting the impact of prolonged hot, dry conditions. The record temperatures of 2016 are only the harbinger of much greater temperature rises to come. It is notable, as well, that 'more than 90% of the total heat accumulated in the climate system between 1971 and 2010 has been stored in the oceans' (Australian Academy of Science, 2015: 9), since this, too, contributes to and reflects the overall warming of the planet.

Rising temperatures translate into rising seas due to melting ice at the poles and in Greenland and mountain glaciers, and increased desertification due to sustained dry periods. Droughts will continue to proliferate and intensify. Plants and animals will die (IPCC, 2014). So, too, will humans. Already this is the world of today in parts of Africa and the Middle East. Things are not going to get any better soon.

The social consequences of the biophysical consequences of climate change are dire. Increased conflict is highly likely as communities struggle to survive, as they move, and as they assert their territorial ownership. It has been calculated that for every half-degree of warming, societies will see between a 10 and 20 per cent increase in the likelihood of armed conflict (Burke et al, 2015). This is violence on a mass scale. Violence will also feature in the street crimes associated with climate change. This, too, is violence on a mass scale but most of this violence consists of crimes within communities rather than between them.

Climate change and crime typologies

Climate change continues to generate shifting ecological conditions that engender considerable anxiety and conflict. Higher temperatures and drought have an impact on food production and thus wellbeing and safety, and affect water-reliant economic sectors, such as power-generation. For example, in a single year in 2003, melting reduced the mass of Alpine glaciers in Europe by one-tenth, and over 20,000 people died in a severe heat wave (EEA, 2010). Collective security will increasingly be tied up with notions of ecological sustainability within a particular social context. Pressures relating to food and water supply, and loss of habitat, will manifest in various class-related processes including certain types of criminality.

Various crimes tied to climate-related events such as food riots and climate-induced migration are very likely to become more prevalent. Some of these, for example, might include looting and blackmarketeering in relation to food products, illegal fishing and killing of birds and land animals, and trafficking in humans and valued commodities such as water and food. Survivalism as well as climate change policy provides the grounding for a suite of new and old crimes – hence, the advent of carbon emission trading fraud into the ranks of officially acknowledged crimes such as murder, assault and rape.

The purpose of Climate Change Criminology is to critically examine the consequences of global warming for the sake of communal security, societal peace, and social and ecological wellbeing. Fundamentally, it is driven by a concern for climate justice. One of the tasks of such research, as Agnew (2011: 27) points out, is to 'examine the impact of climate change on particular types of crime and harmful activity in more detail'. Developing an integrated and detailed picture of environment-related crime and criminality is already a major project of green criminology (South and Brisman, 2013; White and Heckenberg, 2014), and climate change is and should be viewed as one area deserving highest priority.

Typologies of climate-related crimes make reference to diverse situations, settings, offenders and offences. For example, consideration is given to crimes such as water theft for family farm use related to basic survival (caused by lack of rain and changes in temperatures), through to new opportunities for organised crime networks to be involved in activities such as carbon emission fraud and illegal trade in water (created by institutional failures including inability to deal with scarcity) (Johnston et al, 2016; Canepelle et al, 2013; Global Initiative, 2014; Panjabi, 2014).

Suitable crime prevention techniques and approaches to match the nature of the problems foreseen to accompany climate change also need to be developed. A vital component of any criminological project concerned with global warming is an orientation toward building social resilience within and among communities and, as part of this, enhancing the capabilities of institutions and agencies in dealing with the foreseeable and unanticipated consequences of climate change. Much of this, however, depends upon political will and the outcome of ongoing contestations over policy and practice.

Some work at developing concepts and typologies pertinent to analyses of global warming and climate-related crime has already been initiated (Sollund, 2012; White, 2012a; Crank and Jacoby, 2015). For example, one sort of classification relates to the *criminal offences* associated with climate change (White, 2012a). Specific criminal and environmental offences linked to the phenomenon of climate change are categorised according to offences that contribute to climate change, those arising from its consequences, civil unrest and organised criminal activities, and offences pertaining to regulation and law enforcement associated with mitigation and adaptation strategies (see Table 3.1).

It is anticipated that there will be changes in the type, rate and frequency of offences as the climate alters (Bergin and Allen, 2008). Environmental conflicts will largely centre on the allocation and struggle over resources, accompanied by attendant crimes.

Another approach within criminology is to describe climate change-related crime from the point of view of *perpetrators* (White and Heckenberg, 2014). Such analysis includes reference to:

Table 3.1: Crime and climate change

	Subject of offence	Nature of offence
Environmental offences (contributing to climate change)	Forestry	Illegal felling of trees
	Air pollution	Emissions of dark smoke
	Industrial pollution	Unlicensed pollution
	Illegal land clearance	Destruction of habitat and forests
	Clearing native vegetation	Reducing biotic mass
Environmental offences (consequences of climate change)	Water theft	Stealing water
	Wildlife poaching	Illegal killing of animals
	Illegal fishing	Diminishment of fish stocks
Associated offences (civil unrest and criminal activities)	Public order offences	Food riots
	Eco-terrorism	Arson, tree spiking
	Trafficking	Migration and people smuggling
	Violent offences	Homicide, gang warfare
Regulatory offences (arising from policy responses to climate change)	Carbon trading	Fraud
	Carbon offsets	Misreporting
	Illegal planting	Unauthorised use of genetically modified organisms
	Collusion	Regulatory corruption

Source: White, 2012a.

- *crimes by the less powerful* – basic survival (for example, loss of land, lack of rain, change in temperatures), through to illegal migration, foraging for food in reserves, water theft and street riots;
- *crimes by the powerful* – protection of privilege and defence of profit-motive, through to enclosures of land, hoarding of food and other basics, and the establishment of private armies/security;
- *crimes by organised criminals* – new criminal opportunities, such as carbon emission fraud, illegal trafficking of people and substances, dumping of waste, and illegal trade in food and water;
- *crimes by the state* – collusion with powerful interests, denial of human/ecological rights, failure to intervention or regulate, and buying of land for food production/consumption somewhere else.

Further to this classification of climate-related crimes is the notion that a *bifurcation of crime* will likely occur. The rich and powerful will use their resources to secure productive lands, restrict access to food and water, exploit the financial hardships of others, and impose their own coercive rule (private security and private armies is a contemporary growth industry worldwide). Crimes of the less powerful will be crimes of desperation, and child soldiers and armed gangs will likely flourish in conditions of welfare collapse or non-existent government support. Vulnerable people will flee and be criminalised for seeking asylum; others will stay, to fight for dwindling resources in their part of the world. Communities will be pitted against each other, and industries against communities. Law and order will be increasingly more difficult to maintain, much less enforce in other than repressive ways.

Climate change and violent crime

In discussing the consequences of climate change much of the emergent literature has focused on crimes of violence and crimes associated with social conflict. In doing so, recent criminological study has pointed to different types of association between climate change and violence. Much of this has indicated causal relationships between global warming and violent crime, although how robust the evidence is, and whether this will remain so over time remains a significant question, particularly given the longer-term adjustments to climate change that will most likely occur in human communities. Similar to the notion of a crime of passion, climate change violence has been conceptualised (implicitly if not always explicitly) as something that occurs in the heat of the moment – except that rather than 'hot blood' being the driver, it is hot temperatures.

From the point of view of criminology, violence is both ubiquitous and socially patterned (for example, predominantly perpetuated by men) (White and Perrone, 2015). It is also multi-layered in regards context and consequence (Stubbs and Tomsen, 2016). It manifests at the direct face-to-face level as assault and homicide; yet it also takes mass forms such as genocide and 'collateral damage' (in the case of civilian war victims). There are immediate situational triggers that spur people to violence (for example, emotions in the heat of the moment). There are also structural pressures and tensions within which the impetus to action occurs (for example, conflicts related to water and food scarcity). Violence is thus always socially constructed (in terms of legitimacy and with regard to who are the specific victims and perpetrators) and it always involves a combination of personal, institutional and society-wide determinants (White and Perrone, 2015; Stubbs and Tomsen, 2016).

In examining the relationship between climate change and violence, criminological perspectives seek to account for the complexities of the phenomenon by identifying the specific factors which drive climate change-related violence and/or the reasons why certain types of environmental harm persist even when the harm is well known and foreseeable. As with most fields and disciplines, there is a natural diversity of viewpoints within criminology, as different writers and researchers study the world through very different analytical spectacles (White et al, 2017a). These differences are also reflected in the adoption of a wide range of techniques and methodologies in the study of crime including violent crime; from historical document analysis, to surveys and questionnaires, to interviews and field observations (White and Perrone, 2015).

There are three broad levels of criminological explanation: the individual, the situational and the structural (White et al, 2017a). For the first level, the main focus is on the personal or individual characteristics of the offender or victim. This level of analysis tends to look to psychological or biological factors that are said to have an important role in determining why certain individuals engage in criminal activity. For the situational level, the main site of analysis is the immediate circumstances, or situation, within which criminal activity or deviant behaviour occurs. Key concerns are the nature of the interaction between different individuals and groups (including how and to whom labels are applied), the effect of local environmental factors on the nature of this interaction, and the influence of group behaviour and influences on social activity. For the social structural level of explanation, attention is directed at the broad social relationships, power dynamics and major social institutions of the society as a whole. This analysis makes reference to the relationship between classes, genders, different ethnic and 'racial' groups and other social divisions. It also can involve investigation of the operation of specific institutions, such as corporations and nation-states, in the social construction of and responses to crime and deviant behaviour.

The vantage point from which one examines violence – a focus on personal characteristics through to societal institutions – shapes the ways in which issues are conceptualised and responded to. This is a criminological truism that is as relevant to climate change-related violence as it is other types of crime and criminality. Yet the scale of the problem (global warming) and the pervasiveness of its consequences (substantive and widespread climate change) mean that criminology has also had to develop specific concepts to account for and respond to the resultant social and ecological harms.

Dedicated research on the nature of violence points to a wide range of causal factors that range from the macro-social through to the biological (Stubbs and Tomsen, 2016; Roth, 1994). For example, social structural explanations of street violence tend to view the phenomenon in terms of marginalisation of specific population groups (Hagedorn, 2008; White, 2013b). This marginalisation may have a number of interrelated dimensions, including economic (for example, poverty), social (for example, exclusion from mainstream institutions), political (for example, little or no representation) and cultural (for example, minority religious or language group). In effect, brutal social conditions provide the groundwork for angry and aggressive people, whose main resource is their body rather than capital or wages. Different risk factors combine, at different levels and according to different timelines, to collectively influence behaviour (Roth, 1994). Consideration of the roots of violence and its various manifestations leads inexorably to the conclusion that violence can only be diminished or prevented through a multi-pronged approached, backed up by considerable political will and social commitment.

Human behaviour and temperature change

Criminological research exploring the nature and dynamics of criminality associated with climate change has included the examination of the relationship between temperature changes and human behaviour. One issue is whether extreme weather conditions, especially heat waves, are related to increases in aggression and thereby criminal violence (Boyanowsky, 1999; Rotton and Cohn, 2003). Put differently, there appears to be a correlation between high temperatures and human irritability, with one outcome being increased propensity to commit crimes of violence. This is sometimes referred to as the General Affective Aggression Model (GAAM), which proposes that hot conditions raise irritability and may therefore elicit more aggressive responses from people exposed to these more extreme conditions (Anderson, 1989; Anderson et al, 1997).

It appears, for example, that there are increased levels of aggression in hot temperatures, with such aggression having a violent, emotional basis associated with hostility toward a target (Boyanowsky, 1999). This seems to be confirmed in work investigating the relationship between weather and violence in Baltimore, USA, which found that maximum daily temperature was positively associated with total trauma, intentional injury and gunshot wounds presenting to Johns Hopkins Hospital along with total crime, violent crime and homicides in Baltimore City (Michel et al, 2016).

The implications for this are far reaching. For example, a study examining the effect of weather on monthly crime patterns in the United States predicted that climate change will lead to substantial additional numbers of murders, rape, aggravated assaults and robberies, among other serious crimes (Ranson, 2014). Put simply, violence is a 'summer' event and 'hot weather' characteristic. This is reinforced by research that shows that seasonal fluctuations in violence peak during the warmer months of the year (Anderson et al, 1997).

A study in Tangshan, China came to similar conclusions. It found that there was a strong, positive correlation between temperature and both violent and property crimes. Relative humidity was also a factor in crime rates. This study likewise predicted increased rates of rape and violent robbery as temperatures rise over the course of the twenty-first century (Hu et al, 2017).

Other research has further suggested that changes at the individual level – namely, aggression related to heat – may contribute to collective violence during heat waves, such as street riots and mob violence (Boyanowski, 1999). In one meta-analysis that examined multiple types of human conflict, it was estimated that with each degree increase in temperature, there would be a corresponding increase in interpersonal conflict by 2.4 per cent and intergroup conflict by 11.3 per cent (Burke et al, 2015).

Changes to the physical environment, such as the introduction of mist sprays in bus shelters and use of temperature-controlled urban movement corridors could, in this scenario, reduce the effects of heat and, therefore, levels of aggression.

Situational approaches and place-based activities

The focus of situational approaches is on the connections between local weather, indoor/outdoor routines, specific places where people spend their time and with whom, and how this affects their propensity to engage in certain types of crime (Peng et al, 2011). It is suggested that this will vary depending upon ambient temperature and place, and population group. The routine activities theory (RAT) proposes that crime is likely to occur if there is a motivated offender, a suitable target and lack of a capable guardian (Cohen and Felson, 1979). Applied to the relationship between climate change and crime, this explanation suggests that temperature shifts related to climate change may mean that people adjust their typical seasonal routines and thereby the likelihood of crime opportunities (Cohen, 1990).

Ambient temperature is relevant both to daily heat and seasonal fluctuations in climate. For example, examination of daily temperatures and crime events in Philadelphia, USA, found that there were strong associations between higher temperatures and violent crime and disorderly conduct. Interestingly, this study also found that disorderly conduct and violent crimes are highest when temperatures were comfortable, especially during cold months (Schinasi and Hamra, 2017). This makes logical sense in that people would generally be more active (and interactive) when in comfortable rather than bitterly cold conditions. Likewise, rain and snowfall tend to have negative associations with trauma and crime (Michel et al, 2016).

Unsurprisingly, study of seasonal crime patterns in Vancouver, Canada, mirror these findings in that for all crime types the lowest percentage occurs in the winter season. For most crime types, assault and theft, for example, crime counts increase during spring and summer and then decrease again in the autumn. In summer, the key crime hot spots include the city's largest park (Stanley Park), popular beaches and shopping areas (Andresen and Malleson, 2013).

In a different example, in a place that does not feature the kind of weather experienced in Philadelphia or Vancouver, a study in Dallas, Texas, found that higher temperatures may encourage people to seek shelter in cooler indoor spaces, and therefore street crimes and other crimes of opportunity will thereby be subsequently decreased (Gamble and Hess, 2012).

Conversely, research in Beijing has found that while robbery is not correlated with weather, burglary is, insofar as it is correlated with sunlight hours and also varies by the season of the year (Peng et al, 2011).

In a similar vein, research has examined 'weather shocks' in India. This refers to the impact of temperature changes in what are described as harmful degree-months, during which mean temperatures are above 32 degrees centigrade (Iyer and Topalova, 2014). It was found that higher rainfall is associated with significantly lower levels of crime, including violent crimes such as murder and rape. On the other hand, higher average temperatures are associated with higher crimes against public order and crimes against women, particularly rape. Monthly temperatures and levels of precipitation were also seen to have significance in regards to crime rates and types in St Louis, suggesting that climate change may have a significant impact on crime (Mares, 2013).

Whether or not the weather will have such negative and apparently pervasive impacts depends very much on physical aspects of the built environment and social infrastructure in particular localities.

Social strains and communities on the move

General strain theory (a particular theoretical orientation within criminology, see below) has been used to explain the impact of climate change on crime in terms of the factors associated with climate change (such as rising temperatures and extreme weather events) which are, in turn, linked to criminogenic mechanisms such as social and personal strains, reduced social supports and social conflicts. It is argued that these will result in higher levels of individual, group, corporate and state crime (Agnew, 2011).

Agnew's work on general strain theory (GST) reconstituted the concept of strain by going beyond the objective strains identified in early research (such as those events or conditions that were thought to be universal) to include those strains that were stressful or negative for the individual (Agnew, 2006). For example, the closure of a large employer in a small town could be considered an objective strain; however, on closer investigation, some individuals may not be so badly affected or strained by this event (perhaps because other employment opportunities are available to them, or it may give the individual a chance to return to education to retrain in another field). Further, Agnew (2006) identified three categories of strain:

- loss of legal avenues to attain goals (such as loss of secure employment, or autonomy);
- loss of positively-valued stimuli (such as friends, romantic partners, money);

- experiences of negatively-valued stimuli (such as verbal and physical abuse).

According to Agnew and Brezina (2010) strains are most likely to result in criminal behaviour if they are thought by the individual to be (a) insurmountable, (b) unjust, (c), subject to limited social control, and (d) subject to pressure or incentive to act negatively. Within this framework, it is important to note that strains do not inevitably lead to crime or criminality. Some individual- and social-level factors 'immunise' individuals from responding to strain through crime.

The basic proposition of strain theory is that crime is a result of social disjuncture or social processes that represent a *social strain* within a society. Rather than looking solely at aspects of personal psychology or individual biological traits, this approach argues that crime is socially induced, thus locating the cause of crime in social structures and/or value systems that in some way are socially pathological. The pathology is generated from outside the normal life and decisions of ordinary citizens and residents.

Combining observations about different levels of analysis and substantive areas of criminality, Agnew (2011) explicates the impact of climate change on crime in terms of *factors associated with climate change* (rising temperature, rising sea level, extreme weather events, changing patterns of precipitation, habitat change, negative health effects, food/water shortages, loss of livelihood, migration, social conflict). These factors are, in turn, linked to *criminogenic mechanisms* (increased strain, reduced control, reduced social support, beliefs/values favourable to crime traits, opportunities for crime, social conflict). These lead to *higher levels of individual, group, corporate, and state crime.*

More generally, this kind of criminological analysis pitches explanation at a societal level first and foremost. This is also acknowledged in observations by the Intergovermental Panel on Climate Change (IPCC, 2014: 11):

> Climate change is projected to increase displacement of people...Populations that lack the resources for planned migration experience higher exposure to extreme weather events, particularly in developing countries with low income. Climate change can indirectly increase risks of violent conflicts by amplifying well-documented drivers of these conflicts such as poverty and economic shocks.

Events and situations that trigger climate-related migration will create all manner of opportunities for crime and violence, from human trafficking and illegal border crossings to gang stand-over tactics in the acquisition of food and water. Other kinds of violence stem from changing biophysical conditions as well. For example, suicide rates also increase in periods of extended drought and when farms become non-viable (Alston, 2012). Men are disproportionately involved in violence when income and food security is no longer possible.

Mass migrations and the burgeoning growth worldwide of megacities of 20 million people and more are viewed as major factors in increased violence. The megacity is seen not only as a reservoir of inequality, desperation and vulnerability, but a major crucible of crime (Crank and Jacoby, 2015; Agnew, 2011). Insecurities of place and position are exacerbated in the context of failing states and countries that simply do not have the resources to put into human services and social infrastructure (Crank and Jacoby, 2015). Thus, there are various causal factors, such as migration and urban concentration, and control factors, such as vulnerable states and lack of centralised social control, that shape the geopolitical context for climate change in a violent world (Crank and Jacoby, 2015). A form of 'climate apartheid' may well become entrenched as the world's wealthy move into secure residential enclaves; in essence, walled sanctuaries to isolate them from the milling masses of the megacity (Brisman et al, 2018).

Anticipated increases in violence are not simply based upon abstract forward projections. These predictions are derived from analysis of existing trends and practices, from actual known experiences. For example, research has demonstrated increases in reported levels of violence against women in post-disaster communities (Wachholz, 2007). Predicted rises in the number and intensity of natural disasters due to climate change is thereby likely to be correlated with increases in violence against women in those regions that experience extreme weather events. As Wachholz (2007: 178) comments: 'Life for many women after natural disasters is punctuated by violence, and this fact needs to be more deeply integrated into discussions about climate change as well as criminological perspectives on violence against women.' The point is also made that women are not only victims but have shown remarkable levels of resilience and resourcefulness in their responses to climate change (Wachholz, 2007), although gendered-based vulnerabilities (and capacities to respond) are not shared uniformly by women, and ultimately it is the inequalities in power that matter the most (Arora-Jonsson, 2011).

Climate change and carbon emissions crime

The heating up of the planet has also stimulated policy responses that, in turn, are associated with crime and criminality. The introduction of maximum carbon emission caps as part of international agreements on climate change, for example, has opened the door to carbon trading and the commodification of air pollution (Walters, 2013; Walters and Martin, 2013). Countries and companies are set annual emission allowances. Those who meet their targets are given 'carbon credit points' that can be traded as currency on international markets to polluters who exceed their targets. Not only does this not adequately deal with carbon emission production as such (Hansen, 2009), it has also provided opportunity for various types of crime.

For instance, carbon credits are typically 'held' in electronic depositories. As a consequence, hacking and phishing have occurred in multiple national registries (Gibbs et al, 2013). Hacking refers to knowingly accessing a protected computer without authorisation, while phishing involves fraud using account numbers or passwords to fake emails or websites. Credits are stolen electronically and then re-sold on the spot market. Other types of fraud related to government consumption taxes have been undertaken, as have fraud related to the purchase of carbon offset credits issues for emission reduction projects (such as, for example, tree planting projects) (Gibbs et al, 2013).

A big problem with carbon emission trading schemes is lack of guardianship. For instance, such schemes rely upon polluting industries and companies to honestly disclose emissions. But regulatory and policing authorities simply do not have the resources to monitor and ensure compliance, whether in the European Union or in regards to carbon offset projects located in the Global South (Walters and Martin, 2013). Verification is a serious matter and one that is integral to safeguarding against carbon fraud.

This was particularly borne out by the 'Dieselgate' scandal of 2015 involving the Volkswagen company. A respected German car manufacturer, Volkswagen, was found to have fraudulently claimed that its cars complied with emission standards when they had not. What is important is that the issue was not simply a matter of non-compliance. Rather, Volkswagen had installed software in at least 11 million of its cars worldwide – a so-called 'defeat device' – that detected emissions test situations and then automatically scaled down the settings of the engine to reduce nitrogen oxide levels to far below the output generated during normal use. In other words, the company intentionally cheated the regulators by fixing the results of the testing.

The cars in fact produced much more pollution than allowed for, and the deceit was built into the actual car engine design (Spapens, 2018). Lying was the norm in this instance.

When it comes to carbon emission crimes, there is also the issue of carbon colonialism as a form of climate injustice (Martin and Walters, 2013). This relates to interest in the role of forests as carbon sinks (on the part of businesses in developed countries) for which credits might be earned and finance provided to developing countries, particularly biodiverse countries such as in Latin America. The governments of such countries may gain financially from such arrangements, at the expense of local communities. For example, it has been alleged that a Norwegian company operating in Uganda leased its lands for a sequestration project that is said to have resulted in 8,000 people in 13 villages being evicted (Bulkeley and Newell, 2010: 48). The effects of the commodification of carbon thus puts pressure on communities located well away from the originating industries.

Processes of dispossession are fostered by the growth of the voluntary carbon trading market as well (that is, one that is not set up and/or mandated by government). Largely self-regulated, the voluntary market has been linked to a number of instances of deception and bribery. Some involve the distribution of fake carbon offset credits. Others involve potentially large sums of money being paid to intermediaries (including corrupt government officials) who make agreements without the consent or knowledge of local Indigenous communities (Walters and Martin, 2013). Land grabbing is not unknown when it comes to the conversion of traditional lands into profit-making enterprise.

Another form of carbon fraud is the market scam (Walters and Martin, 2013). This involves email and telephone contact in which brokers try to convince clients of the financial benefits of investing in the carbon emissions market. The sales pitch is designed to appeal to those who wish to invest their money ethically in environmentally friendly projects – such as carbon offset schemes. The problem, however, is that the investment schemes themselves may be fake. People are thereby scammed out of their investment dollars, in part precisely because they want to do the right thing. Both legal and illegal actors use basically the same types of arguments (sustainability, ethical behaviour, economic development, technological innovation) to persuade potential clients to invest in the voluntary carbon market (McKie et al, 2015). Ultimately, such market endeavours are problematic regardless of whether immediate client interests are served or not, since the carbon emissions still continue regardless of offsets.

From a critical green criminology perspective, it has been argued that the commodification of carbon and reliance upon markets is in and of itself part of the problem. Specific crimes are inevitable manifestations of 'solutions' that cannot realistically tackle the overarching issues of global warming causation. Carbon markets are, therefore, inherently limited:

> an uncontested, under-researched and unchallenged trade-oriented instrument, embedded as it is in discourses of environmentalism and climate change and granted social and economic visibility by powerful actors, has provided the contexts for fake offsets, fabrication of carbon certificates; bribery of government officials; and the exploitation of Indigenous and poor peoples in developing countries. (Martin and Walters, 2013: 39)

The specific crime and justice problems are generated by a solution that in itself does not fundamentally address the core issue of the day – stopping carbon emissions altogether.

Conclusion

This chapter has presented a variety of explanations and typologies relating to the crime–climate relationship. It is clear that there are many specific causes for particular kinds of crime, and that it is the immediate variables, persons and contexts that shape what occurs, why, where and how. It is also apparent that temperature and climate changes do have an impact on human behaviour, and these are related to broader structural factors such as global warming. There is an interface between structure and agency, and the global and the local, that substantiates commonality (crimes associated with climate change are ubiquitous) yet allows for difference (but how these crimes manifest in practice reflects localised circumstances and social relations).

Government policy and market responses to climate change also become important variables in the rise of new crimes and the movement of criminal networks and individuals into domains that hitherto did not exist. The carbon emissions credit market, for example, is precisely such a phenomenon.

For Climate Change Criminology, it is imperative to keep developing sustained analyses of climate-related crimes. It is also essential to consider the nature of victimhood and who and why certain groups or entities are victimised more than others. A major concern, as well, is to identify the main culprits and perpetrators responsible for the causes of global warming and thereby the consequences of climate change.

FOUR

Climate change catastrophes and social intersections

Introduction

The predictions of catastrophe have been realised in many places around the earth – already. These take the form of sporadic events such as cyclones and droughts. They also feature as longer-term or even permanent changes in living conditions stemming from, for example, rising sea levels. The problem is not 'natural disasters' as such, since these are an inevitable part of habitation on a living planet. Rather, it is the scale, frequency and intensity that matters, as well as the capacity of individuals and communities to predict, adapt to and respond after such events.

This chapter examines the consequences of climate change from the point of view of disasters and their consequences for specific interest and population groups. It does this in several ways. A key focus is the social intersections that become apparent in such events. For example, the climatic and weather events that form the backdrop to present conflicts in places such as Syria are discussed, as are the gendered vulnerabilities evident in disaster situations such as cyclones and tsunami. Social conflicts stemming from climate change are then elaborated as a more general and increasingly likely scenario. In response to real and perceived threats and risk linked to climate change, issues of security are already generating angst among policy-makers and military planners. The securitisation of natural resources, to the detriment of others, is emerging as an important climate-related issue, especially in regard to food, water, land and air quality.

Disasters and criminality

> Disasters are often described as a result of the combination of the exposure to a hazard, the conditions of vulnerability that are present, and insufficient capacity or measures to reduce or cope with the potential negative consequences of

> the hazard. (Official Terminology Guide, United Nations Office for Disaster Risk Reduction, 2018)

Those who are most vulnerable to the effects of climate change are those who are most likely to be vulnerable to events such as droughts, floods and cyclones. The conventional approach to disasters is to see them as 'natural' (and includes such things as earthquakes, volcanoes and floods) or human-caused (relating to fires, explosions and oil spills) (see Picou et al, 2009). In the context of major global changes in climate change, biodiversity and pollution, this presumption may no longer be warranted.

When formulating a definition of environmental victim, Williams (1996) points out that it is usually necessary to exclude those who are more accurately defined as 'environmental casualties', as this relates to those who have suffered as a result of natural disasters. This suffering, it is argued, is the result of chance. However, he goes on to point out that 'Some circumstances that appear natural may, if analysed in greater depth, be a consequence of human acts' (Williams, 1996: 19). As an example, he observes that 'Environmental suffering that has affected many generations, such as iodine deficiency, might not be seen as victimization until power relationships are examined. Why are the communities that suffer iodine deficiency forced to live on land that cannot sustain human life properly?' (Williams, 1996: 19). A similar logic extends to the impact and causes of recent climate change-related events. There is considerable blurring of natural and anthropogenic causes when it comes to human-created increases in global temperature that, in turn, generate massive new 'natural' phenomenon such as Superstorm Sally off the East coast of the US in 2012 or Hurricane Harvey in Texas in 2017. Not all disasters are the same, however.

Slow disasters

Borders mean very little in the case of many environmental harms, especially those pertaining to contamination, pollution and the movement of materials and particles through water and air (White, 2008; Schmidt, 2004; UNEP, 2006). Nor do borders have much material relevance when it comes to environmental harm associated with global warming. Climate change affects us all in different and similar ways, regardless of where we live, regardless of social characteristics.

It has been observed that those most vulnerable to the '*consequences of consequences*' of climate change are people living in poverty, in underdeveloped and unstable states, under poor governance (Smith and Vivekananda, 2007). Indeed, it has been estimated that over half the world's population is potentially at risk.

> There is a real risk that climate change will compound the propensity for violent conflict, which in turn will leave communities poorer, less resilient and less able to cope with the consequences of climate change. There are 46 countries – home to 2.7 billion people – in which the effects of climate change interacting with economic, social and political problems will create a high risk of violent conflict.
>
> There is a second group of 56 countries where the institutions of government will have great difficulty taking the strain of climate change on top of all their current challenges. In these countries, though the risk of armed conflict may not be so immediate, the interaction of climate change and other factors creates a high risk of political instability, with potential violent conflict a distinct risk in the longer term. These 56 countries are home to 1.2 billion people. (Smith and Vivekananda, 2007: 3).

The consequences of global warming will thus have the greatest impact on those least able to cope with climate-related changes, and whose governments are less resilient or have less political will to change. This has huge implications for everyone, including and especially the children and young people living in such circumstances.

Nor is climate change gender neutral. This is particularly apparent when considering continents like Africa where agriculture supports 70 per cent of the population. In the least developed countries, in Africa and elsewhere, 79 per cent of women who are economically active report agriculture as their primary economic activity. Yet only between 10 and 20 per cent of all landholders are women (UNDP, 2013). Women are especially vulnerable to the consequences of climate change, in part due to the prior disadvantages they suffer generally. For instance, compared to men, women have less access to land, financial services, livestock, social capital and access to technology. Impoverishment and lower social status weakens the ability of women to be resilient in the face of the burdens associated with climate change. These are compounded by the extra responsibilities associated with caring work for children, the ill and the elderly. Dramatic changes in temperature, climate and seasons exacerbate existing inequalities and hardships (UNDP, 2013; United Nations Women Watch, 2009).

Women who farm in the developed countries likewise suffer from the consequences of entrenched gender inequalities. A recent study in Australia has shown that a major outcome of years of drought (and subsequent introduction of water saving methods) is an increase in women's labour on and off the farms. It is anticipated that with further global warming, the nature of agricultural labour will continue to change, including greater contributions being asked of farming women. Yet women's labour remains largely taken for granted and is largely invisible in regard to policy development and national responses to climate change (Alston et al, 2018). At the heart of this, is the fact that, while women are active contributors as farmers, they rarely figure in agricultural land ownership. Climate change is leading to changed gender workloads and increased workloads for women, and yet women's input is still being treated as a 'farm survival strategy' rather than a major personal economic contribution by women to the enterprise (Alston et al, 2018: 12). The social costs are immense, especially for the health and wellbeing of both women and men.

These issues and developments are not hypothetical. Increasingly they are manifest in real world situations and real world developments. For instance, the war in contemporary Syria has its origins in a mix of climatic changes, adoption of neoliberal policies and radicalisation of politics (Gleick, 2014). For example, since 1975, Turkey's dam and hydro-power construction has cut water flow to Syria by 40 per cent and drought and poor water management has been drying up water sources everywhere. Between 2003 and 2009 the Tigris–Euphrates basin – comprising Turkey, Syria, Iraq and western Iran – lost water faster than any other place in the world except northern India (Gleick, 2014). Frictions started to emerge as different groups and rural clans laid claim to water resources, and the increasing dictatorship, imposed rule and corruption was met by growing dissent. Meanwhile, Syria's population grew from 3 million in 1950 to 22 million in 2012, further decreasing the country's total per capita renewable water availability (Gleick, 2014). One consequence of this is that the rural unemployed population migrated to the cities, where existing educated youth populations are already congregated. With cyber knowledge and being Internet savvy, many young people could see examples of political reform around the region. They were also experiencing unequal allocation of jobs, wealth, power and enhanced state rule through the military and the police (Gleick, 2014; see also White et al, 2017b).

In the period 2006–2011 Syria experienced multi-season, multi-year periods of extreme drought, contributing to agricultural failures, and further economic and population displacements. The trend toward privatisation of agricultural lands corroded customary law over boundary rights, and more than 1.5 million people, mostly agricultural workers and family farmers moved from rural lands to cities and camps on the outskirts of major cities (Gleick, 2014).

Civil war eventually erupted in 2011, with diverse rebel factions and major political differences, including the opportunism of the so-called Islamic State and their attempts to establish a regional caliphate. War has seen the reduction of many cities to rubble, there are few services outside of emergency provision, and survival is the first priority for those trapped in the conflict zones. The world has been exposed to the worst excesses of human brutality and indiscriminate killing and maiming – from government barrel bombs to jihadist beheadings. There has been the collapse of education and employment for children and young people; and asylum seekers seeking refuge outside the combat zones have been made into global pariahs. This example may well foreshadow similar events in other places in the near future if their circumstances parallel these.

While criminology that deals with climate change can find benefit from engagement in environmental horizon scanning (White and Heckenberg, 2011), so as to anticipate potential environmental issues and crime problems associated with climate change, some attempts to do so have been accused of conceptual over-reach. Thus, in commenting on Farrell's (2012) linking of droughts in the 1980–1984 seasons to the war in the Darfur region of Sudan, Southalan (2013) cautions that complex issues should not be reduced simply or solely to climate change (or specific weather events). Similar reservations may exist in regard to what is occurring in Syria at the time of writing, as described above.

While it is true that such claims require a degree of careful consideration, nonetheless, the association between global warming and changing social, economic and political circumstance is important. They certainly stimulate a series of important questions: do weather-related and resource-control events in Sudan and Syria foreshadow similar events and circumstances in other places around the world? In what ways is this internecine conflict linked to climate change? Is the violence due to similar causes or are there specific drivers? In the light of accelerating global warming, is the fate of these countries to be the fate of others?

There are, as well, other matters that arise from the study of slow crisis scenarios. These relate to the intersection of economic shifts, climatic changes and intergenerational distributions of wealth on a global scale. For example, social inequality looms large in the lives of many young people worldwide (France, 2016; White et al, 2017b; Oxfam, 2018). Under neoliberalism, the main plank of global capitalism, each individual is being forced to fend for themselves and this is elevated to the level of moral good – to fail at getting a job, an income, suitable welfare and an education is construed as personal failure in the marketplace, not a failure of the marketplace. The modern-day credo appears to be: you deserve what you do not get. Such policies and practices contribute to profound ontological insecurities and fears that frequently translate into a 'fortress mentality' (White, 2014). For many, personal security is thus constructed in relation to the notion of 'us' versus 'them' – as witnessed by the treatment of asylum seekers, the unemployed and those vulnerable to precarious life situations.

Social inequality and social exclusion can simultaneously underpin the drift toward radicalisation on the part of young people. The typical characteristics of radicalisation include such things as a sense of injustice or humiliation; response to perceived injustice against a group of people, who are not necessarily related to the protagonists; direct experience of disrespect and oppressive state intervention; a need for identity; and search for defining purpose or goal in life (Walklate and Mythen, 2015). Radicalisation can be reactionary or progressive (Jeffrey, 2010), but ultimately reflects a need to belong – both in terms of belonging in association with like-minded groups and in the sense of belonging to a cause that is bigger than oneself. It is also very much linked to large-scale transformations such as climate change. According to Mary Robinson, President of the Mary Robinson Foundation – Climate Justice, and former Irish President and United Nations Commissioner for Human Rights, 'Climate change is a threat multiplier – it exacerbates poverty and water scarcity, it compounds food and nutrition insecurity and it makes it even harder for poor households to secure their rights', and moreover, 'In a world where climate change exacerbates the stresses of daily life on people already disenfranchised by poverty or social standing, radicalisation is very likely' (Robinson, 2015). The links between inequality, radicalisation and climate change are thus real and pressing. Such realities also complicate matters of climate-induced migration and the re-settlement of population groups, particularly when framed within a security discourse.

Quick disasters

Research and commentary has also paid considerable and increasing attention to traditional natural disasters (White and Heckenberg, 2011; Rodriquez et al, 2007; Heckenberg and Johnston, 2012; UNEP, 2010a; 2010b) or what might be referred to here as quick or event-based disasters. Climate change is especially associated with these sorts of natural disasters, which are projected to increase in intensity and frequency in the foreseeable future. They include phenomena such as floods, cyclones and heat waves.

Study of disasters (both human-created and natural) has revealed substantial instances of criminality (Green, 2005; Thornton and Voigt, 2007). These include crimes pre-disaster (for example, poor construction standards such as omission of steel reinforcing in concrete), during the disaster (for example, looting, rape) and post-disaster (for example, insurance fraud, misappropriation of aid funds). The kinds of crimes associated with disasters include crimes against the person as well as corporate, white-collar and state crimes. Moreover, the scale of recent disasters, such as the 2011 floods in Pakistan, indicate other forms of criminality are associated with these events, including the collapse of public order, enforced climate-induced migration and the prevalence of local gang cultures. Global warming is a powerful driver of natural disasters as climate change fundamentally generates greater propensity toward extreme weather events.

Vulnerabilities to victimisation are not only due to geographical location, as such, but also to other inequalities. For example, many countries have coastal areas that are vulnerable to sea-level rise. The Netherlands, however, has the technological and financial capacity to protect itself to a greater extent than Bangladesh. Thus, not only are poorer countries less responsible for the problem, they are simultaneously least able to adapt to the climate impacts they will suffer because they lack the resources and capacity to do so. This raises three key questions surrounding matters of justice: the question of responsibility (for example, the North owes the South an 'ecological debt'); the question of who pays for action on mitigation and adaptation; and the question of who bears the costs of actions and inactions (see Bulkeley and Newell, 2010).

Disasters also generate other kinds of vulnerabilities, including and especially those based upon gender and age. The very young and the very old are particularly vulnerable to disease, social predation and inability to get out of harm's way. Men and women face different kinds of pressures, risk and vulnerabilities (see Table 4.1). While it may be true that women and children are especially vulnerable to violence, and specifically male violence, during disaster periods, not all men participate in this violence and many are themselves victims to it. Nonetheless, according to Heckenberg and Johnston (2012), women and children are at much more risk of sexual abuse during and after natural disasters than before, and more susceptible to disease and infections, as well as being vulnerable because of gender-specific phenomena such as being pregnant.

Table 4.1: Gender-based vulnerabilities in disaster responses

Issues	Male/Men	Female/Women
Activity	First responders	Forced to stay at home
Risk taking	Risk lives for victims	Risk lives for children
Proximity	Last to evacuate	Forced to evacuate
Assistance	Less assistance	Greater family responsibility
Needs	Finding work/income	Finding food and shelter
Victimisation	Sexual and physical violence	Sexual and physical violence
Perceptions	Seen as threat or perpetrators	Seen as victims
Living arrangements	Living alone	Enforced communal living
Uncertainties	Domestic duties	Head of household duties

Source: Drawing from Heckenberg and Johnston, 2012.

The discourses describing women – as vulnerable or virtuous – also shape how women generally are viewed and portrayed in regard to climate change issues. Too often this framing of the issues leaves begging fundamental questions regarding inequalities of power. They can also gloss over important specificities of context and circumstance (Arora-Jonsson, 2011: 750):

> Marginality needs to be viewed through the power relations that produce the vulnerability in the first place. Different power relations are privileged in different situations and class, gender, ethnicity or nationality assume importance depending on the context. The specificity of vulnerability may differ. A generalized belief in women's vulnerability silences contextual differences. Gender gets treated not as a set of complex and intersecting power relations but as a binary phenomena carrying certain disadvantages for women and women alone.

How best to deal with climate change is therefore partly a matter of understanding the nuances of difference and the contours of inequality across diverse lived situations.

There are hardships faced by all who go through natural disasters. These are immediate and pertain to survival from drowning, cyclonic winds and falling buildings. They are also longer term. Survivors frequently have psychological scars with which to cope as well as re-building tasks and forward planning chores. Lack of resources, community support and empathy from power brokers (witness President Trump's harangue of officials in Puerto Rico post-Hurricane Maria in 2017 [ABC News, 2017]) all factor into the progress or otherwise of post-disaster relief and re-establishment.

Climate change and conflict over resources

Diverse environmental uses have been associated with various social conflicts. One typology of conflict–environmental relationships by Brisman, South and White (2015), for example, identifies four particular categories of concern:

- conflict over natural resource provision;
- conflict over declining resources;
- conflict that destroys environments;
- conflict over natural resource extraction processes.

These may overlap in some instances. Overall, they signal that conflict over resources has several different dimensions (Brisman et al, 2015). Not all of these conflicts are directly caused by or stem from climate change. Most, however, are in some way associated with or relevant to global warming and its impacts. This is not surprising.

Human subsistence is based upon the use of a combination of renewable (for example, freshwater, forests, fertile soils) and non-renewable (for example, oil and minerals) resources, and the ability of the planet to provide a range of naturally provided goods and services. 'Ocean fisheries supply fish that are a *good*, while the stratosphere ozone layer renders a *service* by protecting life from high levels of ultraviolet radiation. Some renewables provide both goods and services: forests supply timber (a good) while also maintaining regional hydrological cycles (a service)' (Homer-Dixon, 1999: 47, emphasis in original).

Climate change affects natural resources as goods and services, especially in conjunction with other ecologically unsustainable practices.

Exploitation of natural resources is a major cause of armed conflict within and between communities and nation-states (Homer-Dixon, 1999; Klare, 2001; 2012; Le Billon, 2012). This is largely due to scarcity of resources, which can arise from depletion or degradation of the resource (supply), increased demand for it (demand), and unequal distribution and/or resource capture (structural scarcity) (Homer-Dixon, 1999). What humans do to the environment is directly implicated in the production of scarcity, and hence conflict. For instance, 'Deforestation increases the scarcity of forest resources, water pollution increases the scarcity of clean water, and climate change increases the scarcity of the regular patterns of rainfall and temperature on which farmers rely' (Homer-Dixon, 1999: 9).

Greenhouse gas (GHG) emissions, a major cause of global warming, are generated by existing industries and result in even further pressures on already vulnerable eco-systems. Arable land and potable drinking water are at a premium under such circumstances. These will be exacerbated under conditions of widescale climate change. Unsurprisingly, then, conflicts will likely become even more evident in relation to struggles related to the necessities of life, territorial claims, the exploitation of natural resources, and the mass movements of people (see Table 4.2).

Confrontations linked to the present realities of the North–South divide, and the legacies of imperialism and colonialism, constitute yet another dimension to the social conflicts mapped out above. Indeed, underpinning many of the conflicts occurring 'elsewhere' (that is, in the non-western world) are processes and decisions made in the metropole – particularly the United States and the European Union, but also, increasingly, China, India and Russia.

Climate change poses risks for food production

> Rural areas are expected to experience major impacts on water availability and supply, food security, infrastructure and agricultural incomes, including shifts in the production areas of food and non-food crops around the world. (IPCC, 2014: 11)

Who sets the overall ecological agenda is fundamental to the conflicts occurring now and into the future. Transnational corporations, in conjunction with hegemonic nation-states and local political elites, are implicated in many of the present changes occurring in global food production and consumption.

Table 4.2: Climate change and social conflict

Source of conflict	Examples	Illustrations
Necessities of life	Food, including land grabs and crop substitution	Food riots particularly in relation to grain prices [Mexico, Haiti, Indonesia, Cameroon]
	Water, scarcity as well as issues of quality and access	Water theft by large companies, including private water corporations [Bolivia, South Africa]
Territorial claims	New territorial claims Receding coastlines and desertification leading to loss of territory	Islands in the South China Sea [China, Vietnam, the Philippines] Waterways and lands in the Arctic [Greenland, Canada, USA, Russia, Norway, Sweden]
Exploitation of resources	Mining and alternative energy operations on prime agricultural land	Fracking and mega-mine operations [USA, Australia, UK]
	Bio-prospecting across the globe	Theft of plants and Indigenous knowledge and techniques under guise of legal patent processes [Brazil, Peru, Colombia]
Movements of people	Climate-induced migration	Sea-rise refugees [South Pacific Islands] Displacement of people due to drought [Horn of Africa]

The exploitation of the world's natural resources by the major transnational corporations occurs through the direct appropriation of lands, plants and animals as 'property' (including intellectual property as in the case of patents). It also occurs through the displacement of existing systems of production and consumption by those that require insertion into the cash–buyer nexus, in other words, the purchase of goods and services as commodities. This has happened in the area of food production as it has in other spheres of human life.

For example, the post-Second World War period saw a major shift in the status of developing countries from exporters of food to importers of food. Africa, for instance, was virtually self-sufficient in grain production in 1950; by 1998 it was heavily reliant upon outside producers. Western Europe, by contrast, had gone from net importer to major exporter of grains. North America, and Australia and New Zealand, systematically increased their share of world grain production over the same period of time (French, 2000).

One result of the shift in the world grain trade is that it transformed countries such as the Philippines from net food exporter to net food importer. The process involved structural adjustment practices, under the auspices of the World Bank and the International Monetary Fund. This consisted of the simultaneous phenomenon of state divestment from agricultural production (for example, lifting of price controls on fertiliser), and trade liberalisation that allowed heavily subsidised US and EU meat and grain producers to flood host markets with cheaper commodities. For example, 'From $367 billion in 1995, the total amount of agricultural subsidies provided by developed-country governments rose to $388 billion in 2004. Since the late 1990s subsidies have accounted for 40 percent of the value of agricultural production in the European Union and 25 percent in the United States' (Bello, 2008). The result has been the collapse of local producer capacities and markets, and the transformation from self-sufficiency among peasant producers to national dependency upon corporate supplied food (Bello, 2008).

What is happening to food generally is symptomatic of how commodification is taking place in regard to all aspects of human life and in all parts of the globe. For example, patent protection ensures that the big agribusiness companies are able to control markets and production processes (White, 2008; Mgbeoji, 2006). This is based upon patents of existing organic materials (that is, through bio-piracy) and technological developments (that is, through genetic modification of organisms). The point is to make direct producers – the farmers – reliant upon commercially bought seeds (and related products such as fertiliser and pesticides). In essence, control is out of the hands of the direct producers, and the product (especially if crops such as soya or corn are grown primarily for biofuels not food) is unrelated to the real need of those consumers positioned outside of the profit maximisation process. The food riot, thus, has its origins in global systems and strategic decisions made in the boardrooms of the rich and powerful. Reliance upon commercial monocultures, in turn, also reduces capacity and resilience in regard to adapting to the consequences of global warming.

Climate-induced migration

> Current estimates of the number of 'climate refugees' and 'environmental migrants' by 2050 range from 25 million to 1 billion people, and the number could soar still higher later in the century if GHG emissions are not seriously reduced. Yet, there is no international agreement on the rights of persons displaced by climate change or the obligations of countries to respect them. (UNEP, 2017: 32)

When subsistence fishing, farming and hunting wither due to overexploitation and climate change, then great shifts in human populations and in resource use take place. The relationship between environmental change, climate-induced displacement and human migration is already generating much angst within western governments and is reinforcing the development of a fortress mentality within particular jurisdictions (whether this is the joined-up countries such as the European Union or discrete nation-states such as Australia and, of course, the United States).

While the phrase 'environmental refugee' is contentious (Castles, 2002), displacement of people due to environmental-related causes has major legal, human rights and national security concerns (McAdam and Saul, 2008; Refugee Studies Centre, 2008). This is not a new problem; such migrations have been experienced in Southern Africa (Singh, 1996) and are presently at the top of the agenda for many Islanders living in the South Pacific.

In the light of climate change, consideration also has to be given to matters such as systemic crop failure, and resultant survival and migration strategies. Changes in local weather conditions affect how people behave psychologically and socially, including participation in activities that may involve poaching and illegal harvesting (Mares, 2010). Climate change induced migration may lead people to either fight over diminished resources in one area (Barnett and Adger, 2007) or leave affected areas, with possible conflict arising in the receiving areas (Reuveny, 2007; Barnett and Adger, 2007).

Moreover, farmers who are forced to leave land that is no longer productive have several immediate issues to grapple with, such as where to live, what to do, how to earn an income, and with whom. For young men in particular, this makes them vulnerable to being recruited into criminal organisations. As one commentator puts it:

> But what happens to young men who no longer have a productive path forward, whether it is on the farm or in the city? They are going to be ripe to be recruited into criminal organizations, whether cartels or human smuggling networks, that can pay them something and give them a sense of status and pride that they don't have starving on a farm. (Oliver Leighton Barrett, retired US Navy lieutenant, quoted in Albaladejo and LaSusa, 2017)

In regions such as South America, Central America and the Horn of Africa, and countries such as Venezuela, Brazil and Somalia, these are present-day and persistent matters of concern. The conundrums of survival mean that at least for some, victimisation caused through climate change could well result in the 'victims' becoming 'offenders' due to the severe restrictions in life options accompanying displacement (Hall and Farrall, 2013).

These particular circumstances, trends and perceptions generate additional realities and responses, including those revolving around migration and security. From the point of view of national interests and international security, for instance, the mass movement of peoples is generally presented as a significant problem (Solano and Ferrero-Waldner, 2008), not least of which because of perceived criminality (and, indeed, perceptions that migrant flows also provide potential space for the movement of terrorist infiltrators). In particular, there is a popular inclination to view third-world ecological ruin as first and foremost a threat to first-world stability and existing wealth. The climate-induced migrant is therefore most likely to be subjected to criminalisation and law enforcement rather than dealt with on the basis of humanitarian issues. As environmental conditions deteriorate due to global warming, the size and extent of migration will be shaped by the combination of geography (for example, places where there is a shortage of fresh water), concern for or abrogation of human rights in potential host countries, and domestic political policy regarding sanctuary for climate-related (and indeed, other) migrants.

It is not only humans who are migrating. Global warming is also radically changing present ecological settings when it comes to the relationship between particular kinds of habitat and particular species of animal and plant. Non-human species are migrating as well (Macaulay, 2016).

The phenomenon of assisted colonisation, which involves the moving of species to sites where they do not currently occur or have not been known to occur in recent history, also signals the nature of the dilemma. This is happening in response to climate change, and is usually directed at species in the wild (for example, see Sutherland et al, 2009).

The movement of non-native species into new ecosystems is well recognised as a major conservation problem (SCBD, 2010). This is evidenced, for example, by the rapid expansion in the numbers of Indo-Pacific lionfish along the east coast of the United States and in the Caribbean which is having a serious impact on native coral reef fish. Similarly, the introduction of the cane toad in Australia has left a devastating impact on native wildlife. The effect of such migrations on food production and farming efforts is considerable. This, too, will compound the problems of those coping with impacts of climate change on agriculture.

For those species unable to move, the situation is increasingly dire. As pointed out by the Intergovernmental Panel on Climate Change (IPCC, 2014), a large fraction of species faces increased extinction risk due to climate change during and beyond the twenty-first century. For example, most plant species cannot naturally shift their geographical ranges sufficiently fast to keep up with current and high projected rates of climate change in most landscapes; most small mammals and freshwater molluscs will not be able to keep up in flat landscapes in this century. It is further observed that 'Future risk is indicated to be high by the observation that natural global climate change at rates lower than current anthropogenic climate change caused significant ecosystem shifts and species extinctions during the past millions of years' (IPCC, 2014: 10). This list of probable mortalities goes on. Marine organisms will face progressively lower oxygen levels and high rates and magnitudes of ocean acidification, with associated risks exacerbated by rising ocean temperature extremes. Coral reefs and polar ecosystems are highly vulnerable. Coastal systems and low-lying areas are at risk from sea level rise, which will continue for centuries even if the global mean temperature is stabilised (IPCC, 2014: 10).

For human and non-human species there are risks and dilemmas regardless of whether they stay put or move on. Either way, there is danger. Insecurity is and will continue to be the hallmark of the next decades and centuries to come.

Securitisation of resources

Diminished human security stems from the biophysical and socio-economic consequences of various sources of threat and damage to the environment, including and especially climate change. The pressures on the essential building blocks of life are complex and contradictory (see Table 4.3). Shortages of food, fresh water, clear air and adequate energy sources can, in turn, trigger criminal activities involving organised criminal networks, transnational corporations and governments at varying political levels. The race is on to secure resources.

While climate change has global consequences, the extent of the impact varies depending on the vulnerability of particular locales, social groups and livelihoods. Diverse circumstances give rise to a range of responses, from the continuation of unsustainable production practices and the systematic hoarding of food, through to widespread social unrest linked to food scarcity and criminality such as individual theft and pilfering.

Environmental security refers to the idea that natural resources such as fresh water, fish, and trees need to be protected and secured for the public benefit of those living within nation-states. The rich and powerful will continue to use their resources to secure productive lands, restrict access to food and water, exploit the financial hardships of others, and impose their own coercive rule (private security and private armies is a contemporary growth industry worldwide). However, the moral and material universe within which these trends occur is one that is generally supportive of this sort of natural resource exploitation. In other words, the ravaging of nature generally takes place with the *consent* of its beneficiaries, among whom are the general populaces of advanced industrialised countries (Agnew, 2013; White, 2014). It is the relative privilege of those in the Global North that outweighs concern for the plight of their neighbours in the Global South, regardless of where each lives, works or engages as part of a community.

Thus, at a concrete level, the social construction of 'security' in an environmental context frequently privileges the rights and interests of the powerful over the public interest. Environmental security is basically a form of *securitisation* that protects financial interests rather than ensuring fair and equal access for all. In pursuit of the ownership and control over natural resources, and to exploit these for particular purposes, governments and companies have singularly and in conjunction with each other worked to break laws, bend rules and undermine participatory decision-making processes. Sometimes this takes the form of direct state–corporate collusion (state–corporate crime); in other instances, it involves manoeuvring by government officials or company executives to evade the normal operating rules of planning, development, and environmental impact assessment (for example, by passing laws allowing 'special treatment').

Demand is escalating worldwide for commodities of all types and increasingly there are scarcities of specific resources, leading to a proliferation of ownership contests. Security is thus also being sought through the appropriation of resources in specific biosocial locations, leading to a proliferation of ownership contests (for example, disputed islands involving China, Vietnam, the Philippines and Japan; re-drawing of boundaries in the Arctic among border states such as Russia, Canada, Norway and the United States). Meanwhile, to guard against immediate food shortages, government-backed agricultural firms in China, South Korea, Saudi Arabia and the United Arab Emirates are already buying vast tracts of arable land in Africa and elsewhere (including for example, Australian dairy farms) to provide food for consumption at home (Brisman, 2013b). The violence of war lurks not far behind the intensified securitisation of nature.

Table 4.3: Pressures on basic essentials of life

Basic essential	Trends	Examples	Impacts	Outcomes
Energy	Decline of traditional fuels Increase in use of alternative energy sources	Drop in coal prices Decline in traditional oil reserves Developments in solar, hydro and wind power	Higher energy prices for consumers Policy settings that signal shift toward renewable energy and energy efficiency	Pursuit of extreme energy sources such as fracking, deep sea oil drilling Biofuels and increased global emissions Resistance to alternative energy targets
Land	Desertification and droughts Less arable land for food production relative to population Loss of habitat and biodiversity	Diminishment of soil health Land grabs by companies and nation-states on a global scale	Less productive food sources Famine Displacement and dispossession of traditional land owners Species extinction and displacement	Greater reliance upon industrial food production Contributions to greenhouse gases via pastoral industry Deforestation and crop substitution
Water	Diminishment of fresh water reserves worldwide Pollution of oceans, rivers and seas	Melting of glaciers and polar ice fields Evaporation due to extreme heat spells Habitat for marine and aquatic life at threat	Thirst and failure to secure enough water for human survival and food production Species extinction and displacement	Water as tradable commodity and source of profit Privatisation of water supply Failure of international protocols and agreements to protect water sources, quality and quantity
Air	Pollution Changes in composition of atmospheric gases due to global warming	Diminishment in air quality in specific locales Diminishment in air quality across the planet due to global warming	Increased breathing and related health problems Detrimental effects for non-human animals and plants	Fresh air as luxury commodity linked to location Higher mortality and morbidity rates

The flexing of military muscle also contributes directly to the problem of climate change. Consider, for example, the ecological costs of securing the climate future, at least from a US point of view: 'the Pentagon is the single largest consumer of oil in the world. There are only 35 countries, in fact, that consume more oil than the Pentagon' (Baer and Singer, 2009: 38). From greenhouse gas emissions to environmental degradation, the operational demands of the military are enormous. The US military, for example, has a heavy reliance upon energy-inefficient equipment and vehicles. The social processes of war are themselves implicated in climate change: 'global warming and war are thus mutually reinforcing, with war and war production fuelling global warming and global warming pushing countries to war' (Baer and Singer, 2009: 39). Responding to this kind of climate-related challenge will require conceptualisations of harm that acknowledge inequality for the evil it is, as well as the evils that stem from perpetuating it.

Conclusion

August 2017 was a month of tragedy and disaster. The main problem was water – this time, in the form of rain. Flooding in Bangladesh, India and Nepal killed an estimated 1,200 people during the region's worst monsoon season in a decade. Although many fewer were killed in Texas during the same period, the deluge unleashed by hurricane Harvey caused damage in the range of US$100 billion. Who knows how many non-human animals and plants were submerged, soaked and devastated by the high winds and incessant downpours.

This was also the month when climate change 'slow crisis' (heating up of the planet) was finally being acknowledged as a contributor to climate change 'quick crisis' (specific immediate disasters). Contemporaneous media commentary put it this way:

> As tropical storm Harvey moved towards the Texas coast last week, few models predicted it would intensify into such a damaging weather system. It then hit an ocean patch in the Gulf of Mexico that remained so hot over the northern winter that it broke temperature records…On the day Harvey hit, the area was around 2.2 degrees hotter than normal. Fuelled by the aberrant water temperature Harvey grew rapidly into a category-four cyclone as it hit the coast. It is now trapped in place over Houston, constantly siphoning energy and moisture from an ocean that scientists

> agree is likely to have been warmed by climate change. (Comment, *Sydney Morning Herald*, Wednesday 30 August)

This all occurred at a time when the USA had formally withdrawn from the Paris climate agreement, when President Trump rescinded regulations that would have made urban development and infrastructure more flood resilient, and the head of the American Environmental Protection Agency, Scott Pruitt, had made it clear that dismantling the EPA's efforts to combat climate change was high on his agenda. Later, in December 2017, the Trump administration dropped climate change from the list of global threats in its new national security strategy (Borger, 2017).

Catastrophe and the responses to it are defined by those most affected. Worldwide, disasters related to climate change have tended to have most impact upon the poor and vulnerable. Those with the capacity to build stronger, higher and better are those most likely to survive. They are also those who have the resources to rebuild and to thrive afterwards. For the rest, the choices are less clear, the options reduced. Those who have, want to retain it. Those who do not have, do what they can to survive. In this gulf between have and have-not lie many struggles and fundamental conflicts. The result is insecurity for all.

FIVE

Climate change victims

Introduction

Social division features greatly in any discussion of climate change justice and victimisation. It is the disadvantaged (those living in poverty), the vulnerable (the very young and the very old) and the dispossessed (Indigenous peoples subjected to colonisation) who are most likely to suffer the worst effects of global warming. These divisions are overlaid by entrenched disparities based upon class division, gender differences and inequalities based upon 'race' (a social rather than biological construction) and ethnicity.

The overarching structural basis for unequal power relations worldwide is global capitalism, a system that is intrinsically based upon exploitation of humans (as workers and consumers) and non-human animals and environmental entities (rivers, trees and mountains). Plundering the planet is ingrained in the political economy of late capitalism. Along with the human victims, there is also destruction of ecosystems, places, and flora and fauna. The core elements of life itself are under attack.

This chapter considers the notion of victimhood as this pertains to climate change. Consideration is given to both human and non-human environmental victims. Special attention is paid to the vulnerability of children and how this fits with notions of intergenerational equity. The particular circumstances and plight of Indigenous peoples globally are also critically examined.

Not all victims or forms of victimisation are considered. Rather, the intent is to broach important areas for investigation by Climate Change Criminology, without implying that specific and additional analysis of phenomena such as gender and victimisation, victimisation related to disability, and other forms of victimisation do not likewise deserve concentrated attention.

Human and non-human environmental victims

Green or environmental victimology refers to the study of the social processes and institutional responses pertaining to victims of environment crime (White, 2015a). Typically, it is humans who are the primary focus of such study (Hall, 2013). Recent criminological commentary, however, has placed attention on non-human animals as 'victims' (Flynn and Hall, 2017) as well as other non-human environmental entities (White, 2018).

For Climate Change Criminology, environmental victimisation is not a solely human or non-human animal experience but incorporates these other considerations as well. Rivers, mountains, animals and plants, and specific ecosystems, for instance, can all be considered 'victims' in particular circumstances (Preston, 2011; Cullinan, 2003). Indeed, more expansive definitions of rights and justice extend the definition of 'victim' to include the non-human across various conceptual domains. An eco-justice perspective frames this in terms of the particular subject or object that is harmed (White, 2013a).

- *Environmental justice* – **the victims are humans**
  Environmental rights are seen as an extension of human or social rights so as to enhance the quality of human life, now and into the future.
- *Ecological justice* – **the victims are specific environments**
  Human beings are merely one component of complex ecosystems that should be preserved for their own sake.
- *Species justice* – **the victims are animals and plants**
  Animals have an intrinsic right to not suffer abuse, and plants to not have their habitat degraded to the extent that it threatens biodiversity.

Environmental victimisation occurs in different forms and takes place in diverse locations. It is ubiquitous although there are important qualitative differences in regard to the nature, dynamics and seriousness of the harm as these pertain to non-human animals, ecosystems, plant species and human populations.

Commentators such as Stone (1972) have employed the term 'natural object' to describe non-living entities such as rivers, mountains and oceans. Fauna, or animal life, is ordinarily dealt with through the use of the term 'animal' (which can be sub-divided into, among other categories, 'native wildlife' and 'threatened species'), while flora (plant life) is ordinarily referred to under the broad category of 'vegetation' (Sankoff and White, 2009; Bates, 2013). An ecosystem has been defined in key international conventions as 'a dynamic complex of plant, animal and micro-organism communities and their non-living environment interacting as a functional unit' (SCBD, 1992). Together these entities comprise what can be described as *non-human environmental entities*. Consideration of the non-human environmental entity incorporates discussion of individual landscape features (such as hills and valleys) and specific living entities (such as flora and fauna), through to particular ecosystems. Any ecosystem is made up of abiotic components (air, water, soil, atoms and molecules) and biotic components (plants, animals, bacteria and fungi) (Merchant, 2005). When destruction, degradation or diminishment of these occurs due to global warming, then this can be seen as a form of climate change-related victimisation.

Defining 'victimhood' is ultimately a matter of perspective and philosophy. As discussed in Chapter Two, for example, ecocentrism refers to viewing the environment as having value for its own sake apart from any instrumental or utilitarian value to humans. A tripartite or composite eco-justice perspective – one that incorporates consideration of humans, ecosystems, and non-human animals and plants – is premised upon enhanced legal and social recognition of non-human interests. Thus, when harmed by human-caused processes or events, the biosphere and non-human biota also can be considered victims (Preston, 2011).

Environmental harm of any kind has traditionally been ignored, downplayed or trivialised, socially and legally, and thus, so too, has its victims (Hall, 2013; White and Heckenberg, 2014). In part this is the result of perceptions of environmental crime as 'victimless' to the extent that 'they do not always produce an immediate consequence, the harm may be diffused or go undetected for a lengthy period of time' (Skinnider, 2011: 2). This is further compounded by the condoning of environmentally harmful activities by governments, industry and in some cases particular communities and society as a whole.

In regard to those non-human environmental entities and humans negatively affected by climate change, this translates into a failure to recognise them as victims of crime. Indeed, one of the lessons of critical victimology is that being and becoming a victim is never socially neutral (Davies et al, 2017; Fattah, 2010). This holds true for climate change-related victimisation as it does for other sorts of victim-making (Flynn and Hall, 2017). An eco-justice approach demands that how humans interact with their environment be evaluated in relation to potential harms and risks to specific creatures and specific places as well as the biosphere generally. This involves critical analysis of human intervention in the affairs of the natural world (White, 2013a).

For example, sudden changes in temperature as well as longer-term shifts in climatic conditions have enormous implications for animals and plants (Sundström et al, 2014). Heat stress increases mortality in animals and can make them less able to withstand disease. Temperature changes will simultaneously change the composition of grass species, thereby affecting food sources for grazing animals. The shortage of adequate supplies of fresh water also has ramifications for the spread of disease and general health and wellbeing.

Climate change is altering the physical and biological world in many ways and non-human environmental entities are not immune to its effects. For instance, the threats to biodiversity are many and profound, including reliance upon genetically modified organisms (GMOs) and monocultures, a situation likely to be made worse by the consequences of climate change (SCBD, 2010). These trends also affect resilience. For instance, 'over the ages farmers have relied upon diverse crop varieties as protection from pests, blights and other forms of crop failure' (French, 2000: 61). Reducing this diversity affects the inbuilt mechanisms that helped to protect the soil and the vitality of the overall agricultural process. Moreover, intensive use of land and soils that rely upon chemical additives to ensure productivity, rather than, for example, traditional methods of crop rotation, further diminishes longer-term agricultural viability. Contemporary farming practices that feature biodiverse fields (based upon many different types of seed crops) have not only been found to be more resilient to frost, drought and variations in rainfall, but to produce more food and cash earnings than that of corn monoculture (Shiva, 2008). Diversity is strength, but the industrialisation of agriculture is pointing us in the wrong direction.

Close scrutiny of the conditions pertaining to the human and non-human reveal instances of shared victimisation, as in the case of climate change, in which many different species and ecosystems are affected, somehow. There are also instances of specific victimisation, as in the case of some plant and animal species being vulnerable to harm but which may be unacknowledged due to remoteness of location or general human de-valuing of species. As with humans, there will be differing degrees and durations of harm, injury and, in some cases, suffering as this pertains to animals and natural objects.

Universal and differential victimisation

> Climate change will amplify existing risks and create new risks for natural and human systems. Risks are unevenly distributed and are generally greater for disadvantaged people and communities in countries at all levels of development. (IPCC, 2014: 10)

Everyone is affected by global warming. As a form of 'universal victimisation', climate change means that we all lose out, regardless of class, gender, ethnicity, race, tribe or caste; and regardless of whose fault it is. As previously noted in Chapter One, Superstorm Sandy in 2012 in the US was not a 'once in a generation' phenomenon. It was simply part of the beginning of the predicted consequences flowing from human-caused global warming.

Yet, there are environmental issues that are specific to particular regions of the world, and the causal processes and effects of climate change will vary according to the peculiarities of each region. For example, huge tropical forests are found in the Amazon basin, an area that encompasses several different countries such as Brazil and Colombia. Such forests also cover parts of South-East Asia, spanning Indonesia, Malaysia, Thailand and Myanmar (Burma), among other countries. What happens to these forests is part of the delicate balance of carbon emission and carbon storage that is so central to global warming. Their specific problem of de-forestation is magnified into our general problem of climate change. We are all implicated in processes that ultimately have consequences for the planet as a whole.

The effects of climate change, while felt by everyone, are not, however, the same for everyone. Claims to a universal victimisation (Beck, 1996) in fact belie crucial differences in how different groups and classes of people are placed quite differently in relation to key risk and protective factors (White, 2008). Social conflict linked to climate change is as much as anything a reflection of social inequality, and not simply determined by changes in environmental conditions.

A lot depends, of course, on where one lives. This has both geographical and economic dimensions. For example, it has been observed that many rich countries are located in the mid to higher latitudes. Poorer countries are concentrated in the lower latitudes, that is, in the hottest parts of the planet. As temperatures rise in the tropics and sub-tropics, people there will suffer heat-related deaths at higher rates than their more geographically and financially privileged counterparts. Even so, an increased number of heatwaves that are simultaneously more intense also means more deaths regardless of geographical location. For example, as pointed out by Liz Hanna, an expert on the impacts of climate change on human health, in the 2003 European heatwave, 70,000 people died in Western Europe and in a 2010 heatwave a further 55,000 people died in Russia and Eastern Europe. The decade 2001–2010 saw a 2,300 per cent increase in heat deaths above the previous decade (quoted in Readfearn, 2017). Regardless of whether this percentage figure is due to better data collection methods or actual increases, this is a lot of people and the problem does seem to be getting worse.

The vulnerabilities to victimisation are not only due to geographical location as such, but also to other inequalities. As noted in Chapter Four, many countries have coastal areas that are vulnerable to sea-level rise but they vary greatly in resources and capacity to respond to the challenges that lie ahead.

In the context of global warming, declining oil resources and food crises puts even more of the world's ecological and economic burdens on the backs of the poor. As Shiva (2008: 5–6) observes:

> First, they are displaced from work; then they bear a disproportionate burden of the costs of climate chaos through extreme droughts, floods, and cyclones; and then they lose once more when pseudo-solutions like industrial biofuels divert their land and their food. Whether it is industrial agriculture or industrial biofuels, car factories or superhighways, displacement and forced evictions of Indigenous peoples and peasants from the land are an inevitable consequence of an economic model that creates growth by extinguishing people's rights.

Various kinds of land acquisitions are having major negative impacts on local people who are losing access to and control over the resources on which they depend, and which are the rightful inheritance of future generations (Duffy, 2010; Bulkeley and Newell, 2010). Peasants, Indigenous peoples, and artisans who live outside the industrialised globalised economy, who have caused the least harm to the earth or other people, are among the most badly affected victims of climate change consequences. Over 96 per cent of disaster-related deaths in recent years have taken place in developing countries. In 2001, there were 170 million people affected by disasters around the world, of which 97 per cent were climate-related (Shiva, 2008: 3).

Differential victimisation associated with climate change reflects social position. The poor and vulnerable suffer from the violence linked with climate change more than the rich and powerful. It is not the affluent who are losing their lands, struggling to make ends meet, and being forced into climate-related migration. Likewise, it is the poorer countries, many of which have contributed the least to global warming processes, which are bearing the brunt of the biophysical changes linked with climate change. Powerful companies and their executives, and hegemonic nation-states and their leaders, are generally immune from the distributional impacts of climate change (that is, instances of harm that are influenced by social situation and ability to marshal needed resources). They are likewise generally freed from having to pay recompense to vulnerable countries and population groups, or funding adaptive measures, even though they are the main contributors to the problem.

Climate change and the world of the young

For children and young people, the present can seem pretty scary as it is already a time when people are fighting and at worst killing each other over water and food. It is a world in which genetically modified organisms promise to feed the masses, yet hunger is more entrenched than ever. It is a world filled with lies and deceit orchestrated by leaders holding the top offices. It is a world rapidly heating up, both literally and metaphorically.

In relation to climate change, the perception and position of children and young people will increasingly hinge upon the distinction between 'the stigmatised' and 'the privileged', particularly as these categories are produced and reproduced on a world scale. For example, the youth who suffer due to extreme weather events, such as floods or cyclones, will be re-presented as 'environmental victims' in the sense of suffering from 'an Act of God'. This is because such events have a tendency to be deemed 'natural disasters', regardless of human interventions (including global warming) that may set these in train.

Conversely, these same young people may be criminalised should they dare to set foot in a boat and attempt to migrate to safer lands and safer climes. The climate-induced migrant is likely to continue to attract negative labels, as the bona fide 'victim' morphs into the 'illegal immigrant'. Again, circumstance and the power to label will dictate master status and key identifiers. Victims are fine when they stay where they are, but are unwanted when they get too close. This process will, yet again, reflect global inequalities and the abrogation of social justice as this applies to certain select youthful population groups (White, 2015b).

Public trust and public interest law have been used selectively worldwide to establish future generations as victims of environmental crime (Preston, 2011; Mehta, 2009). These should now include interests related to the impact of global warming. A vital concept, especially in regard to human interests, is the notion of intergenerational equity, which has three core ideas (Brown Weiss, 1992; see also Brown

Weiss, 2008): conservation of options, conservation of quality and conservation of access.

Conservation of options

Each generation should be required to conserve the diversity of the natural and cultural resource base, so that it does not unduly restrict the options available to future generations in solving their problems and satisfying their own values, and should also be entitled to diversity comparable to that enjoyed by previous generations.

This concept is based on the notion that diversity, like quality, contributes to the robustness of eco-systems and cultural systems alike.

Conservation of quality

Each generation should be required to maintain the quality of the planet so that it is passed on in no worse condition than that in which it was received, and should also be entitled to planetary quality comparable to that enjoyed by previous generations.

This concept relates to ecological sustainability and the importance of maintaining balances as part of ongoing change.

Conservation of access

Each generation should provide its members with equitable rights of access to the legacy of past generations and should conserve this access for future generations.

This concept relates to not degrading what is available and to ensuring effective non-discriminatory access – among the human generations – to the Earth and its resources. This, however, is complicated by the expectation that present generations will be sensitive to the interests of people in the future, at which time there may be many more people populating the planet than at present. Current family and fertility policies and population trends therefore have implications for how access might possibly be construed and provided for under quite different demographic conditions (Schneeberger, 2011).

It is essential to view intergenerational equity as a temporal concept that points in two directions – to the past, and to the future. As members of this present generation we hold the Earth in trust for future generations, while at the same time we are beneficiaries of its resources. Equity must flow to present generations from past generations, while simultaneously present generations must ensure that equity flows to future generations. Moreover, the dynamics of nature (both human and non-human) demands attention to the vagaries of change that naturally occur over time.

The temporal nature of intergenerational equity means there are inherent links between inter-generational equity and intra-generational equity. This is because the obligation is for each generation to pass the planet on in no worse condition than it received it in, and to provide equitable access to its resources and benefits. The planet marks out the scale of the obligation. Therefore, equality of rights extends in time as well as space to embrace both generations and geographical regions (and the people who inhabit these). This observation is particularly relevant to the examination of children and intergenerational equity.

Ecocide as an outcome of the failure to address global warming is not just a theoretical debate about abstract propositions. The casualties of climate change are disproportionately found among the most vulnerable population groups. Intergenerational equity refers to 'vertical equity' (that cuts across generations over time) and to 'horizontal equity' in which equality of rights extends across population groups as well as time.

The health and wellbeing of the next generation is entirely contingent upon how children of the present generation are cherished and nurtured. Climate change challenges the Planet's capacity to do this.

The special vulnerabilities of children to environment-related harms are demonstrated in the following observations.

Children are especially vulnerable

> While acknowledging that childhoods around the world are very different and that children do not comprise a self-evidently unitary group (any more than do 'women' or 'people of colour'), we can still see ways in which the special characteristics of children's biology and development represent a foundation for regarding children as a special category of environmental victims. (Stephens, 1996: 75)

Differential risks

In the use of pesticides to prevent the spread of disease borne by mosquitoes, there are 'hidden' costs that may not be factored in. For instance, children and those with chemical sensitivities will suffer disproportionately if chemicals are sprayed, since they are more vulnerable than others to ill effects arising from the treatment. In such circumstances, the crucial questions are not only 'How many will be harmed?' but also 'Who will be harmed?' (Scott, 2005: 56). To appreciate this, we need to be conscious of differences within affected populations.

Constructing risk

The risk assessment process by which 'safe levels' of exposure to chemicals and other pollutants are assessed is highly problematic, and incorporates a range of ideological and moral assumptions. As Field (1998: 90) comments, 'The use of the apparently reasonable scientific concept of average risk, for example, means that data from the most sensitive individuals, such as children, will not be the basis for regulation, but rather data from the "statistically average" person.' Thus, science provides grounds upon which we may base judgements, but these grounds are not necessarily neutral in terms of social impact.

Bigger risks

'Special attention should be devoted to children because they are generally more vulnerable than adults to environmental hazards. They breathe more air and consume more food and water relative to their size than adults, their bodies are still developing and they have little control over their environment.' (WHO, 2009: 12). The message is that children are not 'little adults' and are especially vulnerable to environmental hazards, to the extent that 'Recent estimates suggest that almost 90% of the global burden of disease from climate change is borne by children' (WHO, 2009: 12).

All children are vulnerable, but some are more vulnerable than others

> 'Each day, the scale of injustice occurring on Indian soil, is catastrophic. Each day, hundreds of thousands of factories fire up without pollution control devices, thousands of Indians go to work without adequate safety protections and over 12 million children between the ages of five and fourteen, spend their days doing labour instead of going to school. Millions of litres of untreated raw effluents are dumping into our rivers and land and millions of tonnes of toxic hazardous waste are simply dumped onto the Earth.' (Mehta, 2009: xviii–xix)

This environment harms children as they grow and work, leaving similar conditions to their children, who will also spend their days at these factories.

While conventionally it is understood that children are more vulnerable to a variety of ailments and environmental risks, rarely are they considered specifically as climate change victims. Yet, as highlighted by Mehta's comment about children in India, children are not being protected very well in practice at all. When it comes to matters specific to the rights of children in regard to intergenerational equity, there are occasionally instances where children's interests (as both vulnerable people and as the future generation) have come to the fore. For example, in *Minors Oposa v Secretary of State for the Department of Environment and Natural Resources*, the issue of intergenerational equity was featured in the Philippines Supreme Court. Two issues in particular had to be decided: whether future generations should have standing; and how to respond to the claimants who in this case were a group of children, and who sought an order to the government to discontinue existing and future timber licence agreements. 'The claimants alleged that deforestation was causing environmental damage which affected not only young but also future generations and they sought to establish standing for both present and future generations' (Schneeberger, 2011: 26). The Supreme Court held that standing be granted to the claimants and that they had adequately asserted a right to a balanced and healthful ecology.

Beyond this specific case, however, there is little evidence of any serious shift toward protecting children's rights to intergenerational equity at either domestic or international level around climate change issues. The International Criminal Court is not really designed to hear such matters (Hall, 2013), and when it comes to environmental victims generally there are considerable ambiguities over the adoption of a narrow or broad definition of victim, including reference to suffering due to immediate harm and the substantial impairment of rights generally (Skinnider, 2011; Hall, 2013; Jarrell and Ozymy, 2012). Existing laws and court decisions tend to be inadequate to the task of considering generalised harms (such as those stemming from global warming), since they tend to be applied in relation to specific victims and specific perpetrators (Brisman, 2013b). More broadly, international and domestic laws relating to rights matters and to climate change tend to be hamstrung by the political economic context within which they are situated. The powerful continue to get their way.

Yet, among those most vulnerable to the consequences of climate change, now and into the future, are our children. Many children suffer today from polluted air and water, extreme weather events, poverty, exploitive and unhealthy labour conditions, and the effects of toxins in their bodies even before they are born. Current inequities in access to the planet's environmental resources are being compounded by lack of due care for what is left. Meanwhile, the activities of the extraction and waste industries serve to further exacerbate and accelerate global warming. This occurs in a political context within which de-regulation and inaction form the essence of the governmental climate change paradigm.

Indigenous people and climate injustice

> This is your island and you grow old and you have children.
>
> Then for thousands and thousands of years your children have told the story of you: our ancestor who's buried here on the island.
>
> We don't write our stories. Our stories are the headstones. Our stories are the trees. Our stories are the caves.
>
> Your whole sense of spirituality, your whole sense of who you are is connected there.
>
> Now imagine that island is sinking under the water and there is nothing you can do about it. Where is your sense of identity? Where is your connect to country? What have you become now?
>
> (Getano Bann, Torres Strait Islander, quoted in Marciniak, 2016)

At the heart of colonialism and imperialism is land. The imposition of colonial power was and still is intrinsically a matter of resource colonisation. This is a phenomenon that has affected many different Indigenous peoples in places such as South America, North America and Australasia, as well as the native inhabitants of Africa, Asia and beyond. The taking of land has been central to dispossession and maltreatment of Indigenous peoples across many continents and over a period of several centuries. It continues today (Gedicks, 2005; Short, 2016).

Global warming likewise affects the health and wellbeing of Indigenous people worldwide. It does so in several interrelated ways. The causes of climate change include activities such as deforestation, which in turn is due to crop substitution, mining operations and cattle farming. These kinds of intrusions on and desecrations of their lands directly affect the Indigenous way of being.

In the United States, for example, the Chippewa people have fought against mining operations on their lands, knowing that mining on their ceded lands would lead to environmental destruction of the land and water, thereby destroying their means of subsistence (Clark, 2002). As with similar events elsewhere, such contamination of the natural world constitutes an assault that goes to the heart of Indigenous culture and identity. These kinds of struggles are symptomatic of a long historical process of internal colonisation of which confiscation of land and natural resources has been a central feature. Prior ownership rights, interests and knowledge of Indigenous inhabitants were totally ignored and were deemed irrelevant by the invading states. The broad ethos was that the 'natives' and their lands were there to be exploited.

What is at stake is fundamental to the identity and social lifeblood of Indigenous communities. This is because of the dynamic and vibrant relationship between local Indigenous communities, and the land upon and within which they live. Central to this is the idea of 'land' or 'country' (Graham, 2008; Connell, 2007), which also extends to that which lies within. The Maori relationship with Nature, for example, has been expressed as follows:

> Indigenous peoples throughout the world have strong connections to the flowing freshwater of rivers. For instance, Maori – the Indigenous peoples of Aotearoa New Zealand – view many rivers as tupuna (ancestors) and invoke the name of a river to assert their identity. There is a deep belief that humans and water are intertwined as is encapsulated in common tribal sayings such as 'I am the river and the river is me' and 'The river belongs to us just as we belong to the river.' (Morris and Ruru, 2010: 49)

The special relationship between Indigenous communities and land/ Nature finds expression in a number of different places and ways worldwide, a point made by Suzuki (2010: 71) when he observes:

> Whether it's in the Amazon, the Serengeti, or the Australian outback, Aboriginal people speak of Earth as their mother and tell us we are created by the four sacred elements: Earth, Air, Fire, and Water. I realized that we had defined the problem incorrectly. I had pressed for laws and institutions to regulate our interaction with the environment when, in fact, there is no environment 'out there', separate from us; I came to realise that we *are* the environment.

It is thus not a question of humans owning the land, or the land owning humans – it is far deeper than this. These expressions of connection and interrelationship have profound implications for understanding and responding to desecration of Indigenous lands and waters.

For Climate Change Criminology, these observations alert us to the fact that climate injustice is uniquely experienced by Indigenous communities. That is, the specific material and cultural positioning of Indigenous people within certain landscapes is vital to understanding the nature of their victimisation. Unsurprisingly, declarations on the rights of Mother Earth stem in part from the efforts of Indigenous peoples worldwide to gain international recognition and acknowledgement of the Earth–people connection (UN Economic and Social Council, 2010). The Earth is experienced as sacred and vital, a source of spiritual strength and wholeness, and part of a harmonious unity between land and human. They identify *with* Nature, and in so doing do not see themselves as separate *from* Nature.

The unnatural causes of global warming simultaneously undermine Indigenous existence. The Alberta tar sands in Canada stand as a monument to the scale and impact of harm wrought by ecologically disastrous processes of energy extraction. The project is based upon efforts to extract and refine naturally created tar-bearing sand into exportable and consumable oil. One result of the project is a wide range of different types of harm to the ecosystem, animals and humans. For local Indigenous people, it constitutes a form of genocide, as their life and connection to the lands is severed (Crook and Short, 2014; Short, 2016).

In the Amazon regions of Brazil and Colombia, land clearance is happening due to forestry, agricultural exploitation, cattle farming, mining, oil and gas installations and hydroelectric dams (see Boekhout van Solinge, 2008a; 2008b; 2010; Khagram, 2004). For Indigenous inhabitants, this is having particularly devastating consequences materially and spiritually.

One hallmark of the colonial other is dispossession (of land, of knowledge). The other is disregard for welfare and wellbeing. Consider, for example, that the Arctic region is inhabited by some four million people including more than 30 Indigenous peoples. Eight states – Canada, Denmark/Greenland, Finland, Iceland, Norway, the Russian Federation, Sweden and the United States – have territories in the Arctic region. While ostensibly a pristine environment, and while local peoples rely upon traditional food sources, numerous pollutants have been having an impact on the Arctic and the people and animals that live there for decades (UNEP, 2007; EEA, 2010). This pollution originated elsewhere, especially in industrial heartlands such as the US, but the effect has been devastating. In some parts of the Arctic, for example, breastfeeding mothers have been advised to supplement breast milk with powdered milk in order to reduce exposure to noxious chemicals. All of this is compounded by the effect of melting Arctic ice and permafrost, as food sources and long established traditions become that much more difficult to sustain.

In a similar vein, rising sea levels are posing immediate problems for Indigenous and traditional peoples across the Pacific and Indian oceans. As alluded to at the beginning of this section, the swamping of island homes is in essence a form of genocide – the wholescale destruction of a people through the destruction of their land and life. Relocating people away from their ancestral homeland is not the answer, for Indigenous peoples depend on their land for spiritual wellbeing (Tekayak, 2016b). To separate the people from their country is in effect to kill both.

Indigenous people are not passive in the face of such atrocities. For several decades now they have been fighting back, with both local resistance and active participation at international forums on climate change (Etchart, 2017). Among the demands of Indigenous people are assertions of their choice not to allow unfettered 'economic development', especially when the costs are so high. For Climate Change Criminology this, too, is important. For it highlights once again the significance of self-determination for Indigenous people. Colonisation provides the lived and historical context within which struggles for self-determination occur. An anti-colonisation stance also frames the basis for possible alliances between environmentalists and Indigenous activists. At the heart of the struggles is the question of territory, and who controls what happens on the land as well as beneath the surface. Land rights are vital to Indigenous people wherever they live.

Respecting the basic principles of Indigenous criminology (Cunneen and Tauri, 2016), Climate Change Criminology has to likewise be open to the knowledge, experiences and stories from Indigenous communities. Understanding fully the impacts of climate change involves diverse ways of seeing the world around us, including through the eyes of Indigenous people. There is much to learn from those whose Earth connections date back long generations. Responding to the causes and consequences of climate change must also involve supporting Indigenous efforts to 'speak truth to power'. Let Indigenous people speak for themselves and respect them when they do. Fundamental to this support is also the idea that research and action must contribute to community empowerment if it is to be real and meaningful (Cunneen and Tauri, 2016).

Schneeberger (2011), in discussing the reverence afforded the Earth by Indigenous cultures and their strongly embedded equity considerations (related to the passing on of environmental goods and services to the next generations), suggests that this can be linked to climate science and climate modelling into the next few centuries. Here, again, the issue of intergenerational equity is relevant. For if intergenerational equity is indeed the goal then action is justified now in addressing cumulative emissions. Failure to enact scientific and evidence-based policy relating to carbon emissions is a failure to protect present and future generations. Present day scientific evidence also provides the objective basis for charges of ecocide, that is, demonstrable long-lasting serious environmental harm. This is particularly relevant to island communities such as Tuvalu, the Maldives, Kiribati and the Marshall Islands, where the consequences of climate change are both present and dire. The causes of their plight originate elsewhere, and it is here that the solutions must also be found.

Conclusion

This chapter has explored several issues pertaining to climate change victims. Each section deals with a specific victim category – non-human environmental entities, children and young people, and Indigenous communities. Each grouping has its own specific histories, stories and issues. What perhaps unites the discussion is an underlying emphasis on adopting an ecocentric perspective that incorporates social and ecological justice.

From a human perspective, ecocentrism attempts to strike a balance between the need to utilise resources for human survival, and the need to develop rules that facilitate the benign use of the ecosphere. Thus, for example, ensuring the preservation of biocentric values (such as providing for the widest possible spectrum of species within a forested area) becomes integral to maintaining long-term human needs (such as the continued existence of clean air, unpolluted rivers and fertile soils). To do this means minimising the victimisation of both the human and the non-human – in essence, to assert a form of *ecological citizenship*.

In practice this means that present generations ought to act in ways that do not jeopardise the existence and quality of life of future generations. It also means that we ought to extend the moral community to include non-human nature. By doing so, we enter a new politics of obligation:

> In ecological thought, human beings have obligations to animals, trees, mountains, oceans and other members of the biotic community. This means that human beings have to exercise extreme caution before embarking upon any project which is likely to have the possibility of adverse effects upon the ecosystems concerned. (Smith, 1998: 99)

This particular notion of ecological citizenship thus centres on human obligations to all living things, and the need to carefully assess the impacts of human activity across the human and non-human domains. The connections to climate justice are obvious.

SIX

Carbon criminals

Introduction

What distinguishes critical criminology from mainstream criminology is its concern with structures of power. These are seen to be institutionalised in particular ways, and to reflect social interests that oppress specific categories of people. In other words, critical criminology is premised on the idea that the present operation of the criminal justice system is unfair and biased, and operates in ways that advantage certain groups or classes above others (McLaughlin, 2010). Given policy and practice developments in regard to climate change, it is unsurprising that Climate Change Criminology shares several essential concerns with critical criminology more generally.

The focus of analysis for critical criminology is both the crimes of the powerful and the crimes of the less powerful. In examining the crimes of the powerful, attention is directed at issues relating to ideology (especially, the nature of 'law-and-order' politics, which focuses primarily on street crimes), political economy (the social impacts of privatisation and market forces), and the state (dictatorial and top-down rather than democratic modes of rule, and criminal actions by the state itself). The structural context of crime in relation to capitalist development and institutional pressures is viewed as central to any explanation of crimes of the powerful (Russell, 2002). For the powerful, there are pressures associated with the securing and maintenance of state power and specific sectional interests in the global context of international trade and transnational corporate monopolisation (Coleman et al, 2009).

This chapter asks the question, 'Who is responsible for climate change?' In answering this, it frames the issues in terms of crimes of the powerful (especially corporate and state crime). Systemic destruction of the environment is discussed in terms of global capitalism. The agents of this destruction are particular transnational corporations. The chapter raises the issue of responsibility and accountability, arguing that specific perpetrators can be identified and should be considered 'criminal' in the light of their acts and omissions.

Capitalism and the growth imperative

The systemic pressures associated with the global capitalist mode of production inevitably lead to the exploitation of humans, eco-systems and species, and the degradation of the environment via pollution and waste, as well as global warming and climate change. The problem is the dominant political economic system. Environmental 'crimes' are committed in the pursuit of 'normal' business outcomes and that involve 'normal' business practices (Rothe and Friedrichs, 2015; Tombs and Whyte, 2015; Rothe and Kauzlarich, 2016). This can be distilled down somewhat by reference to specific industries, such as the 'dirty industries' of coal and oil and how they engage in particularly damaging practices. But the overarching imperative to expand and increase production and consumption nonetheless obtains for all industries plugged into the global capitalist mode of production.

The specific organisational form that global capitalism takes is that of the transnational corporation. These act and operate across borders, and involve huge investments of resources, personnel and finances. They are also amalgamating (via mergers and take-overs) and expanding (via horizontal and vertical integration of business operations). Their 'crimes' are occasionally explicit and legally acknowledged (as in the case of BP and the Gulf of Mexico oil spill in 2010). More often than not, the social and ecological harms associated with transnational corporations (TNCs) are not criminalised.

Some writers see the corporate form as intrinsically criminogenic (Glasbeek, 2004; Bakan, 2004). In this view, the corporation has been designed precisely in order to first, facilitate the gathering of investment capital for large-scale ventures by the selling of shares in the companies. Originally investment was nearly always associated with the expansion of production. Today, most investment is speculative (in futures, options and shares themselves). Second, the corporation allows the separation of the corporate identity from that of the shareholder. If the venture succeeds, the shareholder gets dividends and the shares tend to rise in value; if the venture fails leaving large debts, this is nothing to do with the shareholder, who has no responsibility.

The duty of company directors is to maximise the interests of shareholders (that is, to increase their return on investment). They have no duty to advance, or even consider, any other interest, economic or social. There may be talk of a triple bottom line in which accounts seemingly balance the economic, the social and the environmental, but the reality is that profit is the only meaningful measure of corporate success.

The first duty of the corporation, therefore, is to make money for shareholders and thus for executives and managers to always put their corporation's best interests first. This makes them ruthless and predatory, and always willing to externalise costs and harms, regardless of the lives destroyed, the communities damaged and the environments and species endangered (Bakan, 2004). Morality, in this context, is entirely contingent upon local social, economic and regulatory conditions. Where corporations can get away with immoral cost cutting, profitable activities that are nonetheless harmful to others, and give them market advantage, they will. This impulse to place profit before anything else is ingrained in the nature of global capitalist competition. There is thus an identifiable nexus between capitalism as a system, and environmental degradation and transformation.

In essence, the competition and pollution and waste associated with the capitalist mode of production have a huge impact on the wider environment, on humans and on non-human species (for example, in the form of pollution and toxicity levels in air, water and land). At the heart of these processes is a political culture which takes for granted, but rarely sees as problematic, the proposition that continued expansion of material consumption is not only possible *ad infinitum* but will not harm the biosphere in any fundamental way. Built in to the logic and dynamics of capitalism is the imperative to expand (Foster, 2002), a tendency that is reinforced and facilitated by neoliberal ideologies and policies. Ecocidal destruction is thus ingrained in the present political economy.

Possessive individualism is the essence of the model, in which self-interest is the main motivator as each business positions itself in competition with others in order to survive (Mcpherson, 1977; Harvey, 2005). Specific decisions are made in the light of particular self-interests, and notions such as universal human interests and ecological justice are subsumed under a business model that relies upon dog-eat-dog (or the larger fish eating the smaller fish).

While a system can be seen to be to blame for environmental degradation (in the sense of being instrumental), it is nevertheless perplexing when it comes to assigning specific responsibility. Systems are deemed to be blameworthy, but they are not responsible insofar as there is no single 'controlling mind'. Systems may be subjected to social and moral condemnation, but there is no single perpetrator as such. Yet, on reflection, we know that 'something is wrong' and that this occurs within the overarching parameters of global capitalism. The net result of this situation is systemic damage for which no one wants to claim responsibility, be held accountable or provide compensation.

Commodification

In the capitalist mode of production (which dominates on a world scale), goods and services are produced for exchange on the market. These goods and services are *commodities* in that they are produced not for their immediate use-value, but for their exchange-value (that is, the monetary equivalent they fetch on the market). Although these commodities possess qualitatively distinct use-values (for example, shoes, sandwiches, sun cream), in addition they express quantitatively distinct exchange-values (that is, dollar value). As Marx (1954: 45) points out: 'As use-values, commodities are, above all, of different qualities, but as exchange-values they are merely different quantities.' What counts for business, therefore, is the exchange-value of the commodity, for this is where the realisation of profit occurs.

Profit comes from the process of production itself. The total value of a commodity is made up of the expenditure of capital in the production of a good or service, plus a surplus value that is added. Labour power possesses the exceptional quality of being able to produce more value than is necessary to reproduce it. Simply stated, labour is the only thing in the production process that can be exploited (as distinct from machinery and raw materials which constitute 'fixed' or constant capital). The total value of a commodity is greater than the elements that combine to produce it (that is, constant capital, and 'variable' capital as represented in the wages paid for the use of workers' labour power). The source of surplus value therefore lies in the surplus labour power that is expended by the worker, for which they are not paid. The product of this surplus labour ultimately translates into profit for the capitalist (Mandel, 1968; Onimode, 1985).

The sphere of production worldwide is dominated by the production of commodities, the advance of technology and bio-technologies, and the exploitation of labour in the service of mass production of goods and services that, in turn, demand a high turnover rate. Extensive and intensive forms of consumption are essential to the realisation of surplus value – that is, profit depends upon a critical mass of buyers purchasing the mass-produced commodities. Economic efficiency is measured by how quickly and cheaply commodities can be produced, channelled to markets, and consumed. It is a process that is inherently exploitative of both humans and nature (Pepper, 1993), and that has a huge impact on the wider environment, humans and non-human animals (for example, in the form of pollution and toxicity levels in air, water and land). These same processes pose major threats to biodiversity and the shrinking of the number of plant and animal species generally.

Expansion of material consumption is built in to the logic and dynamics of capitalism (Foster, 2002), a tendency that is reinforced and facilitated by neoliberal ideologies and policies. Commodification refers to the transformation of use-value into exchange-value, as more and more aspects of social life and environment are commercialised, and 'worth' is gauged by how much something, including basic necessities such as water, sells for on the commodity markets. The monopolisation of control over production (and thereby consumption) by corporate conglomerates has ensured that private interests dominate over public interests in the use and re-use of natural resources.

Under capitalism there are constant pressures to increase productive forces and a tendency toward repeated crises (as witnessed by the Global Financial Crisis of 2008). Capital is constantly seeking new areas for investment and consumption in order to maintain and increase profit rates. Thus, every aspect of human existence is subject to transformation insofar as capital seeks to create new forms of consumption (for example, fads, fashions) and the transformation of existing use-values into exchange values through commodification of all types of human activity and human requirements (for example, water, food, entertainment, recreation). The four elements – water, air, earth (land) and fire (energy) – are thus ever more subject to conversion into something that produces value for private interests. Capitalism is always searching for things that can be transformed from simple use-values (that is, objects of need) into exchange-values (that is, commodities produced for exchange). This extends to 'nature' as it does to other kinds of objects.

For example, what may have been formerly 'free' (for example, drinking water), is now sold back to the consumer for a price (for example, bottled water or metered water). What is most important here is that this insinuates that water is only seen as valuable once it has been commodified. Effectively, consumption has been put at the service of production in the sense that consumer decisions and practices are embedded in what is actually produced and how it is produced (see Table 6.1). Yet it is through consumption practices, and the cultural contexts for constantly growing and changing the forms of consumption, that production realises its value.

Commodity production and consumption takes place within a global system that is hierarchical and uneven. In the area of energy, for example, the oil and gas companies have long dominated and have held major sway in terms of government policies regarding carbon emissions as well as renewable energy sources. Who controls energy supplies (as evident in several wars in the Gulf region of the Middle East, as well as Russian exploits in Eastern Europe) also dominates politically and economically. Energy provision grants profit and power.

Table 6.1: Commodification of nature

Production and nature	Consumption and nature
Exploitation of workers and of nature that transforms each into a commodity	Circuits and processes of exchange that realise the monetary value of exploitation
Surplus value as source of profit [access to relevant labour pools]	Profit as realisation of surplus value [markets for commodities]
Scarcity as source of profit [access to natural resources and exploitable animals and plants]	Waste related to and as source of profit [cost minimalisation, recycling, externalisation of costs and harms]

Source: White, 2015b.

Sovereignty is itself historically and socially constructed through the prism of colonialism and imperialism, with certain nation-states holding greater power and resources (including military might) than others. The relationship between local, national, regional and global interests is construed within diverse social and political formations (for example, United States, European Union, Association of South-East Asian Nations, African Union), but these, in turn, reflect the continuing legacy of a world divided into the 'haves' and 'have-nots'. The contours of this division are dictated by the strength of ownership and control over the means of production exerted regionally and globally by particular nation-states in conjunction with and in the interests of particular corporations. At the top of the hierarchy of nation-states is the United States.

The appropriation of nature does not merely involve the turning of natural resources into commodities for the global market but also frequently involves capital actually remaking nature and its products biologically and physically. It has been observed, for instance, that 'A precapitalist nature is transformed into a specifically capitalist nature' (O'Connor, 1994: 158) in the form of genetic changes in food crops, the destroying of biological diversity through extensive use of plantation forestry, and so on. Indeed, the industrialisation of agriculture (incorporating the use of seed and other patents) is one of the greatest threats to biodiversity as it is one of the leading causes of erosion of plant genetic and species diversity. The basic means of human life is being reconstituted and re-organised through global systems of production (Croall, 2007; 2013) and in many cases the longer-term effects of new developments in the food area are still not known.

The capitalist accumulation process is one driven by the fundamental imperative to continually extend the horizons of *productive labour* (the source of surplus value) and *productive consumption* (related to the realisation, and further creation of surplus value) (see Table 6.2).

Table 6.2: Productive and unproductive labour and consumption

Politics of labour	Politics of consumption
'Productive labour' based upon profit, private ownership of means of production and extraction of surplus value	*'Productive consumption'* based upon profit, exchange-value of commodities that are capitalistically produced
Versus	Versus
'Unproductive labour' based upon need and ownership of own means of production and collective ownership of resources	*'Unproductive consumption'* based upon need and satisfied via self-sufficiency, state provision and/or cooperatives

Source: White, 2017b.

Increasing the production of surplus value by labour – the source of profit – demands constant changes to the ways in which labour is exploited, and in the things which can be transformed from simple use-values (that is, objects of need) into exchange-values (that is, commodities). The first can be achieved via changes in the organisation of work, by manipulation of the conditions within specific workplaces, and by transforming previously unproductive or non-capitalist forms of activity into sites of productive labour (for example, family farming and subsistence farming into agribusiness). The second can be achieved by not only subsuming previously non-capitalist activities into capitalist forms of production, but also by expanding capitalist commodity consumption into new spheres of activity. The exploitation of humans and the exploitation of the natural world are inextricably bound up in this process.

Yet it is via consumption practices, and the cultural contexts for constantly growing and changing forms of consumption, that production realises its value. Consumerism is the name given to a process in which certain habits of consumption are generated by the pursuit of profit. The process involves the transformation of the production of goods and services according to the dictates of exchange, rather than simply immediate use. It involves the incorporation of certain kinds of consumption, over time, into the unconscious routines of everyday life. For instance, it has been observed that the 'reproduction of the commodity of labour-power is increasingly achieved by means of capitalistically produced commodities and capitalistically organized and supplied services' (Mandel, 1975: 391). This takes the form of precooked meals, ready-made clothes, electrical household appliances and so on, goods which previously would have been produced by family members as immediate use-values (and to which contemporary community farms and local self-help environmental groups are, in part, responding and objecting). What is important is that consumerism is driven by private interests, rather than communal or state concerns. It is based upon private investments by individuals or private companies in production, in distribution services, in entertainment and shopping complexes, in food outlets and restaurants, in leisure pursuits and in financial services (Bocock, 1993).

Systemic obligations to expand require that natural resources such as water are themselves subject to varying processes of commodification, rather than being a right for citizens. One consequence of commodification is that the distribution of goods and services using market mechanisms is privileged, rather than, for instance, being based upon communal and ecological assessments of need. In this context, and somewhat perversely, scarcity of, for example, clean drinking water, makes the natural commodity even more valuable to the owner. Scarcity thus equates to high profit levels.

The nature of capitalist production and consumption also effectively severs the connection between consumption and waste. The commodity appears as outside human agency – as alienated from production as such. This is also evident in a culture of disconnection that marks the relationship between consumer and producer (O'Brien, 2008). Thus, there is no sense of communal ownership in relation to the costs, as well as the benefits of the exploitation of human and natural resources (Pepper, 1993). This extends to temporal aspects of commodification as well, insofar as a process of cultural infantilisation reduces the ability of adults to effectively direct their attention forward into the future and thereby face the consequences of their present actions, now (Brisman and South, 2014).

One impact of unsustainable environmental practices is the increased pressure on companies to seek out new resources (human and non-human) to exploit as existing reserves dwindle due to over-exploitation and contamination from already produced waste. Under capitalism there are constant pressures to increase its productive force and thus a tendency toward cyclical crises of over-production and under-consumption. What makes both labour and consumption 'productive' from the point of view of capitalism is whether such activity directly contributes to a profit-making process.

To make and/or to consume something yourself (whether at the individual, cooperative or societal levels) and to so do on the basis of need (rather than for profit or artificially manufactured desire) is the exception. Rather, goods and services tend to be produced in the context of privately owned and managed businesses, for the purpose of generating profits for the private shareholders. Similarly, consumption tends to be based upon capitalistically-produced goods and services (that is, goods and services sold in a buyer–seller nexus) rather than homemade goods and services (for example, vegetables from your own garden, hand-sewn shirts). Small alternative forms of non-capitalist production and consumption exist (for example, community gardens, local exchange trading systems (LETS), and small-scale residential cooperatives), but the general pattern is dominated by profit-making exchanges. Periodic economic crises lead to system transformations toward ever more commodification of basic necessities – food, water, air and energy. Living outside of polluted areas of a city carries with it premium housing costs for the privilege of breathing (relatively) fresh air. Prevailing wind patterns separate out the dirty air and the clean air, and suburbs align to this in accordance with wealth. Meanwhile, entrepreneurs in Australia have recently celebrated their success in selling canisters of clean, fresh Australian air to buyers in India, China and Vietnam. The air is 'harvested' in the New South Wales Blue Mountains, a World Heritage-listed area recognised for its eucalyptus forests, waterfalls and beautiful landscapes (Caisley, 2018: 5). We can now buy bottled air, much as we buy bottled water. Rather than fixing the problem (namely, pollution) through spending on infrastructure and governmental regulation, this type of fix (that is, using the market) benefits selected consumers and makes money for the few.

For the past 30 years, this commodification of nature has occurred within a particular political economic context. Neoliberalism describes a broad political and economic orientation that places greatest emphasis on the individual, responsibility for one's own actions, and accountability for the consequences of these actions, within the institutional framework of strong private property rights and unfettered commodity markets.

Neoliberalism ostensibly favours market forces over state intervention, and it views inequality as a natural outcome of competition between individuals. At an abstract level, each person is seen to be personally responsible for their own welfare and life chances. In practice, economic power tends to already be monopolised and concentrated in ways that foreclose any possibility of fair or free competition. The main policy and practical trends associated with neoliberalism include reduced trade protection, user-pays, privatisation and de-regulation (Harvey, 2005).

> Institutionally the policies and ethics of neo-liberalism are reflected in reliance upon the market for the allocation of goods and services, the shrinking of the welfare state, assertion of the role of the state as 'night watchman' (albeit with little government oversight for those at the top), and an emphasis on strong law and order and defence of private property (that includes strict control over those at the bottom). (White, 2015b: 219)

Historical analysis demonstrates empirically that social inequality is intrinsic to the capitalist system (Piketty, 2014). This has been exacerbated and further entrenched over several decades of aggressive neoliberalisation, involving the collusion of international corporate elites working in conjunction with high-level political leaders in the USA and other hegemonic nation-states (Beder, 2006). Neoliberal 'free trade' policies are linked to the commodification of a wider range of services and products that were formerly state-owned and operated ostensibly for public benefit. Education, water and power, for example, are being sold by governments to private concerns as profit-making enterprises. This is yet another instance in which the consumption relations of ordinary citizens are being transformed in ways which reduce the possibility of democratic participation in decision-making and the imposition of public controls over how resources are managed and consumed.

Capitalist responses to climate change

The global capitalist system is simultaneously the major impediment to structural changes necessary to tackle global warming at all levels, since the lifeblood of this system is economic growth over and above ecological sustainability. The tendency of the capitalist mode of production is to fragment nature and exploit resources in their specificity (that is, as coal, as water, as trees) to the detriment of the ecological whole. This has been described as a 'metabolic rift' between economy and ecology, between the dominant forms of human production (organised capitalistically) and nature (evident in ecological destruction) (Foster, 2002; Crook and Short, 2014). The dynamics of this mode of production also prevent it from structurally accommodating systemic solutions and remedies to climate change (Crook and Short, 2014).

Powerful enterprises substantially own and control the bulk of the world's resources (including natural, financial and technical capital). There is no 'free market' as such. Land, water, food and energy are under the control of a small and shrinking number of private firms, and the community outside is both growing and increasingly powerless in the face of this concentrated ownership. One consequence of this concentration of power is that the carbon emitting industries have continued to exercise considerable economic and political clout, especially in resource-dependent economies such as Australia and Canada.

Exploitation of natural resources is big business, and big business ensures that its interests (that is, private interests) are protected across many different spheres of activity. This is evident for example in ongoing natural resource developments in which oil and coal industries, the 'dirty' industries, are privileged still: where coal-seam fracking is allowed to pose a threat to prime agricultural land; in the advent of deep-drill oil exploration and exploitation, and, similarly, mega-mines and open-cut mining; and also in the continued resistance by powerful businesses to global agreements on carbon emission reductions and use of carbon taxes.

Given that the largest private corporations are economically more powerful than many nation-states, and given that they own and control great expanses of the world's land, water and food resources, individually and collectively they are a formidable force. On occasion, as well, they may combine their collective muscle to influence world opinion or global efforts to curtail their activities. For example, analysis of how big business has responded to global warming reveals a multi-pronged strategy to deter or defer action on climate change (Bulkeley and Newell, 2010). Some of these include:

- challenging the science behind climate change;
- creating business-funded environmental non-governmental organisations (NGOs);
- emphasising the economic costs of tackling climate change;
- using double-edged diplomacy to create stalemates in international negotiations;
- using domestic politics (particularly in the United States) to stall international progress;
- influencing the climate change negotiations through direct lobbying.

Climate change is also dealt with by focusing on the economic potentials of 'dirty industry' development, and the employment and financial costs of their demise, rather than their impacts on global warming. This is highlighted, for example, in the active governmental and political defence of the Alberta Tar Sands project, one of the most polluting and carbon charged developments in the world (Klare, 2012).

The big companies also have the support of political stooges such as US President Donald Trump and the former Prime Minister of Australia, Tony Abbott. The latter once extolled the virtues of coal by saying that:

> Coal is good for humanity, coal is good for prosperity, coal is an essential part of our economic future, here in Australia, and right around the world.
>
> Coal is essential for the prosperity of the world.
>
> Energy is what sustains our prosperity, and coal is the world's principal energy source and it will be for many decades to come.
>
> [W]e think that coal has a big future as well as a big past. (Abbott, quoted in Massola et al, 2014)

This statement was made just a few weeks before the Intergovernmental Panel on Climate Change (IPCC) released its 2014 report. According to the IPCC (2014: 5, emphasis added):

> Total anthropogenic greenhouse gas emissions have continued to increase over 1970 to 2010 with larger absolute increases between 2000 and 2010, despite a growing number of climate change mitigation policies... *Increased use of coal* has *reversed* the long-standing trend of gradual decarbonization (that is, reducing the carbon intensity of energy) of the world's energy supply.

The science tells us that coal is, in fact, 'bad' for humanity. In the light of the existing scientific evidence on global warming, continued encouragement of such activities represents intentional harm that is immoral and destructive of collective public interest in the same moment that particular industries and companies benefit.

When climate change is acknowledged, the response tends to be framed in technical rather than political terms. For example, the notion that business can profit by protecting the environment (Baer and Singer, 2009) is frequently linked to the idea of technological fixes in relation to climate change, such as the development of hybrid cars, more technologically efficient appliances, and use of compact fluorescent light bulbs. Burying the problem is also touted as a solution – whether this is radioactive waste or carbon pollution. The politics of climate change has mainly focused on debates over taxes (such as carbon taxes), which technologies to adopt (such as nuclear energy), and fiscal constraint (since budgets are limited), rather than the overarching causes of global warming per se.

Responding to the grand scale of the problem as a technical issue has likewise been embraced by those supporting geo-engineering solutions over and above stopping the carbon emissions themselves (Brisman, 2015). For example, there are proposals for deliberate large-scale intervention in the climate system so as to moderate the problem of global warming. According to Hulme (2014: 2–3), geo-engineering technologies are united in their ambition to deliberately manipulate the atmosphere's mediating role in the planetary heat budget: 'They aim to do one of two things: either to accelerate the removal of carbon dioxide from the global atmosphere; or else to reflect more sunlight away from the Earth's surface and so to compensate for the heating of the planet caused by rising concentrations of greenhouse gases.'

At its heart, energy production and consumption is centre stage in climate change, both as a source of the problem and as part of the response through mitigation and other measures.

Large-scale mitigation involving geo-engineering has two key dimensions according to Redgwell (2012: fn11):

1. carbon dioxide removal – ocean iron fertilisation to enhance plankton growth and absorption by the oceans of CO_2 from the atmosphere, and the construction of mechanical filters to remove CO_2 from ambient air;
2. solar radiation management – releasing aerosols into the stratosphere or constructing solar arrays in outer space to reflect solar radiation back into space, and enhancing the reflectivity of clouds.

As Redgwell (2012: 28) also notes:

> Such responses include use of carbon capture and storage (CCS), greater energy efficiency, increased use of renewable energy (for example, wind, wave and solar), and alternative energy sources (for example, biofuels). Many of these responses are technology-driven, in particular the increased

> focus on CCS, and do not necessarily reflect a move to reduce carbon dependency.

The latter observation is particularly instructive in that it highlights both the continuing reliance upon carbon and the successful efforts of those reliant upon the carbon economy to maintain the status quo.

It is 'the market' which has skewed production and its harmful emissions to the Third World for the sake of First World consumers. Simultaneously, it is the 'market' that is now being seen as the solution to global environmental problems such as climate change. Resolution of the problems arising from commodification are now seen to involve commodification of the solutions – for instance, in the form of carbon emission trading (see Chapter Three). Given the vested interests involved in protecting and maintaining existing inter-state inequalities, as well as those associated with particular industries (such as oil and coal), the critiques of carbon emissions trading schemes, in practice, could be anticipated in advance. For example, as much as anything, carbon emission trading favours the polluter and the practice of polluting (Shiva, 2008; Hansen, 2009).

Much public debate has occurred over the regulation and reduction of carbon emissions (Martin and Walters, 2013). At the heart of the matter is the fact that carbon emissions are directly contributing to global warming, and that without adequate mitigation and adaptation strategies the problems associated with climate change will get worse before they get better. The urgency surrounding the reigning in of carbon emissions has been matched by the audacity of businesses in lobbying to defend their specific economic interests, whether in relation to taxes, mine permits or pollution thresholds.

Given the vested interests involved in protecting and maintaining existing inter-state inequalities, as well as those associated with particular industries (such as oil and coal), the stifling of carbon emissions has been slow and well below what is needed to counter present global warming trends (IPCC, 2013). Private profits continue to dominate public interests, usually with government collusion. Prohibition and restriction strategies are basically off the agenda.

Business as usual

Rather than tackling global warming, quite the opposite has been happening at a systems level. While some capitalist enterprises have embraced 'green capitalism' and new technologies that are meant to be more environmentally benign, the overarching trend has been a continued reliance upon the 'old' extraction industries such as coal, gas and oil. These are being supplemented by newer forms of energy extraction, the so-called 'extreme energy' industries. This refers to novel forms of ecologically unsound energy extraction: mountain-top removal, deep-water drilling and hydraulic 'fracking' (Crook and Short, 2014).

In the neoliberal universe, the global status quo is protected under the guise of arguments about the 'national interest' and the importance of 'free trade', which usually reflect specific sectoral business interests. This is most evident in state support in countries like the United States, Canada and Australia for the oil, gas and coal industries, deep-drilling oil exploration and mega-mines.

Developments in Asia also provide a case example of what is wrong. For example, the World Bank (hardly an enemy of the transnational corporation) recently voiced its concern about developments in south and south-east Asia through its president, Jim Yong Kim and senior climate change official John Roome. The problem relates to climate change and the fact that many countries were on track to build hundreds more coal-fired power plants in the next 20 years. According to Roome, 'If all of the business-as-usual coal-fired power plants in India, China, Vietnam and Indonesia all came online that would make up a very significant part – in fact almost all – of the carbon budget. It would make it highly unlikely that we would be able to get to 2C' (quoted in Goldenberg, 2016). Such developments make a mockery of the 2016 Paris talks about cutting greenhouse gas emissions and undermine the idea that de-escalating the Earth's rising temperature is do-able.

Climate vandals engaging in ecocide

Given the stakes involved, should the impending destruction of ecosystems, and the human collateral damage associated with this, be thought of as a form of environmental genocide – ecocide? If so, then it is state leaders and government bureaucrats, as well as corporate heads and key shareholders, who should ultimately be held responsible for this crime.

The carbon footprint of countries such as the United States is often cited as evidence of the privileges and advantages of people living in these countries, and therefore their collective responsibility for the lion's share of carbon emissions (Levene and Conversi, 2014). Likewise, the consumption habits of those in the so-called affluent countries have been linked to expanded production of carbon emissions across the globe in order to satisfy US consumer demand (Lynch and Stretesky, 2010). To blame the 'consumer' in this instance is, however, misleading. First, there is massive disparity in wealth and consumption within highly unequal societies such as the US. Second, and what is more important, the system as a whole is precisely structured and designed to enhance commodity production, consumption and the realisation of value through the cash nexus. The system functions in accordance to the dictates of those who effectively plan and control social production.

As already noted, pockets of alternative forms of production exist, in the form of cooperatives and communes, but these are overwhelmed by the dominant commodity-based system of production and consumption. This also applies to much of the so-called 'sharing economy', particularly as manifest in phenomena such as Airbnb (private rental of units and houses) and Uber (private hire of vehicles), which are less about peer-to-peer sharing, recycling and cooperative structures (the original vision and intent of some sharing economy proponents), than atomised profitmaking that collectively undermine worker wages and conditions, while simultaneously affecting the established housing rental market and taxi services. The general point is that decisions of what and how to consume are still largely taken out of the hands of the ordinary person. It is mandated 'from above' (even if the 'above' is a mathematical logarithm designed to profit the originators of an online service, such as access to Uber cars). These decisions are taken in the crucible of global capitalist competition and monopoly, and as such, are themselves dictated by the systemic imperatives of the global capitalist mode of production.

A dilemma for both criminology and social action around climate change is that there are nonetheless big differences between systems and perpetrators. *Systems* may be deemed to be blameworthy, but not to be responsible. As such, they may well attract social and moral condemnation, can be analysed in terms of their social, economic and cultural dynamics, and be challenged through social transformation and revolutionary change. They are not able to be prosecuted for their crimes, however. Here, it is *perpetrators*, specific individuals and companies who can and should be deemed responsible in the eyes of the law. Accordingly, the focus and discourse shifts in this section from structure (global capitalist mode of production) to agency (corporate bosses and state officials), since the latter can be specifically assessed in terms of conduct, intent and liability. What happens to agents within a system also ultimately has an impact on the structure of the system as a whole and so is important in its own right.

In criminological terms, the crimes of the powerful can be distinguished on the basis of particular sets of actors and institutions (Rothe and Kauzlarich, 2016). These actors and institutions interact across interrelated sectors. The criminality of the powerful includes:

- corporate crime (large businesses and industry conglomerates);
- state crime (government agencies and officials);
- state–corporate crime (collusion between companies and states);
- international financial institutions crime (arising from the activities of agencies such as the International Monetary Fund and the World Bank);
- organised crime (organised criminal networks including Mafia and Yakuza);
- militia and insurgency crime (rebel groups, religious-based fanatics).

A key defining feature of crimes of the powerful is that such crimes involve actions (or omissions and failures to act) that are socially harmful and carried out by elites and/or those who wield significant political and social authority in the particular sectors or domains of their influence.

The destruction of the environment in ways that differentially, unequally and universally affect humans, eco-systems and non-human species can be conceptualised criminologically as a specific type of crime – namely, ecocide. A key feature of this crime is that it occurs in the context of foreknowledge and intent. That is, ecocide arising from global warming, while marked by uncertainty in regard to specific rates and types of ecological change, is nonetheless founded upon generalised scientific knowledge that profound change is unavoidable unless carbon emissions – the key source of global warming – are not radically reduced, now.

Ecocide describes an attempt to criminalise human activities that destroy and diminish the wellbeing and health of ecosystems and species within these, including humans (see Chapter Two). Climate change and the gross exploitation of natural resources are leading to the general demise of the ecological status quo – hence increasing the need for just such a crime. This requires a major shift in collective thinking about climate change issues: 'For realization of a strong public support and mobilization, there is a need for a cultural transformation where ecologically harmful acts are viewed not as economic issues but as criminal ones' (Tekayak, 2016a: 65).

From an eco-justice perspective, ecocide involves transgressions that violate the principles and central constituent elements of environmental justice, ecological justice and species justice (White, 2013a). At the core of the climate change problem are carbon emissions. If carbon emissions are at the forefront of the causes of global warming and subsequent climate chaos, then the obvious question is why continue to emit such dangerous planet-altering substances into the atmosphere.

Introducing ecocide as a crime against humanity would mean that 'individuals in a position of superior or command responsibility will be criminally liable if they carry out an activity covered by such a provision, disregarding knowledge or intent' (Hellman, 2014: 278). Ecological destruction accompanying natural resource extraction such as the oil and gas industries, coal mining, logging and so on could be proceeded against on the basis of such an international law of ecocide. Such a law would create prohibitions as well as obligations, and cover persons having superior responsibility in a corporation and in government (Higgins, 2012).

Not all 'carbon crimes' are attributable to the powerful. Everyday citizens are implicated in activities that contribute to global warming through the embedded experiences and habits of everyday consumer life (Agnew, 2013). So, too, those committing 'real crimes' likewise can be viewed as affecting the climate. For example, street crimes, such as burglary, theft, criminal damage and crimes against the person are estimated to account for some 1 per cent of total UK emissions (Pease and Farrell, 2011: 157). Crimes committed, as well as emissions generated by criminal justice institutions responding to crimes committed, are part of recent calculations into the size and nature of the carbon footprint in England and Wales (Skudder et al, 2016). Such crimes – of 'ordinary' people and 'criminal elements' – tend to be related, however, to the dominant mode of production and/or arise from class inequalities (White, 2008). Their origins lie in structures over which the participants have little or no direct control.

Criminal activities of another kind also constitute a distinct class of 'carbon crimes'. For example, Mafia investment in the wind power sector in Italy has involved fraudulently skimming money from alternative energy subsidies, with developers playing a central bridging role between legitimate and criminal interests. Related to this is corruption of public officials (Caneppele et al, 2013), although these crimes stem, in part, from the regulatory systems put into place that allow certain activities to go forward while not threatening the existing status quo whatsoever. They are crimes associated with new economic projects and directions, the origins of which stem from limited state responses to climate change challenges.

The big players on the carbon emissions stage remain those of the transnational corporation and the nation-state. The 'choices' ingrained in environmental exploitation (of human beings and of the non-human world) stem from systemic imperatives to exploit the environment for production of commodities for human use. Consumerist ideology and practice has simply become part of a taken-for-granted common sense, especially among the affluent (Agnew, 2013; Tombs and Whyte, 2015). To tackle climate change means challenging ingrained assumptions, presumptions and ways of being. Carbon emissions that lead to global warming occur in the pursuit of 'normal' business outcomes and involve 'normal' business practices. This has to change for global warming to be adequately addressed.

Conclusion

The problem with trying to tackle corporate harm is that virtually every act of the corporate sector is deemed, in some way or another, to be 'good for the country'. This ideology of corporate virtue, and the benefits of business for the common good, is promulgated through extensive corporate advertising campaigns, capitalist blackmail (vis-à-vis location of industry and firms) and aggressive lobbying of government and against opponents. Anything which impedes or opposes business-as-usual is deemed to be unreasonable, faulty, bad for the economy, not the rightful domain of the state, will undermine private property rights, and so on.

In other words, the prevailing view among government and business is that, with few exceptions, the 'market' is the best referee when it comes to preventing or stopping current and potential environmental harm. Powerful business interests (which, among other things, provide big financial contributions to mainstream political parties) demand a 'light touch' when it comes to surveillance of, and intervention in, their activities. In this framework, the state should not, therefore, play a major role in the regulation of corporate activities beyond that of assisting in the maintenance of a general climate within which business will flourish.

To address corporate harm, then, requires a political understanding of class power and a rejection of formally legal criteria in assessing criminality and harm. It is therefore from beginning to end a political process. As such, it implies conflict over definitions of conduct and activity (for example, as being good or bad, harmful or not so harmful, offensive or inoffensive), over legitimacy of knowledge claims (for example, media portrayals, expert opinion), and over the role and use of state instruments and citizen participation in putting limits on corporate activity (for example, via regulations, public access to commercial information).

SEVEN

Criminal justice responses to climate change

Introduction

Global warming is rapidly changing the ecological and social landscape of the planet. These changes are profound and far-reaching. From the point of view of Climate Change Criminology several questions warrant close consideration. Answers to these questions also have implications for how to interpret the role and actions of different elements of the criminal justice system.

With regard to mitigation, for example, the issue is what can be done to reduce the contributing causes of climate change. The obvious and science-based answer is to diminish greenhouse gas emissions (GHG). This could and arguably should involve the *criminalisation* of carbon emissions and the forced shutdown of dirty industries.

With regard to adaptation, the issue is what can be done to enable communities and species to adapt and survive climate change? One answer is, at the very least, to ensure that harm is explicitly acknowledged in public policy. This could and should involve recognition of *victimisation* and some type of compensation and reparation.

This chapter provides an overview of how criminal justice institutions are responding to climate change. This entails description of court cases intended to bolster the reduction of carbon emissions and the overall role of climate change litigation in the pursuit of climate justice. The greening of the institutions of criminal justice (police, courts, prisons, community corrections) also is examined. So too is the role of the police in dealing with environmental protest and direct action, as is the place of climate change victims in the wider criminal justice narrative. The chapter concludes by raising issues pertaining to the holding to account of those who do most to cause and perpetuate global warming.

Litigation in support of climate justice

Climate change litigation involves cases being brought before administrative and judicial bodies that raise issues of law or fact regarding the science of climate change and climate change mitigation and adaption efforts (UNEP, 2017). Over the past few years several key trends have been identified in climate change litigation (see Table 7.1). While most of these cases are civil and rarely criminal, they nonetheless are directed at addressing the ecocidal tendencies associated with climate change. To that end, they deal with matters of fundamental ecological and social harm – key considerations of Climate Change Criminology.

Climate change litigation may have implications for national policies and practice relating to mitigation, or be directed to addressing issues pertaining to specific projects such as expansion of airports and coal mines. In many instances, the defendant has been a government. Where corporations have been targeted for legal action, the impetus has been

Table 7.1: Trends in climate change litigation

Legal trend	Substantive issues
Holding governments to their legislative and policy commitments	Holds governments accountable for climate-related commitments, including those made through international climate agreements
Linking the impacts of resource extraction to climate change and resilience	Attempts to compel alternative approaches to natural resource management to those which involve emissions due to combustion of extracted fossil fuels or that impair resiliency and adaptive capacity
Establishing that particular emissions are the proximate cause of particular adverse climate change impacts	Seeks to establish liabilities that generate emissions with full knowledge of those emission's effects on global climate
Establishing liability for failures (or efforts) to adapt to climate change	In the light of improvements in technical understandings of climate science, seeks to assign responsibility where failures to adapt result in foreseeable, material harms
Applying the public trust doctrine to climate change (that is, certain natural and cultural resources must be preserved for public use, and the government owns and must protect and maintain these resources for the public's use)	The state has a responsibility for the integrity of a nation's public trust resources for future generations, and thus to principles of intergenerational equity

Source: Drawing upon United Nations Environmental Programme, 2017.

twofold: first, holding corporations to account for harms stemming from their activities (for example, after-the-fact use of torts and criminal law); and second, viewing corporations as agents for achieving a safe climate future (for example, using company and securities law to highlight disclosure requirements regarding foreseeable climate risk and viewing climate obligations as linked to director duties and liabilities) (Haines and Parker, 2017). Most countries have experienced little or no climate change litigation; the majority of cases have involved advanced capitalist countries, in jurisdictions such as the United States, Australia, the United Kingdom and the European Union. Some of these cases are considered further below.

At an international level, it has been observed that '[a]ccess to information, obligations to exercise due diligence and regulatory regimes that make corporations responsible for their actions are all important to the quest for climate change justice' (Mascher, 2016: 69). Yet, this rarely occurs in practice, and much more is needed if substantive change is to happen. Meanwhile, governments still tend to be the main targets for legal action.

Action against corporations is rhetorically supported in calls for the enactment of the international crime of ecocide, as well as in recommendations put forward by the International Bar Association (Mascher, 2016). This can also manifest concretely in present-day legal proceedings, mainly but not exclusively in US cases brought against corporations in the fossil fuel sector (UNEP, 2017). There are exceptions to this trend however. For example, at the time of writing, a legal case in the Philippines is investigating the liability of 50 of the largest fossil fuel companies for violating the human rights of Filipinos as a result of catastrophic climate change (Commission on Human Rights of the Philippines, 2016). Important issues include making actors accountable for action in one country, which may cause harmful consequences in another (that is, international law and global processes), as well as how to hold any one corporation responsible for its relatively small contribution to a global crisis caused by many (Howard, 2016).

The Council of Europe (2012: 12) recently observed that, '[c]urrently, no comprehensive legally binding instrument for the protection of the environment exists globally'. Even the Aarhus Convention (The Convention on Access to Information, Public Participation in Decision-Making and Access to Justice in Environmental Matters (adopted in Aarhus, Denmark, on 25 June 1998)) only offers procedural rights, not the right to a healthy environment as such. Moreover, it is the impact of the environment on the individual rather than protection of the environment itself with which instruments such as the European

Convention on Human Rights and the European Social Charter are concerned.

Nonetheless, a wide range of regulatory and civil laws are being mobilised around climate change, as well as potential use of criminal law. The US Environmental Protection Agency, for example, has explicit powers to deal with those polluting the atmosphere, including actions that contribute to global warming. In *Massachusetts v EPA* (Environmental Protection Agency), a US Supreme Court decision (2007), the EPA was found to have the legal authority under the Clean Air Act (1963) to regulate GHG emissions. Whether it will or not and to what extent is still questionable. Meanwhile, Schapiro (2014: 181) has noted important issues pertaining to liability law and compensation: 'There is also the big payout liability factor, identified by the global insurance giant Lloyd's of London, of companies being held accountable for the economic consequences of climate change.'

A recent 2015 climate case *Urgenda v State of the Netherlands* saw a non-government organisation (Urgenda) file a lawsuit against the government of the Netherlands to the effect that the state is acting unlawfully by falling short of its current emission reduction target. The District Court agreed with the plaintiff that 'given the high risk, the current insufficient emission reduction targets, and the fact that an early and speedy reduction of the emissions increases the chance to avoid dangerous climate change, the state has a "serious duty of care to take measures to prevent it"' (Lambrecht and Ituarte-Lima, 2016: 61). The Dutch state is appealing the judgment and, even if successful, questions can be asked about the substantial investment in time and money for such cases and whether the benchmarked reduction of emissions (in this instance 25 per cent reduction) is sufficient anyway (Lambrecht and Ituarte-Lima, 2016).

In Australia, by contrast, similar suits have met with little success. For example, the Federal Court recently dismissed cases involving the Carmichael Mine in Queensland, both in regards to Native Title determinations and claims that burning coal and climate pollution would be inconsistent with international obligations to protect the Great Barrier Reef (Briggs, 2016; Kos, 2016a). Another suit hinging upon coal's contribution to 'dangerous global warming' was also recently brought against the Alpha coal mine in central Queensland. This case proceeded through the Land Court, Supreme Court and Queensland Court of Appeal, with the result that the claim was dismissed and the instigating conservation group was ordered to pay court costs (Smail, 2016; Kos, 2016b). Peculiar interpretations of legal responsibility and environmental impact were evident. For example, the Court accepted the 'market substitution' argument that a particular mine will have 'no net impact' on global GHG levels and thus no impact on climate change because the same quantity of coal could be supplied by others (Bell-James and Ryan, 2016). This reasoning obscures any responsibility that individual actors have to mitigate climate change by attributing all responsibility to an aggregated 'market' that is ultimately unaccountable (Bennett, 2016).

As discussed in Chapter Five, the notion of intergenerational equity refers to the concept that all generations are partners caring for and using the Earth and that every generation needs to pass on the Earth and its natural and cultural resources in at least as good condition as they received them (Brown Weiss, 2008; Lawrence, 2014). The notion of 'carrying capacity' of the planet (that is, its ability to sustain a given amount of human, plant and animal life) has been suggested as criteria against which harm can be measured, and criminalised (Mares, 2010). This also makes sense if framed within the twin concepts of ecocide and intergenerational equity. That is, intergenerational equity considerations can be gauged according to the strength of the carrying capacity at any one time, and fundamental or serious diminishment of this can be construed as a form of ecocide.

At a strategic level, however, there is still a long way to go. Without widescale change, climate change will continue to accelerate, with disastrous consequences for all. The devastation of natural resources, especially deforestation, and the continued reliance upon energy sources that we know contribute to global warming, are directly contributing to ecocide. There is foreknowledge of the harm, and we know who the perpetrators are. Unfortunately, the law and litigation tend to take a long time (as well as using considerable financial and human resources). This, too, becomes part of the equation of whether or not, and how best strategically to use legal mechanisms to foster mitigation and enhance adaptation.

Time itself therefore becomes a strategic tool in the hands of activist and carbon criminal alike. There are certainly considerable ramifications associated with the length of time it takes to make important decisions concerning climate change (particularly in the context of real world urgency and political-economic developments). This is, however, a two-edged sword. Add in the delay associated with appeal, and there is the potential strategic use of courts on behalf of both climate change activists (wishing to delay a mining project, for instance) and climate change contributors (for example, using the law to fob off potential brakes on their activities). These observations once again reaffirm the legal arena as a major site of contestation and political struggle.

Compensation suits involving Chevron in Ecuador illustrate the levels of harm perpetrated by such corporations as well as the clash of basic social interests between corporations and the public good. They also indicate the instrumental use of the law to protect elite interests. Thus, in August 2016, United States Court of Appeals for the Second Circuit in New York upheld a decision by US District Judge Lewis A Kaplan, who found that an Ecuadorean judgment that ordered the collection of $9 billion from Chevron Corporation for rainforest damage was obtained through bribery, coercion and fraud, and therefore invalid (Los Angeles Times, 2016). Chevron, which struck a deal to buy Texaco in 2000, has long argued that a 1998 agreement Texaco signed with Ecuador after a $40 million clean-up absolves it of liability. Nonetheless, in 2011, a judge in Ecuador issued an $18 billion judgment against Chevron in a lawsuit brought on behalf of 30,000 residents. The judgment was for environmental damage caused by Texaco during its operation of an oil consortium in the rainforest from 1972 to 1990. In 2014, Ecuador's highest court upheld the verdict but reduced the judgment to about $9.5 billion. This decision has now been invalidated by a foreign court – in the USA – a decision which thereby signals that powerful corporations can avoid legal accountability anywhere in the world if they have the legal and financial resources to do so.

New concepts of harm, as informed by ecological sciences and environmental values, will inevitably be developed as part of any legal reform process, and these can contribute towards climate justice ends. A good – and positive – illustration of this was provided in an English court case involving six Greenpeace activists (McCarthy, 2008). The six had been charged with criminal damage after being involved in scaling and defacing a chimney at a plant at Kingsnorth, Kent, in a location earmarked for the development of a new generation of coal-fired plants. At the conclusion of the eight-day trial, the jury decided that the activists had been justified in causing damage to the coal-fired power station due to the larger threat of global warming. The jurors thus accepted the defence arguments that the six defendants had 'lawful excuse' (under the Criminal Damage Act 1971) to damage the property at the power station to prevent even greater damage caused by climate change. For Climate Change Criminology such cases go to the heart of the changes needed today if planetary wellbeing is to be secured.

Greening justice initiatives

In recent years there has been a growth of ecological awareness, alongside the emergence of environmental sustainability initiatives, within criminal justice institutions around the world. This is partly driven by cost-cutting imperatives, but it also reflects concern to address the obvious deleterious effects on the environment of activities stemming from the operation of criminal justice institutions and agencies (White and Graham, 2015). 'Greening justice' encompasses a variety of initiatives and actions within criminal justice that advance a more sustainable relationship between humans and the environment (Graham and White, 2015). Fundamentally, it implicates practitioners, offenders and communities in efforts to reduce the social, economic and ecological costs of crime and criminal justice.

Changes within policing, courts, prisons, offender supervision and community reintegration reflect aspects of this phenomenon (see Table 7.2). Again, the motivations will vary, as will the impacts. Not everything that is done is driven by climate change concerns to either mitigate or adapt to global warming. Nonetheless, in many instances the outcomes do precisely that, albeit in their own limited way.

The financial and other benefits of 'greening justice' need to be interpreted carefully and contextually (White and Graham, 2015). Yet, the advent and spread of 'greening justice' projects is not insignificant in terms of justice operations and staff and offender experiences. In other words, 'greening justice' initiatives *can* make a positive difference, for some, in particular places, and under specific circumstances.

Yet, as with most criminal justice institutions there are countervailing processes and contradictory policies. For example, making prisons more efficient in regards energy use and reliance upon locally grown foods matters little when it comes to the big picture of climate change if this only provides more money and impetus to build more prisons. Climate Change Criminology would therefore agree entirely with the following sentiment.

> There are strong reasons – in terms of both ecological and social justice – to not build more prisons. In a criminal justice context, it is not only about doing more with less, it is about doing less. Indeed it is a truism that the most sustainable building is the one that is never built. It is entirely contradictory to the core notion of 'sustainability' to see claims about 'greening justice' that interpret it as justifying penal expansionism. Similarly, one of the paradoxical harms

> which may potentially be produced from the emergent 'greening justice' evolution is the reification of a new generation of 'green eco-prisons' as an ideal type, and through this a further legitimation of the penal project, rather than its transformation or abolition. In our view, true sustainability hinges upon the impetus to decarcerate, diminish in size and de-commission, restricting the use of confinement as a genuine last resort. (White and Graham, 2015: 860)

As so often is the case, however, broad policy prescriptions of this type may not suffice to stem the 'law and order' brigade, particularly if and when mass migration is perceived to pose a threat to internal order. Indeed, the imposition of concentration camps as preferred measures to contain the asylum seeker may be mollified somewhat by rhetorical appeal to 'greening justice' aspects of camp design and oversight. This is hardly reassuring to those seeking social *and* ecological justice.

In a world that is rapidly subject to the vagaries of climate change, more and more attention will be placed upon the natural environment and the Nature–human relationship. To 'save the planet' every workplace will be modified and every worker exhorted to 'do their bit'. Saving the planet, however, also has other dimensions that likewise present interesting dilemmas for agents of the state. This is nowhere more apparent than with respect to the role of the police, not as recyclers but as enforcers of law.

Policing and environmental conflict

Actions for change on climate change issues will require that concepts such as human rights, ecological citizenship and the global commons be developed in ways that assert the primacy of climate justice over narrow sectional interests. For this to occur there is a need for strong action within civil society to progress a more radical social change agenda. As part of this, criminologists (among others) must insist upon the protection of democratic spaces within which popular struggles can occur, given the powerful social interests opposed to needed climate change solutions.

Social conflict inevitably means police intervention – of some kind, however. The policing of public order represents distinct challenges for the police, operationally in terms of choice of tactics and strategies, and politically with regard to the social environment within which events take place. Such policing is highly visible, and has a high impact.

Table 7.2: Greening justice

Domain	Objectives	Examples	Initiatives
Policing	• Reduce carbon footprint • Increase energy efficiency • Waste minimisation	• Reduction in fleet and car sizes, more bicycle and foot patrols • Use of solar, wind and hydro energy • Paper recycling	• Hong Kong – 'green police initiative' designed to raise consciousness
Courts	• Reduce environmental impact of courts • Conserve resources and reduce pollution • Adjudication practices that involve doing environmental good	• Proximity of court buildings to allied criminal justice institutions • Multiple purpose building such as co-located support services • Diverting offenders to environmentally focused projects	• New York State – electronic filing systems
Corrections	• Penal architecture • Reduce energy and resource consumption • Preparing prisoners for green-collar jobs • Sustainability awareness training for staff	• Reducing the size of prisons and prison populations • Recycling of paper • Prison gardens • Engagement in external conservation projects	• Washington State – 'sustainability in prisons project'
Community Corrections	• Engagement in environmental projects • Young offender programmes that lead to environment-related jobs • Reintegration through use of green technologies	• Maintaining footpaths and tree planting • Waterway clearance and habitat vegetation management • Activities that include building greenhouses, solar panel installation, hydroponics	• United Kingdom – 'offenders and nature schemes'

Source: Drawing from White and Graham, 2015.

Failure to prevent violence through police inaction, or escalating violence through police intervention, are constant dilemmas faced by the police as they respond to specific kinds of events and situations. This includes responding to situations generated by climate change – food riots, conflicts over water, protests against carbon emissions from coal-powered plants, and the list goes on.

The assumptions about the policed, the techniques and style of intervention, and the operational strategies employed in dealing with events such as riots all affect the course and consequences of these events. The policing of demonstrations in recent years, for example, has been accompanied by critical examination of policing practices, including police violence and over-reaction, whether this be Melbourne, Seattle or Genoa. Three main interrelated strategic areas for protest control have been identified: *coercive* strategies (for example, use of weapons and physical force), *persuasive* strategies (for example, discussion between police and protestors), and *information* strategies (for example, widespread information gathering before, during and after a protest) (Della Porta and Reiter, 2006). Years of experience with demonstrations, across many different national contexts, have been consolidated into forward planning and preventative work that draws upon coercive, persuasive and information strategies. Simultaneously, protest movements likewise have learned from experience how to maximise their political impact, even if this, at times, leads to conflict with the police.

It would seem that 'low profile' policing and good respectful practice is generally more effective than a coercive paramilitary style of policing (Stott et al, 2007; Baker, 2003). Reaching for the 'big stick' may in fact antagonise protagonists and generate the kinds of violence that good policing is meant to minimise. Again, police stereotypes and attitudes toward 'hooligans' have been shown to influence how the police contribute to the conflict, including the escalation of conflict (Reicher et al, 2004). Could the same be said about police stereotypes of climate change activists and protestors?

Good practice in public order policing is hard to separate from political pressures to operate in particular ways. Further issues of public order policing relate to matters such as the influence of the wider political environment on specific event policing, the tensions between paramilitary styles and peacekeeping modes of operation, and the precipitation and amplification of violence due to the policing approach adopted. Whether it is policing of 'hooligans', anti-globalisation protests, climate change activists or rioters, the method of intervention has practical as well as symbolic purchase.

For example, a comparison of public order policing in Canada and Bolivia around anti-globalisation demonstrations provides disturbing evidence of the politicisation of policing to the detriment of good policing practice. It is argued that police tactics are increasingly being influenced by transnational political agendas, which are about avoiding embarrassment, instead of using the most appropriate, effective and non-violent methods (Sheptycki, 2005). In contrast to the 'negotiated management' policing that is adopted in many other public order situations, in the specific case of anti-globalisation events the emphasis tends to now be on escalated use of force and extensive coercion. This, in turn, has major implications for public order policing in other areas, and the relationship between police and the policed in future planned and spontaneous events.

Not all climate change-related policing deals with street level disorder stemming from climate justice protests and activism. Policing, as well, deals with investigation and prosecution of environmental offenders. How they do so is of course another major concern of Climate Change Criminology, especially in regards the largest perpetrators of climate change harm – corporations and governments.

Global issues demand global responses. This pertains to policing as much as it does to laws, policies and overall environmental strategies. Dealing with global warming, and the specific contributing factors to global warming (including both legal and illegal carbon emissions, legal and illegal logging practices, systematic reductions in biodiversity via extensive reliance on genetically modified organisms, extinction and endangering of species, and so on), ultimately will call forth concerted coercive action to combat environmental harm. The role and capacities of the police are essential in this regard. One thing is crystal clear. More thought has to go into how best to organise environmental law enforcement and its effectiveness in relation to the regulation and policing of climate change mitigation and adaptation measures.

Ultimately, environmental law enforcement will require collaboration between different nation-states and police services. It may well also require the setting up of some form of planetary police, preferably backed up by an International Environment Court (or equivalent) with requisite United Nations support. This is especially so if we are to adequately deal with environmental matters such as those pertaining to the international spaces of our oceans (for example, pollution, concentrations of plastic, illegal fishing, transference of toxic materials). Understanding the complexities of environmental issues is an important step in forging a transnational value system protective of specific biospheres, nonhuman animals and human interests.

Climate change and victim issues

Another dimension of criminal justice relates to matters of how best to respond to victims and victimisation. In part, criminal justice responses will be initially dictated by existing laws. Being viewed as 'victim' has several dimensions including whether or not their rights have been violated in some way through someone else's acts (or omissions).

In respect to environmental rights for example, existing laws and conventions do acknowledge such rights to some extent. For example, *Principle 1 of the Stockholm Declaration* stressed that 'Man [sic] has the fundamental right to freedom, equality and adequate conditions of life, in an environment of a quality that permits a life of dignity and well-being, and he [sic] bears a solemn responsibility to protect and improve the environment for present and future generations' (quoted in Council of Europe, 2012: 11).

Yet, as noted above, the Council of Europe (2012: 12) has also observed that 'Currently, no comprehensive legally binding instrument for the protection of the environment exists globally.'

In the context of major global shifts in climate change, biodiversity and pollution, this presumption may no longer be warranted. So too, the general and unequal impact of climate change highlights the limitations of more narrowly defined legal remedies based upon existing human rights law. The fact is that those least responsible for, and least able to remedy the effects of, climate change are worst affected by it.

The seriousness, or lack thereof, of how environmental victims are treated is reflected in how the UN *Declaration of Basic Principles of Justice for Victims of Crime and Abuses of Power* has been interpreted and used in practice, with much less attention being given to those suffering abuse of power compared to traditional crime victims. Indeed, Fattah (2010: 56) makes the telling comment that:

> the new victimologists have been extremely selective in the types of crime they denounce and the groups of victims whose cause they champion. They chose to focus their attention and to concentrate their political efforts and action on traditional crime and its victims, on crimes that cause individual harm rather than ones that cause collective harm. As a result, victims of white-collar crime and its depredations have been once again relegated to the shadow, to the background.

Replace the phrase 'white-collar crime' with 'ecocide' or 'climate injustice' and the result is pretty much the same. This is a situation that Climate Change Criminology wants to change.

Consider again, for example, the place and plight of children in the light of the threats and risks posed by global warming (White, 2015b).

From the point of view of intergenerational equity, the problems are more than apparent.

- Many children worldwide have not had adequate access to their rightful Earth legacy: present discriminations and environmental injustice constitute violations of intergenerational equity (unequal inheritance from 'past' generations).
- Suffering and harm is evident among children today, as are the heightened risks and vulnerabilities (inequities within the 'present' generation).
- Future harms are already well known, particularly in relation to climate change and threats to biodiversity (putting at jeopardy 'future' generations).

At a strategic and symbolic level, efforts to widen the parameters of legal application and political debate about these issues might be informed by appeal to the *UN Declaration of Basic Principles of Justice for Victims of Crime and Abuse of Power* (1985). This is essentially a non-binding 'soft law' instrument. Nonetheless, it is concerned with the infliction of harm on individuals and groups, broadly defined, rather than violations of national criminal laws per se. That is, it is concerned with 'those who suffer damage' (Hall, 2013). Tied into the notions of ecocide and intergenerational equity, this notion of victimhood could well provide the grounding for taking the interests and needs of children seriously.

There is, however, still a need to elaborate and codify the relevant norms of intergenerational equity – in order to reduce the ambiguities about expected behaviour and define cooperative behaviour from uncooperative behaviour. Here, again, the concept of 'ecocide' finds purchase as one means to emphasise the *seriousness* and *urgency* of the problem, and the pressing need for *action* and *redress*.

Addressing intergenerational equity in practice will require much more consideration of specific legal issues – including and especially the crime of ecocide and how best to deal with environmental destruction and degradation. There are also issues relating to how victims and victimhood are to be conceptualised and represented, and how compensation, remediation, rehabilitation and restoration are to be accomplished.

The place of the non-human environmental entity also requires further critical scrutiny, particularly in the light of legal developments that grant some specific rights. For example, a recent decision by India's Minister of the Environmental and Forests to ban dolphin shows is significant, with the Central Animal Authority issuing the statement that 'Cetaceans...should be seen as "non-human persons" and as such should have their own specific rights' (Bancroft-Hinchey, 2013).

On another front, the intrinsic rights of nature have also been acknowledged in specific laws recently passed in New Zealand. These pertain to Te Urewer (land) and Te Awa Tupua (water). The laws acknowledge *this* land and *this* river as having their own mana (its own authority) and mauri (its own life force). In a similar vein to developments in Ecuador and Bolivia, the landscape/river is personified – it is its own person and cannot be owned – and this is established through legislation that establishes their status as a legal person. This means that nature (in its various manifestations) is recognised as a subject within law. In the case of the *Te Urewera Act 2014*, the land is to be preserved in its natural state, introduced plants and animals exterminated, and the Tuhoe people and the Crown are to work together in a stewardship role. Similarly, the *Te Awa Tupua Act 2016* grants legal recognition to the Whanganui River and provides for a co-management regime involving the Whananui Iwi and the Crown.

To be granted rights is to simultaneously establish the conditions of victimhood insofar as rights can be violated and thus wrongs committed against the rights-holder. This is an important development, although in and of itself a rights-based argument is not essential in supporting a call for the recognition of the non-human as a victim of harm (Flynn and Hall, 2017).

Holding to account those responsible

While we are all implicated in the wrongs contributing to climate change, particularly in regards to consumption in the affluent west (and as demonstrated in Chapter Six, some are more culpable than others), it is time to criminalise these carbon criminals.

Most fundamentally, the fight for climate justice must involve assertion of democratic control over land, air, water and energy. This means divesting the present 'owners' of their private property and re-asserting communal control. Just a handful of transnational corporations contribute a significant proportion of the world's carbon emissions. These companies are responsible for more GHGs than most countries.

Apportioning responsibility

The question is not only who is to blame for global warming but how do we allocate blame? There are a series of overlapping issues here that need to be unpacked. These revolve around acknowledgement of both nation-states and corporations as the major contributors to the problem, assessment of the criteria used to apportion responsibility and costs, prior and ongoing knowledge of the harm, ability to pay, and the beneficiaries of past damaging activities (White, 2017b).

Contribution to the problem

The matter of who is responsible for global warming is generally framed in terms of the 'polluter pays principle' (those who pollute should rectify the mess) and historical wrongs (stemming from the industrial revolution onwards). To some extent this is simply an issue of measurement, that is determining who has contributed the most carbon emissions over time. It is also, however, a matter of context.

From an historical perspective, roughly 75 per cent of total anthropogenic CO_2 emissions from 1750 to 2005 were produced by the developed world (defined in this instance as OECD North America and Europe, Eastern Europe, Former USSR, Japan, Australia and New Zealand), which is also responsible for at least 60 per cent of current GHG emissions. Into the future, however, emissions will mainly come from the developing world's collective emissions, especially China and India (Page, 2008).

Foreknowledge and precaution

Matters of foreknowledge have both an historical and a horizon dimension. Looking backwards, questions can be asked as to who made the decisions, when and under what circumstances. For example, it was not until the 1990s that generalised knowledge about climate change and carbon emissions was available. Therefore, it is argued that responsibility should not be attributed prior to this date (Page, 2008). Is 'excusable ignorance' actually justified, however, especially if the scope of the damage and the looming problems are so large?

For crimes such as ecocide the question of intent (or 'conditional liability') is over-ridden by considerations of the magnitude of the harm. Thus, it is proposed that ecocide be considered a 'strict liability' offence, and that offenders are punished accordingly (Higgins, 2012). Additionally, as a crime against peace, the penalty and response must be proportionate to the offence, which translates into the use of higher-end sanctions.

From both a policy and a legal perspective, however, the determination of environmental harm is nonetheless contingent upon where thresholds are set (for example, when pollution is deemed to be harmful enough) and where responsibilities allocated (for example, who the designated responsible officer is within a company). It has been noted that 'life without emitting is not possible. Every human must breathe and has to use some amount of energy for heating and nutrition purposes' (Baatz, 2013: 95). Pollution is therefore inevitable. The questions of how much and what kind of pollution is 'acceptable' and who, specifically, is 'responsible' require precise answers if prosecution is to happen. Without clear guidelines and rules in place, this will be difficult to obtain.

Knowledge of harm runs into the future as well as taking into account past actions. Existing mechanisms of regulation are patently inadequate. From the point of view of the precautionary principle, activities that involve additional carbon emissions ought to be banned now, rather than assessed after the fact. The trend, however, is in the opposite direction. It is notable, for example, that things have got much worse *since* official recognition of global warming: 'In the 25 years since nations resolved to act in 1992, the level of atmospheric carbon dioxide has continued to climb ever more rapidly. It is now well clear of 400 parts per million everywhere in the world – 45 per cent higher than in pre-industrial times' (Boyer, 2018: 14).

This is continued harm in the face of foreknowledge, and continued resistance to change in the midst of international agreement that there is, indeed, a problem needing redress.

Ability and responsibility to pay

Who should pay for climate change adaptation and mitigation measures is partly based upon the implicit assumption that those with the ability to solve environmental problems were also responsible for their emergence. Even if this is not always the case empirically (some present-day countries are wealthy but this was not founded upon industrial growth), there is reason to favour such payments insofar as climate change is a global phenomenon that affects every place on the planet. Insofar as this is the case, then those with the resources need to pitch in to a greater extent than those without, for the benefit of all.

There is also the argument that those countries that have most benefited from past industrialisation should also bear the burden of compensation. Taken together, it is argued that there is a broad convergence of reasons why certain countries should pay more: 'Developed countries were *causally responsible* for climate change; they are the main *beneficiaries* of activities that cause climate change; and they have the *ability* to tackle the causes and effects of climate change' (Page, 2008: 564 – emphasis in original).

Assigning proportional payments is, however, a complicated task and various complex formulae have been theorised (Baatz, 2013; SEI, 2018). Such calculation takes into account factors such as the benefits associated with emissions, over distinct time periods, as well as the damages associated with emissions from certain periods (Meyer and Roser, 2010). What is important, however, is that such accounts seem to largely ignore political economy and the dominance of the capitalist mode of production. Instead, class politics is refracted through the lens of nation-state responsibilities. Moreover, the discussion tends to be pitched around compensation rather than regulation and control. Little is said about democratisation of those decisions – about air, water, land and energy – which are most fundamental and decisive in determining the fate of the planet.

Countries consist of citizens and residents who have differential access to the levers of power, and who command uneven access to and mobilisation of resources. It is governments of nation-states that bear responsibility for climate change policy, but they do so in the context of the interpenetration of corporate and state power. Critical discussion of responsibility, accountability and prosecution must privilege these factors and relationships. What is most important is that there is a need to shift the primary focus from states (countries) to incorporated entities (that include both private and state corporations). A certain level of specificity is possible insofar as the extent of harm and foreknowledge of the harm can be pinpointed to particular states and companies, at particular times.

For instance, quantitative analysis of historic fossil fuel and cement production records of the 50 leading investment-owned, 31 state-owned, and nine nation-state producers of oil, natural gas and cement from 1854 to 2010 showed that they produced 63 per cent of cumulative worldwide emissions of industrial carbon dioxide and methane (Heede, 2014). The largest investor-owned and state-owned companies produced the most carbon emissions. It is also known that more than half of all industrial emissions of carbon dioxide have occurred since 1986, when the risks of global warming were becoming better known. These same major entities possess fossil fuel reserves that will, if produced and emitted, intensify anthropogenic climate change.

GHG emissions come from a variety of sources and include direct emissions, indirect emissions that arise as a consequence of a corporation's activities, and other indirect emissions from sources not owned or controlled by a corporation but which occur as a result of its activities (Mascher, 2016). The largest 500 companies account for over 10 per cent of total GHG emissions produced each year, and 31 per cent of GHGs emitted globally each year is attributed to the 32 energy companies among the top 500 companies (Mascher, 2016). We know who the main culprits are.

Yet, internationally most political attention is still on nation-states and as articulated in the Paris Agreement, interpreting and putting into practice the notion of 'common but differentiated responsibility' (United Nations, 2015). Environmental activists are pressuring nation-states to accept their fair share of the financial burden in countering global warming, for needed expenditures on both mitigation and adaptation strategies (see SEI, 2018). Many of the wealthy nation-states are, however, running huge budget deficits and accordingly are disinclined to spend money outside of their own domestic sphere. Simultaneously, major tax cuts, such as occurred in 2018 under the Trump administration in the United States, privileges the corporate sector and the wealthy, thus contributing to overall budget shortfalls. It is already the case that transnational corporations pay little or no tax, and many shift money around globally to avoid tax – as demonstrated in the Panama and the Paradise Papers that deal with the clandestine financial wheeling and dealing of the world's elite (see for example, Alberici, 2018a; 2018b). Corporations must be held to account, not only nation-states.

Intervention and social action

There are several ways in which to frame climate change intervention and the prevention of environmental harm (White, 2008). One approach is to chart existing environmental legislation and provide a sustained socio-legal analysis of specific breaches of law, the role of environmental law enforcement agencies, and the difficulties of and opportunities for using criminal law against environmental offenders. Another approach places emphasis on social regulation as the key mechanism to prevent and curtail environmental harm, including attempts to reform existing systems of production and consumption through a constellation of measures and by bringing non-government and community groups directly into the regulatory process. A third approach presses the need for transnational activism, with an emphasis on fundamental social change. What counts is engagement in strategies that will challenge dominant authority structures and those modes of production that are linked to environmental degradation and destruction, negative transformations of nature, species decline, global warming and threats to biodiversity.

In many cases, social movements are seen to be vital in dealing with instances of gross environmental harm in the legal, regulatory and social action spheres (Brecher, 2015; Stilwell, 2018). The emphasis on social reform or social transformation is certainly not necessarily mutually exclusive. They can feed into each other, and occur simultaneously. The global nature of the biggest environmental problem of this era – climate change – means that inevitably our collective survival will require planetary cooperation and worldwide action. True eco-security can only be achieved when specific groups of people are not made insecure through displacement (physically and in terms of livelihood) and when universal rather than sectoral interests become the measure of what is right and good (for example, notions of ecological citizenship).

Environmental reform and transformative change is only possible insofar that powerful class forces and state power is confronted directly and indirectly. This is because dealing with environmental risk and harms demand action that gets to the source of the problems and the imperatives that drive environmental degradation and global warming. Systemic problems require answers that transcend the existing system. The status quo must change. The question is how is this to be achieved?

There is no one answer to this question. Instead, progress toward significant social change demands multiple actions across multiple domains. History teaches us that momentum for revolutionary transformation must incorporate many different interest groups (in alliance formally or in united front), pursuing the struggle from within existing state and civil institutions, as well as fighting against the powerful elite. The matrix of an action plan against climate change (see Table 7.3) must therefore include activities and responses that involve the law and legal change, environmental law enforcement activities, courts and adjudication processes, and direct social action. Efforts to highlight ecocide and intergenerational equity assume the politicisation of legal systems and the necessity of the internationalisation of legal action. Meanwhile, activist challenges must address the skewed nature of state–corporate cooperation, overcome the fortress mentality of ordinary citizens fostered by populist rhetoric and sectional interests, and garner support from those sceptical of any form of contemporary politics, including climate change politics.

This matrix of activity represents many contemporary struggles and actions, some of which are increasingly central to criminological endeavours. From public criminology (Kramer, 2013b) to NGO collaboration with state environmental law enforcement agencies

(White, 2012c; Pink and White, 2016), from the focus on ecocide (South, 2012; Higgins, 2010; 2012) through to the role of environment courts (Walters and Westerhuis, 2013), the strategic message is that intervention counts, and that it counts along many different frontiers of engagement. In this process everyone has a part to play.

Conclusion

This chapter has provided a brief review of climate change developments involving institutions of criminal justice. The discussions have exposed a number of topic areas warranting much further discussion and debate – including strategic uses of the law, adoption of greening strategies within institutional settings, conflicting demands on and models of policing in regards climate change activism, victim recognition and acknowledgement within formal systems of criminal justice, and the complications associated with assigning blame and responsibility to real world actors such as corporations. Climate Change Criminology seeks answers to such questions and dilemmas, all the while participating in activities and movements in support of the climate justice goal.

As reinforced in this chapter, an action plan against climate change must include activities and responses that involve the law and legal change, environmental law enforcement activities, courts and adjudication processes, and direct social action (White and Kramer, 2015). Ultimately, however, this will also require action in and around the exercise of state power as well – since the carbon vandal more often than not acts with direct and indirect state support, through government policy decisions and via laws and courts that are skewed in pro-business directions. Bias in the system demands taking a stand against that bias. The place and role of the criminologist in pursuit of climate justice, therefore, can never be politically neutral.

Table 7.3: An eco-justice action plan

	Short-term	Medium-term	Long-term
Law and legal reform	Innovative application of existing laws eg: public interest, public trust, human rights Strengthen protocols within existing Conventions eg: transnational organised crime	Strengthen acknowledgement of victims' rights and interests eg: Environmental Victims Charter Legitimise NGO status vis-à-vis legal standing generally, and acting on behalf of environmental victims eg: 'surrogate victims' (that is, humans acting on behalf of non-human environmental entities)	Systematic criminalisation of environmental harm eg: education combined with urgency for action Establishment of new international convention on environmental crime eg: defining environmental crime, including ecocide
Environmental law enforcement	Strengthen collaborative networks involving key environmental law enforcement agencies, NGOs and academics eg: regular meetings, workshops and conferences, sharing of information, provision of training sessions and training materials Establish environmental crime task forces to tackle specific types of environmental crime eg: key government agencies across relevant operational areas	Establish National Environmental Security Taskforces eg: permanent operational bodies at the national level Strengthen research and intervention capacity in non-government sectors eg: research institutes, Interpol internships, NGO exchanges	Establishment of international eco-police, with dedicated specialist skills and capacities to investigate and prosecute environmental crime eg: international 'green police' service
Courts and adjudication	Expansion of specialist environmental courts and tribunals eg: New South Wales Land and Environment Court Internationalisation of judicial training programmes eg: UK magistrates training	Special court of International Criminal Court eg: operationalisation of existing powers Systematic review of sanctions and remedies eg: restorative justice, reparative justice, public trust	Establishment of International Environmental Court eg: equivalent status to International Criminal Court Integrated Eco-Justice System eg: protection of victim rights, global eco-policing, effective sanctions and remedies
Social action	Rhetorical and symbolic construction of climate change as 'crime' eg: climate scientists and criminologists speaking out Carbon emission protests and renewable energy advocacy eg: anti-coal marches and demonstrations (eg: campaigns such as blockadia)	Collaboration with state environmental law enforcement agencies eg: participation in National Environmental Security Taskforces Further internationalisation of and collaboration across NGO activist networks eg: climate justice alliances	Establishment of permanent environmental justice people's tribunal eg: regular global events Ongoing critical intervention around state policies and international conventions eg: climate change mobilisations Making national economies climate-safe eg: conversion to low carbon technologies, more efficient use of energy, reduced demand

Source: White and Kramer, 2015.

EIGHT

Criminological responses to climate change

Introduction

This chapter provides a short conclusion to this book by summarising the main propositions and areas of concern for Climate Change Criminology. The chapter emphasises the role of criminologists as public intellectuals and political activists, and the necessity that there be stewards and guardians of the future. This translates into prioritising research, policy and practice around climate change themes – so that we collectively address the key problem of this age, flowing into the future.

For criminologists, ultimately this means that we need to go beyond parochial viewpoints and those perspectives that frame harm in terms of national or regional interests. Our loyalty has to be to the planet as a whole, rather than being bound by a narrow prescriptive patriotism based on nation.

Indeed, the role of criminology itself is brought into question around these issues. In conventional terms, criminology as a field could end up simply as handmaiden to a repressive state if its proponents uncritically accept narrowly conceived national security and environmental securitisation agendas. This would translate into defence of dirty industries, resource protection internally and externally, and collusion of criminologist against climate change activists (perhaps under the rubric of fighting against 'eco-terrorism'). The focus of Climate Change Criminology takes us into completely opposite directions.

Constructing the issues

There are a series of systemic contradictions that underpin global warming. The treadmill of production embodies a tension or 'metabolic rift' between economy and ecology. Productivist and consumerist ideologies and practices ensure continued economic growth at the expense of ecological limits (Stretesky et al, 2014; Brisman and South, 2014). These limits are now being reached, and global warming is exacerbating the situation.

Existing harms are perpetrated via a series of feedback loops that are, in turn, generated in the first place as politically and economically 'safe' responses to climate change. This occurs because 'non-reformist reforms' preferred by powerful government and business interests (such as proposals for deep earth repositories for carbon storage) override those that would actually address the key ecological problems underlying climate change (such as keeping the coal in the ground). The result is that not enough is being done to combat global warming.

To be effective, therefore, responses need to address deep-seated inequalities and trends within the treadmill of production that go to the heart of ownership, control and exploitation of resources, and human relationships with nature. Adequate responses to climate change demand a transformation of basic concepts of ownership and the relationships underpinning these. The public interest and accountability for harm need to take precedence over sectional interests and existing private controls over resources that affect us all.

Yet, in countries like Australia, and indeed many other advanced capitalist countries, climate change is not *the* topic of the day. Although climate change features regularly in commercial media reports, its news value is still relatively low compared to other stories, events and trends.

The discourses surrounding climate change tend to revolve around three aspects: loss, solutions and expertise. First, there is acknowledgement that climate change is 'real' with consequences that are 'unreal'. While a small minority of political leaders still dispute this claim, most are thoughtful and reasonable enough to accept climate change as fact not belief. Any sense of loss, however, is usually projected to somewhere else and into the future. It is neither here nor now. There is little urgency in tackling the problem of climate change or the problems stemming from global warming. Debates over partisan political issues such as leadership and taxes, and concrete issues such as the costs of energy, continue to dominate the political agenda.-

Second, any proposed solutions to climate change, from a policy perspective, are sold to the public as being relatively painless. Reducing carbon emissions by enacting legislation supportive of electric vehicles, for example, is a process of phasing in the new in ways that do not radically unsettle present-day consumption patterns. Moreover, individuals are frequently exhorted to 'do their part' by reducing their reliance upon plastic bags, eating less animal products and utilising public transport. Such solutions ignore the question of loss, both to others already experiencing the harsh realities of rising seas and escalating temperatures and to oneself as a potential victim. Massive changes to the Earth's climate system do not equate to massive shifts in government policy or mainstream western lifestyles. Business as usual simply finds new avenues by which to profit and grow.

Third, the most favoured solutions are those that present themselves as technical rather than social, political or economic solutions. Rather than changing systems, the point of departure is to focus on innovation and the 'silver bullet'. Specifically, technology itself is sold as the best or only way in which to tackle global climate change. This involves western wizardry of the most ingenious kind. Spray the atmosphere with sulphur dioxide in order to reflect back the sun's rays. Foster ocean algae blooms to do a similar thing. Such solutions offer false promise, they fail to address the fundamental causes of global warming, and if implemented they are imposed by those doing the most damage in the first place. What is important is that these kinds of solutions are once again universalised and exported by the Global North. The voices, opinions and interests of the Global South are thereby, once again, marginalised and ignored. So too are solutions that address the issues – such as stopping deforestation and planting multiple crop varieties – that resonate with and are responsive to the needs of local communities worldwide.

State–corporate interests define environmental risk and harm in ways that prop up existing profit-based modes of production (and consumption). In so doing, transgressions against particular groups of people, specific environments and other species occur as a 'natural' consequence of systemic pressures and elite choices. Exploitation of both the human and the non-human is built into the very fabric of dominant constructions of biosecurity and national interest. There is then a close relationship between state power and class power (White, 2014; Kramer, 2013b). Wealth, power and influence are not pluralised, but are increasingly concentrated into fewer and fewer hands, typically in the form of the transnational corporation. The state is not independent of the general power relations of a society, and therefore the exercise of state power generally reflects the interests of those who have the capacity to marshal significant economic resources (for example, large mining companies, agricultural corporate giants).

Nonetheless, there is a relative autonomy to state power insofar as the nation-state must rule in favour of the system as a whole (which periodically means intervention in the affairs of specific companies). Likewise, for the sake of the wider political economy the nation-state has an interest in maintaining a modicum of public order (which may require addressing the most obviously harmful social and environmental practices of private business). The state in a capitalist society is a capitalist state. Its effectiveness in most liberal democratic countries rests, in part, however, upon maintaining the illusion of neutrality, impartiality and plurality, and sustaining this through implementation of basic safeguards for individual human rights, baseline welfare and educational provision, democratic elections and environmental protection. Where these collapse, the result is dictatorship and more blatant self-serving activity on the part of state and corporate elites. Capitalism does not require democracy, liberal or otherwise. The experiences and lessons of China and Russia, where one party and strongmen dominate is to some extent being replicated in the Philippines and even the United States in 2017–2018 as populism gives free rein to the demagogue.

What gets socially defined as climate injustice is contingent upon the capacity of sectional interests to first garner consensus about how to interpret what is happening, and second, to secure measures for generalising and implementing action against what is deemed to be 'harmful' behaviour, primarily via the state. To date, material differences in social power, and in social and ecological interests, mean that state action is skewed in favour of powerful individuals and companies. This is supported by employment of techniques of neutralisation, aggressive contrarianism and outright government fiat. Most of the harm the powerful do, therefore, is not defined as such. Additionally, harm can be rendered invisible to the extent that it is externalised to more vulnerable population groups that do not have the social power to match that of the powerful. Bio-insecurity (for the many), state action (on behalf of the few) and the corporate colonisation of Nature (for the sake of profit) are interconnected.

Key aspects of climate change criminology

From the point of view of Climate Change Criminology, identification, investigation and responsiveness to climate-related harm are fundamental concerns. Harm related to climate change has many different aspects pertaining to matters of time, space and scale. For example, it may be specific to local areas (such as threats to certain species, like coral in the Great Barrier Reef) yet manifest as part of a general global pattern (such as being an effect of widescale temperature changes affecting coral everywhere). It may be non-intentional (in the sense of being a by-product of some other agenda) or premeditated (insofar as the negative outcome, for some, is foreseen). The demise of the polar bear due to the impact of global warming in the Arctic is an example of the former. The displacement of local inhabitants from their land due to carbon sequestration schemes is an example of the latter. Analytically, therefore, it is important to acknowledge and capture the nuances and subtleties of harm and harm production in any study of climate change causes and effects.

A 'crime'-focused analysis of climate change naturally tends to frame issues around specific crime determinants. For example, the climate change–crime nexus can be described in terms of crimes that arise as a consequence of climate change, as well as in terms of those crimes that lead to or cause climate change (see Table 8.1). Such an approach, while useful in pinpointing aspects of criminality and criminogenic causes, nonetheless fails to fully get to the heart of the issues surrounding climate change insofar as climate change expresses particular social, economic, cultural and political relations on a grand scale. Indeed, global warming is best seen as a structural phenomenon that cannot be explained solely or simply in criminological terms – it is fundamentally about power, interests and resources.

Table 8.1: The climate change–crime nexus

Consequences of climate change for crime	Causes of global warming as a crime
Human behaviour and temperature change eg: increased aggression linked to hot temperatures *Place-based activities affected by weather patterns* eg: places with higher rainfall have lower rates of violent crimes *Social strains arising from biophysical changes* eg: less food availability linked to increased social conflicts	Activities of the powerful drive global warming eg: carbon emissions as part of normal business practices State–corporate crime as a form of ecocide eg: intentional and systematic destruction of environments *Contrarianism as denial of harm and criminality* eg: neutralisation techniques that forestall mitigation and adaptation strategies

Source: Drawing from White, 2017c.

Given the structural nature and determinants of climate change (and responses to climate change), a crime focus alone is not sufficient in either understanding its harms or addressing its causes and consequences. In other words, a topic-based focus is valuable in its own right for exposing important issues, but generally has limited answers to the big questions surrounding climate change, culpability and consequence. In a similar vein, a criminal justice solution to the complex problems associated with global warming is simply not possible.

Higher order theoretical explorations, therefore, must accompany the topic-based investigations. Any strategic response must necessarily be a multi-pronged, multi-disciplinary and multi-agency in nature. Criminology can contribute to this, but in doing so it must incorporate certain critical elements. This is precisely the intent of Climate Change Criminology as a conceptual framework and action model.

Climate Change Criminology, as outlined in Chapter One, brings together a range of propositions that are intended to elaborate a critical and holistic approach to the dilemmas and challenges posed by global warming. Throughout this book, these themes or pillars (see Table 8.2) have been interwoven into a narrative that attempts to provide insight and exposition across various domains of endeavour and different topics of concern. Fundamental to this project is the notion of climate justice, an ideal that encompasses care and concern for the human and the non-human. Transgressions against humans, ecosystems and non-human environmental entities (biotic and abiotic) are deemed morally problematic and in most instances 'bad' if the effect is to destroy, diminish or degrade environmental functioning and services at the expense of overall quality of life. Climate change poses the biggest threat in this regard.

A fifth and vitally important pillar is therefore needed to counter this threat.

Social action and agitation

> Climate Change Criminology involves and supports public engagement and social interventions that challenge the status quo by focusing on climate justice for humans and non-human environmental entities.

The attainment of climate justice necessarily involves support for and engagement in mass political and social movements. These need to be directed against the forces, discourses and policies that stymy needed mitigation and adaptation measures. They also have to be informed by values, language and tactics that reflect a vision of hope, resilience and equality in regard to the future. For criminologists this propels us directly into the realm of public criminology (Loader and Sparks, 2011; Kramer, 2013a; 2013b). Climate Change Criminology is about speaking out about issues that matter.

As the key propositions illustrate, Climate Change Criminology has to be broad-based in terms of empirical remit and interdisciplinary in its conceptual orientation. Its wide scope also means that there is far too much for any one person or team to do – it will always be a collective project unable to be 'owned' by this or that individual or group of researchers. The limitations of this book reside not only in word count, but in the sheer breadth and depth of thinking, hard work and creativity required to adequately summarise and analyse all that needs to be done. As well, much more is required if we are to map out a systematic and coherent pathway for climate change activism, professional engagement and social change movements.

Moreover, the wide reach of its topic concerns means that there is much scope within Climate Change Criminology for collaboration (within criminology and across disciplines and fields), consolidation (of existing criminological writing as well as specific climate change related research) and innovation (as newly emergent trends and issues demand novel ways of thinking and acting). There is much to be done.

A vital concern that should also influence the direction and uptake of Climate Change Criminology is the question of time. This has two pertinent aspects in regard to research and intervention. First, there is a growing urgency for critique and activism in the light of receding deadlines for the prevention of further global warming. Global warming is accelerating, and in-built biophysical feedback loops (such as melting ice sheets), mean that it is likely to happen even faster than it already is today as time goes by. Policy-set targets (rather than science-derived evidence) by the Intergovernmental Panel on Climate Change that attempt to keep the planet's temperature under two additional degrees in fact required changes 'way back then'; yet, even now the world continues to struggle to slow down the carbon emissions that have contributed to current increases. Time, in this sense, is running out.

Second, it needs to be recognised that there are different timescales driving different activities. The politics of time is inherent in the time it takes to pursue climate change litigation, to change domestic policies in favour of renewable energy and to organise campaigns to keep the coal in the ground. Each endeavour to save the world takes precious time that we are steadily and rapidly losing out on. The idiocy of the likes of Donald Trump and Tony Abbott – among the foremost of climate change contrarians – has real and pertinent effects. Specifically, their interventions delay and prevent precisely the action that is needed now to counter global warming and its consequences. Fools are killing the planet and all are suffering because of it.

Table 8.2: Five pillars of Climate Change Criminology

Pillar	Theme	Concepts	Examples
Crime and harm	Climate Change Criminology views criminality in terms of criminal and/or harmful behaviour that contributes to the problem of global warming and that prevents adequate responses to climate change related consequences	*Malum prohibitum* crimes that are criminal not because they are inherently bad, but because the act is prohibited by the law of the state *Malum in se* conduct assessed as inherently wrong by nature, independent of regulations governing the conduct	Harms such as carbon emission fraud currently defined as unlawful and therefore punishable Harms currently condoned as lawful, such as carbon emissions stemming from coal-fired power stations, but which are nevertheless socially and ecologically harmful
Global connectedness and eco-justice	Climate Change Criminology is informed by a global perspective that views the world as an interconnected whole in which acts and omissions in specific locales have social and ecological ramifications for what occurs elsewhere on the earth	*Ecology*: the complex interactions of non-human nature, including its abiotic components (air, water, soils) and its biotic components (plants, animals, fungi, bacteria) *Eco-justice*: the relationship of humans generally, to the rest of the natural world, and includes concerns relating to the health of the biosphere, and more specifically plants and animals that also inhabit the biosphere	All living things are bound together and environmental matters are intrinsically global and transboundary in nature Importance of democratic conceptions of perception, knowledge and social interest, and the contributions to global knowledge (including adaptive and preventative responses to climate change) emanating from the vulnerable, the dispossessed, the disadvantaged and the ignored

Pillar	Theme	Concepts	Examples
Causes and consequences	Climate Change Criminology examines the causes of global warming, which continue to be in play even with scientific evidence and foreknowledge of its impacts, and explores the diverse consequences of climate change	*Perpetrators*: issues of culpability, accountability and responsibility *Victims*: humans, ecosystems and plant and animal species and individuals	Analysis of the causes of climate change, from a criminological perspective, focuses on who is doing what in causing the problem and/or making it worse Attention on the consequences of climate change, and differential and universal victimisation
Power and interests	Climate Change Criminology focuses on the role of contemporary political economic systems and of the powerful in creating the conditions for further global warming while abrogating their responsibilities to deal with the substantive changes and suffering arising from climate change	*Climate justice*: fundamentally concerned with the intersection of environmental destruction and degradation, and the social injustices arising from this *Ecocide*: destruction and diminishment of environments stemming from systematic human interventions that pollute and destroy	Power and interests underpin both the representation of climate change issues and the material aspects of climate change Concern is with who is causing and benefiting from harmful activities, and who is suffering from their consequences
Social action and agitation	Climate Change Criminology involves and supports public engagement and social interventions that challenge the status quo by focusing on climate justice for humans and non-human environmental entities	*Democratisation* of mitigation and adaptation strategies that are premised upon universal human and ecological interests *Multiple sites of intervention*, including in and against the state	Rallies, protests and public/social media forums in opposition to hegemonic policies and institutions Cross sectoral and cross-class collaborations in support of climate justice goals and objectives

Contesting the future

> Let's be clear about what this means: Given what we know and have known for decades, to willfully obstruct any serious response to global warming is to knowingly allow entire countries and cultures to disappear. It is to rob the poorest and most vulnerable people on the planet of their lands, their homes, their livelihoods, even their lives and their children's lives – and their children's children's lives. For money. For political power. These are crimes. They are crimes against the Earth, and they are crimes against humanity. (Stephenson, 2014: 3)

How we respond to climate change is intrinsically a process that involves contests over morals, values and perspectives that, in turn, determine how diverse groups construct the problem and what to do about it. The endeavour of Climate Change Criminology should be to create the conditions for a future that is more forgiving and generous rather than exploitive of humans, environments and animals. Empowerment is the necessary counterweight to the powers that pull us ever more into scarcity, barbarism and ecocide.

Dominant power structures are hegemonic at an international scale and at the level of the nation-state; however, they are not monolithic. The state itself, for example, is a site of social struggle over policies as well as enforcement practices. From this perspective, the specific roles of non-state actors in lobbying, regulation and enforcement around environmental issues are especially important. Accordingly, resistance to state and class power in the context of global capitalism is also an integral part of social and ecological dynamic of exploitation. If the state is implicated in the source of the problem (via state–corporate collusion in environmentally destructive activities), then this has ramifications for strategies designed to diminish environmental harms. In the end, effective intervention around climate change frequently demands action in collaboration *with* and *against* the state.

In the midst of despair over contemporary politics and climate change trends, notions such as ecological stewardship, ecological sustainability and ecocide nonetheless still provide conceptual challenges to the status quo. Activist environment groups – local through to global – are confronting the dangers and immoralities of 'industry' and 'government'. There may be no 'enemy' as such, but there are multiple sources and places of conflict and contestation. Each place and each struggle carries import for the planet as a whole. The problem is universal; but resistance, too, is everywhere.

This is not a time for subtlety, as President Trump has made abundantly clear. Rather this is an era of massive and rapid change. In this context, bold ideas and extravagant critique are needed and essential, as is mass activism and social transformation. This is the promise and commitment of Climate Change Criminology.

Most fundamentally, the fight for climate justice must involve assertion of democratic control over land, air, water and energy. This means divesting the present 'owners' of their private property and re-asserting communal control.

Climate change is everyone's business. For the sake of ourselves and our children and the non-human environmental entities with which we share the planet, we must all become guardians of the future. This is not a commissioned role, in the sense that the Hungarian Parliament has a 'Commissioner for Future Generations' (Schneeberger, 2011). This is an activist role. Forestalling future harms associated with climate change demands more than exposing corrupt institutions and systemic inequalities and abuses of power. It requires ongoing political engagement in the form of public criminology. It also requires professional expertise in areas where criminology may well add value to the climate change story.

For criminologists, the role responsibilities are clear. We need to engage ourselves as public intellectuals and in political action, to assume the mantle of stewards and guardians of the future, and to prioritise research, policy and practice around climate change themes. The biggest issue in the history of humankind demands nothing less than this.

Intervention in relation to climate change involves drawing upon of a wide variety of sources (for example, cross-disciplinary, multi-jurisdictional, cross cultural) to investigate matters such as conflicts over resources, climate-induced migration, and the social effects of radical shifts in weather patterns. Information and data that is collated can be analysed and interpreted in the light of broad eco-global criminological considerations (for example, transgressions against humans, ecosystems and animals), as well as specific patterns of environmental victimisation involving particularly vulnerable groups (for example, women, children, disadvantaged groups, ethnic minorities). Steps can be taken to theorise the findings in relation to anthropogenic causes (for example, human responsibility for harm, specific perpetrators and degrees of culpability). All of these have been identified herein as crucial tasks of Climate Change Criminology.

Climate change and the gross exploitation of natural resources are leading to the general demise of the ecological status quo – hence increasing the need for the crime of ecocide (Tekayak, 2016b). If carbon emissions are at the forefront of the causes of global warming, then the obvious question is why continue to emit such dangerous planet-altering substances into the atmosphere. Introducing ecocide as a crime against humanity would mean that 'individuals in a position of superior or command responsibility will be criminally liable if they carry out an activity covered by such a provision, disregarding knowledge or intent' (Hellman, 2014: 278). Ecological destruction accompanying natural resource extraction such as the oil and gas industries, coal mining and logging could be proceeded against under an international law of ecocide.

As discussed in Chapter Seven, from a Climate Change Criminology perspective, to effectively combat global warming requires a series of interrelated developments. These need to occur over the short term, medium term and long term, and involve interventions across various areas of criminal justice (White and Kramer, 2015). For example, with respect to law and legal reform, the kinds of measures that are needed include innovative use of public litigation and public trust laws as well as the establishment of a new international convention on climate justice that incorporates the crime of ecocide.

Embedding the 'Oxford Principles' for the governance of geoengineering projects is also important (Oxford Geoengineering Programme, 2017; see also Asilomar Scientific Organizing Committee, 2010), although some question whether geoengineering solutions and democracy can go hand-in-hand (Szerszynski et al, 2013). The principles include:

- geoengineering to be regulated as a public good;
  public participation in geoengineering decision-making;
- disclosure of geoengineering research and open publication of results;
- independent assessment of impacts;
- governance before deployment.

So-called 'technical solutions' to climate change involve remediation technologies (such as carbon dioxide removal) and intervention technologies (such as solar radiation management). Control over and deployment of these must involve a broad range of participants, countries, experts and interests (Asilomar Scientific Organizing Committee, 2010). Decisions in this domain are too important to be left in the hands of dominant nation-states and corporations that more often than not are self-serving of narrow sectional interests.

In regard to law enforcement, policy should be directed at strengthening collaborative networks involving key environmental law enforcement agencies (government as well as NGOs), and establishing permanent operational bodies at the national level to tackle environmental security issues, such as the INTERPOL 'National Environmental Security Taskforce' (NEST) model (Higgins and White, 2016). For courts and adjudication, measures could include the expansion of specialist environment courts and tribunals at the national domestic level, accompanied by the establishment of an international environment court (or its equivalent, such as an environmental division of the International Criminal Court).

Fundamentally, however, policy change and reform in relation to global warming is bounded by one essential consideration – politics. This, too, is reflective of the conditions which created the problem in the first place, and which require radical transformative change if global warming is to be substantially addressed. The nation-state remains an essential platform for concerted action to deal with the causes of environmental harm, as well as mitigating the worst symptoms of such harm. The global nature of the problem – climate change – means, however, that inevitably our collective survival will require planetary cooperation and worldwide action. For Climate Change Criminology, this is best undertaken under the guidance of an eco-justice framework, rather than protection of existing privilege or 'might makes right' strategies. The latter strategies only lead to further violation of rights, and the downward spiral to our mutual destruction.

Electing and appointing people who continue to deny the basic realities of global warming and whose first acts are to tear down the institutions of environmental regulation and law enforcement are fundamentally backward steps that put one and all into jeopardy – yet with the 2017 election of President Donald Trump, this is exactly what happened. In the light of this, it is undoubtedly a time when citizens must be even more active politically in support of sensible climate change policies. There is much to defend and protect. There is much to struggle for and against. How people intervene and interact in the political life of their society, however, is also complicated by the undermining of the ordinary conventions of truth and knowledge. At the time of writing, President Trump, the most powerful person on the planet, tweets daily and the world listens attentively. In this post-fact era, the veracity of what is said seems to matter less than the attention that his comments garner. Evidence and contradiction matter nought. Saying something thus appears to trump the something that is being said. The medium is indeed the message insofar as what counts is presence, not content. A criminology for the future thus also requires media literacy and a search for truth that is not side-tracked by trivialisation, slander and bullying. This, too, is part of the challenge and struggle for climate justice.

Responses to climate change ecocide must be built upon solid foundations and involve many diverse sets of actors. Fundamentally the fight for climate justice must involve assertion of democratic control over land, air, water and energy. This means that the pursuit of climate justice will necessarily involve pushing the boundaries of the status quo, especially given the centrality of demands such as the communal appropriation of 'private property'.

Accordingly, it is only the expression of 'people's power' that will ensure that the decisions about land, air, water and energy are distributed more fairly. The essence of the struggle is to transform as well as challenge, to democratise through resistance, and to change institutions as well as criticise them. Pushing the pause button on climate change inevitably demands diverse forms of participatory resistance, and the realisation that it was the militancy of the women's liberation movement, the civil rights movement, and the anti-slavery movement that enabled some to claim their freedom and their legitimate place in society. Radical action is likewise urgently needed given the rapid ticking of the climate change clock.

Joining up diverse social forces (for example, farmers, Indigenous people, students, environmentalists) in support of climate justice goals and objectives is therefore essential, as are rallies, protests and active social media use that provide opposition to hegemonic policies and institutions. While tactics might differ, the important thing is to agree on common objectives, regardless of disagreements over how to attain these. The more specific the objectives, the more scope there is to build communities of practice around particular initiatives. Consider for instance the key demands (abridged) of the Climate Justice network (Global Campaign to Demand Climate Justice, 2018):

1. fight for the transformation of energy systems;
2. fight for food sovereignty, for peoples' rights to sufficient, healthy and appropriate food and sustainable food systems;
3. fight for peoples' rights to sufficient, affordable, clean, quality water;
4. fight for just transitions for all workers beginning with those in the dirty and harmful energy industries;

5. fight for people's safety and security of homes and livelihoods from climate disasters;
6. fight for the social, political, economic, cultural and reproductive rights and empowerment of all our people and communities;
7. fight for mobilisation and delivery of climate finance by all states;
8. fight for reparations for climate debt owed by those most responsible for climate change;
9. fight for an end to deception and false solutions in mitigation and adaptation;
10. fight for an end to policies, decisions and measures by governments, elites, institutions and corporations (domestic, regional and global) that increase the vulnerabilities of people and planet to impacts of climate change;
11. fight to stop the commodification and financialisation of nature and nature's functions;
12. fight for an international climate agreement that is rooted in science, equity and justice.

The first demand actually translates nicely into movements away from centralised energy systems to de-centralised systems that are also community-run for community benefit. Solar power at the local level is one example of such initiatives. More generally, each demand also carries with it the potential to make things better. In this regard, activism can be informed by an emphasis on the positive aspects of change – clean air makes us feel good! From Beijing to Hamburg, Bangkok to Sydney, many will appreciate the benefits that flow from this.

In a similar vein, the '350.org' campaign (350.org, 2018) has three clear demands: keep carbon in the ground; help build a new, more equitable zero-carbon economy; and pressure governments into limiting emissions. Three basic principles inform the work of this campaign:

> Principle 1
> We believe in climate justice.
> Principle 2
> We're stronger when we collaborate.
> Principle 3
> Mass mobilisations make change.

Taking a stand involves deciding whose side you are on, who you can work with, and what the specific objectives of the campaign are.

Criminologists have an important role in these political processes and in taking part in grounded alliances of activists, academics and advocates around climate change issues.

Conclusion

This book has provided an argument for and introduction to Climate Change Criminology. In so doing, it has covered a wide variety of topics, from climate change victims to carbon criminals, ecocide as a climate crime to heat and criminality. As stated at the outset, the intention is to open up debate and to welcome future dialogue. For Climate Change Criminology, this is only the beginning.

Yet we need to talk about the End.

Capitalism (and the capitalist class) is incredibly resourceful as well as a gross user of resources. At the moment, the costs and penalties of climate change are being shunted to those who are not privileged by the power structure. In due course, however, no one can escape the catastrophic events, collapsing economies, the food and water scarcities, and the desperations of survivalism. This is acknowledged by the leading figures of mainstream economics, politics and international relations. It is the topic of much discussion within military hierarchies and public policy forums. Shifting the deckchairs only has momentary purchase, before they too are lost to the overwhelming seas. Our doom, ultimately, is their doom.

Regardless of what we think or do, the Earth is resilient, with or without humans, and is forever changing. The task ahead is to make sure that we – the vast majority of humanity and the rest of the inhabitants and ecosystems of the biosphere – are part of its future, for a future it will have regardless of whether we survive or not.

Earth will abide. Climate Change Criminology is about helping to shape the terms and conditions under which it does so. Fundamentally, it is about us, and the interests and social forces that oppose us – past, present and future.

References

350.org (2018) 'Overview' and 'Principles'. www.350.org.

Aall, C. (2014) 'Sustainable tourism in practice: Promoting or perverting the quest for a sustainable development?', *Sustainability*, 6: 2562–2583.

Abbot, T. (2017) 'Address to the Global Warming Policy Foundation', 10 October, Westminster, London. Transcript, http://tonyabbott.com.au/2017/10/transcript-hon-tony-abbott-mp-address-global-warming-policy-foundation-westminster-london/#.

Abboud, A. (2013) 'The market versus the climate', *The Conversation*, 5 June.

ABC (Australian Broadcasting Corporation) (2015a) 'Southeast Asia's haze: Find out what is behind the choking smoke covering Indonesia, Malaysia and Singapore', *ABC News*, 19 October.

ABC (Australian Broadcasting Corporation) (2015b) 'South-East Asian haze strikes the Pacific as fires exceed greenhouse gas output of the US', *ABC News*, 22 October 2015.

ABC News (Australian Broadcasting Corporation) (2017) 'Hurricane Maria: Donald Trump snaps at Puerto Rico capital's mayor on emergency aid criticism', ABC News, 1 October 2017.

Agnew, R. (2006) *Pressured into Crime: An Overview of General Strain Theory*. Los Angeles: Roxbury.

Agnew, R. (2011) 'Dire forecast: A theoretical model of the impact of climate change on crime', *Theoretical Criminology*, 16(1): 21–46.

Agnew, R. (2012) 'It's the end of the world as we know it: The advance of climate change from a criminological perspective', in R. White (ed) *Climate Change from a Criminological Perspective*. New York: Springer.

Agnew, R. (2013) 'The ordinary acts that contribute to ecocide: A criminological analysis', in N. South and A. Brisman (eds) *Routledge International Handbook of Green Criminology*. London: Routledge, pp 58–72.

Agnew, R. and Brezina, T. (2010) 'Strain theories', in E. McLaughlin and T. Newburn (eds) *The SAGE Handbook of Criminological Theory*, London: SAGE, pp 96–113.

Akella, A. and Cannon, J. (2004) *Strengthening the Weakest Links: Strategies for Improving the Enforcement of Environmental Laws Globally*. Washington, DC: Center for Conservation and Government.

Albaladejo, A. and LaSusa, M. (2017) 'The Perfect Storm: How climate change exacerbates crime and insecurity in LatAm', *Insight Crime*, 25 September, https://www.insightcrime.org/news/analysis/perfect-storm-climate-change-exacerbates-crime-insecurity-latin-america-caribbean/.

Alberici, E. (2018a) 'Tax-free billions: Australia's largest companies haven't paid corporate tax in 10 years', *Australian Broadcasting Corporation (ABC) News*, 14 February.

Alberici, E. (2018b) 'There's no case for a corporate tax cut when one in five of Australia's top companies don't pay it', *Australian Broadcasting Corporation (ABC) News*, 14 February.

Alston, M. (2012) 'Rural male suicide in Australia', *Social Science and Medicine*, 74: 515–522.

Alston, M., Clarke, J. and Whittenbury, K. (2018) 'Contemporary feminist analysis of Australian farm women in the context of climate changes', *Social Sciences*, 7(16), doi:10.3390/socsci7020016.

Anderson, C. (1989) 'Temperature and aggression', *Psychological Bulletin*, 106(1): 74–96.

Anderson, C. and Anderson, K. (1998) 'Temperature and aggression: Paradox, controversy, and a (fairly) clear picture', in R. Green and E. Donnerstein (eds) *Human Aggression: Theories, Research, and Implications for Social Policy*. San Diego, CA: Academic Press.

Anderson, C., Bushman, B. and Groom, R. (1997) 'Hot years and serious and deadly assault', *Journal of Personality and Social Psychology*, 73(6): 1213–1223.

Andresen, M. and Malleson, N. (2013) 'Crime seasonality and its variations across space', *Applied Geography*, 43(1): 25–35.

Arora-Jonsson, S. (2011) 'Virtue and vulnerability: Discourses on women, gender and climate change', *Global Environmental Change*, 21: 744–751.

Asilomar Scientific Organizing Committee (2010) *The Asilomar Conference Recommendations on Principles for Research into Climate Engineering Techniques: Conference Report*. Washington, DC: Climate Institute.

Athanasiou, T. (1996) *Divided Planet: The Ecology of Rich and Poor*. Boston, MA: Little, Brown and Company.

Australian Academy of Science (2015) *The Science of Climate Change: Questions and Answers*. Canberra: Australian Academy of Science.

Baatz, C. (2013) 'Responsibility for the past? Some thoughts on compensating those vulnerable to climate change in developing countries', *Ethics, Policy and Environment*, 16(1): 94–110.

Baer, H. and Singer, M. (2009) *Global Warming and the Political Economy of Health: Emerging Crises and Systemic Solutions*. Walnut Creek, CA: Left Coast Press.

Bakan, J. (2004) *The Corporation: The Pathological Pursuit of Profit and Power*. London: Constable.

Baker, D. (2003) 'Policing industrial disputation: Lessons from the Lyttleton Picket Line Tragedy', *New Zealand Journal of Industrial Relations*, 28(3): 258-269.

Bancroft-Hinchey, T. (2013) 'India: Dolphins declared non-human persons', 5 August, Pravda.ru, www.pravdareport.com/science/earth/05-08-2013/125310-dolphins_india-0/.

Barclay, E. and Bartel, R. (2015) 'Defining environmental crime: The perspective of farmers', *Journal of Rural Studies*, 39: 188–198.

Barnett, J. and Adger, W. (2007) 'Climate change, human security and violent conflict', *Political Geography*, 26: 639–655.

Bates, G. (2013) *Environmental Law in Australia*. Sydney: LexisNexis Butterworths.

Beck, U. (1996) 'World risk society as cosmopolitan society? Ecological questions in a framework of manufactured uncertainties', *Theory, Culture, Society*, 13(4): 1–32.

Beder, S. (1997) *Global Spin: The Corporate Assault on Environmentalism*. Melbourne: Scribe Publications.

Beder, S. (2006) *Suiting Themselves: How Corporations Drive the Global Agenda*. London: Earthscan.

Beirne, P. (2014) 'Therocide: Naming animal killing', *International Journal for Crime, Justice and Social Democracy*, 4(3): 50–67.

Beirne, P. and South, N. (eds) (2007) *Issues in Green Criminology: Confronting Harms Against Environments, Humanity and Other Animals*. Collumpton: Willan.

Bell, S., McGillivray, G., Pedersen, O., Lees, E. and Stokes, E. (2017) *Environmental Law* (9th Edition). Oxford: Oxford University Press.

Bell-James, J. and Ryan, S. (2016) 'Climate change litigation in Queensland: A case study in incrementalism', *Environmental and Planning Law Journal*, 33: 515–537.

Bello, W. (2008) 'How to manufacture a global food crisis: lessons from the World Bank, IMF, and WTO', *Transnational Institute*, 16 May, www.tni.org/detail_page.phtml?&&act_id=18285.

Bennett, K. (2016) 'Australian climate change litigation: Assessing the impact of carbon emissions', *Environmental and Planning Law Journal*, 33: 538.

Bergin, A. and Allen, R. (2008) *The Thin Green Line: Climate Change and Australian Policing*. Canberra: Australian Strategic Policy Institute.

Berry, T. (1999) *The Great Work: Our Way into the Future*. New York: Harmony/Bell Tower.

Bisschop, L. (2015) *Governance of the Illegal Trade in E-Waste and Tropical Timber: Case Studies on Transnational Environmental Crime*. Farnham: Ashgate.

Bocock, R. (1993) *Consumption*. London: Routledge.

Boekhout van Solinge, T. (2008a) 'Crime, conflicts and ecology in Africa', in R. Sollund (ed) *Global Harms: Ecological Crime and Speciesism*. New York: Nova Science Publishers.

Boekhout van Solinge, T. (2008b) 'The Land of the Orangutan and the Bird of Paradise under Threat', in R. Sollund (ed) *Global Harms: Ecological Crime and Speciesism*. New York: Nova Science Publishers.

Boekhout van Solinge, T. (2010) 'Equatorial deforestation as a harmful practice and a criminological issue', in R. White (ed) *Global Environmental Harm: Criminological Perspectives*. Cullompton: Willan.

Boekhout van Solinge, T. and Kuijpers, K. (2013) 'The Amazon rainforest: A green criminological perspective', in N. South and A. Brisman (eds) *Routledge International Handbook of Green Criminology*. New York: Routledge.

Borger, J. (2017) 'Trump drops climate change from US national security strategy', *Guardian*, www.theguardian.com/us-news/2017/dec/18/trump-drop-climate-change-national-security-strategy.

Borras Jr., S., Franco, J. and Wang, C. (2013) 'The challenge of global governance of land grabbing: Changing international agricultural context and competing political views and strategies', *Globalizations*, 10(1): 161–179.

Boyanowsky, E. (1999) 'Violence and aggression in the heat of passion and in cold blood', *International Journal of Law and Psychiatry*, 22(3–4): 257–271.

Boyd, D. (2003) *Unnatural Law: Rethinking Canadian Environmental Law and Policy*. Vancouver: University of British Columbia Press.

Boyer, P. (2012) 'Wake up call from real world', *The Mercury*, Tasmania, Australia, 23 October, pp 14–15.

Boyer, P. (2014) 'Keeping up appearances is really a complicated business', *The Mercury*, Tasmania, Australia, 12 August, pp 12–13.

Boyer, P. (2018) 'El Nino weather event puts gloss on another stinker of a year', *The Mercury*, Tasmania, Australia, 16 January, pp 14–15.

Brecher, J. (2015) *Climate Insurgency: A Strategy for Survival*. Boulder, CO: Paradigm Publishers.

Bricknell, S. (2010) 'Environmental crime in Australia', *Australian Institute of Criminology (AIC) Reports Research and Public Policy Series* 109. Canberra: AIC.

Briggs, C. (2016) 'Australian Conservation Foundation's case against $16b Adani Carmichael mine project dismissed', *Australian Broadcasting Corporation (ABC) News* [online], 29 August, www.abc.net.au/news/2016-08-29/adani-carmichael-mine-court...case/7795192.

Brisman, A. (2012) The cultural silence of climate change contrarianism. In R. White (ed) *Climate Change from a Criminological Perspective*. New York: Springer, pp 41–70.

Brisman, A. (2013a) 'The violence of silence: Some reflections on access to information, public participation in decision-making, and access to justice in matters concerning the environment', *Crime, Law and Social Change*, 59(3): 291–303.

Brisman, A. (2013b) 'Not a bedtime story: Climate change, neoliberalism, and the future of the arctic', *Michigan State International Law Review*, 22(1): 241–289.

Brisman, A. (2015) 'Environment and Conflict: A Typology of Representations', in A. A. Brisman, N. South and R. White (eds) *Environmental Crime and Social Conflict*. Farnham: Ashgate.

Brisman, A. and South, N. (2013) 'Resources, wealth, power, crime and conflict', in R. Walters, D. Westerhuis and T. Wyatt (eds) *Emerging Issues in Green Criminology*. Basingstoke: Palgrave Macmillan.

Brisman, A. and South, N. (2014) *Green Cultural Criminology: Constructions of Environmental Harm, Consumerism, and Resistance to Ecocide*. London: Routledge.

Brisman, A., South, N. and White, R. (2015) 'Toward a criminology of environment–conflict relationships', in A. Brisman, N. South and R. White (eds) *Environmental Crime and Social Conflict: Contemporary and Emerging Issues*. Farnham: Ashgate.

Brisman, A., South, N. and Walters, R. (2018) 'Climate apartheid and environmental refugees', in K. Carrington, R. Hogg, J. Scott and M. Sozzo (eds) *The Palgrave Handbook of Criminology and the Global South*. Palgrave Macmillan, pp 301–321.

Brook, D. (1998) 'Environmental genocide: Native Americans and toxic waste', *American Journal of Economics and Society*, 51(1): 105–113.

Brown, D. (2010) Is climate science disinformation a crime against humanity?, *Guardian*, 3 November, www.theguardian.com/environment/cif-green/2010/nov/01/climate-science-disinformation-crime.

Brown Weiss, E. (1992) 'Intergenerational equity: A legal framework for global environmental change', in E. Brown Weiss (ed) *Environmental Change and International Law: New Challenges and Dimensions*. Tokyo: United Nations University Press.

Brown Weiss, E. (2008) 'Climate change, intergenerational equity, and international law', *The Vermont Journal of International Law*, 9: 615–628.

Bulkeley, H. and Newell, P. (2010) *Governing Climate Change*. London: Routledge.

Burdon, P. (2010) 'Wild law: The philosophy of earth jurisprudence', *Alternative Law Journal*, 35(2): 62.

Burdon, P. (2015) 'Wild law: A proposal for radical social change', *New Zealand Journal of Public and International Law*, 13(1): 157.

Burger, M., Gundlach, J., Kreilhuber, A., Ognibene, L., Kariuki, A. and Gachie, A. (2017) *The Status of Climate Change Litigation: A Global Review*. New York: United Nations Environment Programme.

Burke, M., Hsiang, S. and Miguel, E. (2015) 'Climate and conflict', *Annual Review of Economics*, 7(1): 577–617.

Burrell, A., Gay, S. and Kavallari, A. (2012) 'The compatability of EU biofuel policies with global sustainability and the WTO', *The World Economy*, 35(6): 784–798.

Butcher, B. and Stilwell, F. (2009) 'Climate change policy and economic recession', *Journal of Australian Political Economy*, 63: 108–125.

Caisley, O. (2018) 'Fresh air proves a hit, sales aren't inflated', *The Weekend Australian*, The Nation section, 17–18 February, p 5.

Caneppele, S., Riccardi, M. and Standridge, P. (2013) 'Green energy and black economy: Mafia investments in the wind power sector in Italy', *Crime Law Social Change*, 59(3): 319–339.

Carrington, K., Hogg, R. and Sozzo, M. (2015) 'Southern criminology', *British Journal of Criminology*, 56(1): 1–20.

Castles, S. (2002) Environmental change and forced migration: Making sense of the debate. *New Issues in Refugee Research, Working paper* 70. Geneva: Evaluation and Policy Analysis Unit, United Nations High Commissioner for Refugees.

Chambers, D. (2011) 'Policing and climate change', *The Australian Journal of Emergency Management*, 26(3): 52–59.

Charles, C., Gerasimchuk, I., Birdle, R., Moerenhout, T., Asmelash, E. and Laan, T. (2013) *Biofuels – At What Cost? A Review of Costs and Benefits of EU Biofuels Policies*. Manitoba: International Institute for Sustainable Development.

Clark, B. (2002) 'The indigenous environmental movement in the United States', *Organization and Environment*, 15(4): 410–442.

Cohen, E. (1990) 'Weather and crime', *British Journal of Criminology*, 30(1): 51–64.

Cohen, L. and Felson, M. (1979) 'Social change and crime rate trends: A routine activity approach', *American Sociological Review*, 44(4): 588–608.

Cohen, S. (2001) *States of Denial: Knowing about Atrocities and Suffering*. Cambridge: Polity Press.

Colangelo, A. (2016) 'Warm August arrives in Australia as 2016 tipped to hit new highs', *The New Daily*, 16 August, https://thenewdaily.com.au/news/national/.

Coleman, R., Sim, J., Tombs, S. and Whyte, D. (eds) (2009) *State Power Crime*. SAGE, London.

Commission on Human Rights of the Philippines (2016) *Petition: To the Commission on Human Rights of the Philippines Requesting for Investigation of the Responsibility of the Carbon Majors for Human Rights Violations or Threats of Violations Resulting from the Impacts of Climate Change*. Case No.CHR-NI-2016-0001. Quezon City: Commission on Human Rights of the Philippines, www.greenpeace.org/seasia/ph/PageFiles/105904/Climate-Change-and-Human-Rights-Complaint.pdf.

Connell, R. (2007) *Southern Theory: The Global Dynamics of Knowledge in Social Science*. Sydney: Allen and Unwin.

Constitution of the Republic of Ecuador 2008, Article 71.

Convention on biological diversity (with annexes), concluded at Rio de Janeiro on 5 June 1992, registered ex officio on 29 December 1993

Council of Europe (2012) *Manual on Human Rights and the Environment* (2nd edn). Brussels: Council of Europe Publishing.

Crank, J. and Jacoby, L. (2015) *Crime, Violence, and Global Warming*. London: Routledge.

Croall, H. (2007) 'Food crime', in P. Beirne and N. South (eds) *Issues in Green Criminology: Confronting Harms Against Environments, Humanity and Other Animals*. Cullompton: Willan.

Croall, H. (2013) 'Food crime: A green criminology perspective', in N. South and A. Brisman (eds) *Routledge International Handbook of Green Criminology*. London: Routledge.

Crook, M. and Short, D. (2014) 'Marx, Lemkin and the genocide–ecocide nexus', *The International Journal of Human Rights*, 18(3): 298–319.

Cullinan, C. (2003) *Wild Law: A Manifesto for Earth Justice*. London: Green Books, in association with The Gaia Foundation.

Cunneen, C. and Tauri, J. (2016) *Indigenous Criminology*. Bristol: Policy Press.

Davies, P., Francis, P. and Greer, C. (2017) *Victims, Crime and Society: An Introduction*. London: Sage.

De Lucia, V. (2015) 'Competing narratives and complex genealogies: The ecosystem approach in international environmental law', *Journal of Environmental Law* 27: 91.

Della Porta, D. and Reiter, H. (2006) 'The policing of global protest: the G8 at Genoa and its aftermath', in D. Della Porta, A. Peterson and H. Reiter (eds) *The Policing of Transnational Protest*. Farnham: Ashgate.

Donnelly, B. and Bishop, P. (2007) 'Natural law and ecocentrism', *Journal of Environmental Law*, 19(1): 89.

Duffy, R. (2010) *Nature crime: How we're getting conservation wrong*. New Haven, CT: Yale University Press.

Edwards, M. (2017) 'Humans driving climate change 170 times faster than natural forces, scientists calculate', *Australian Broadcasting Corporation (ABC) News*, 13 February, www.abc.net.au/news/2017-02-13/humans-accelerating-global-warming-anthropocene-equation/8265326.

EEA (European Environment Agency) (2010) *EEA Signals: Biodiversity, Climate Change and You*. Copenhagen: European Environment Agency.

Etchart, E. (2017) 'The role of indigenous peoples in combating climate change', *Palgrave Communications*, Vol 3, https://ssrn.com/abstract=3024581 or http://dx.doi.org/10.1057/palcomms.2017.85.

Farrell, S. (2012) 'Where might we be headed? Some of the possible consequences of climate change for the criminological research agenda', in S. Farrell, T. Ahmed and D. French (eds) *Criminological and Legal Consequences of Climate Change*. Oxford: Hart.

Farrell, S., Ahmed, T. and French, D. (eds) (2012) *Criminological and Legal Consequences of Climate Change*. Oxford: Hart Publishing.

Fattah, E. (2010) 'The evolution of a young, promising discipline: Sixty years of victimology, a retrospective and prospective look', in S. Shoham, P. Knepper and M. Kett (eds) *International Handbook of Victimology*. Boca Raton, FL: CRC Press.

Field, R. (1998) 'Risk and justice: Capitalist production and the environment', in D. Faber (ed) *The Struggle for Ecological Democracy: Environmental Justice Movements in the US*. New York: Guilford Press.

Fisher, D. (2010) 'Jurisprudential challenges to the protection of the natural environment', in M. Maloney and P. Burdon (eds) *Wild Law – in Practice*. London: Routledge.

Flynn, M. and Hall, M. (2017) 'The case for a victimology of nonhuman animal harms', *Contemporary Justice Review*, doi: https://doi.org/10.1080/10282580.2017.1348898.

Foote, K.J., Joy, M.K. and Death, R.G. (2015) 'New Zealand dairy farming: Milking our environment for all its worth', *Environmental Management*, 56(3): 709–720.

Foster, J. (2002) *Ecology Against Capitalism*. New York: Monthly Review Press.

Foster, J. (2007) 'The ecology of destruction', *Monthly Review*, 58(9): pp 1–14.

France, A. (2016) *Understanding Youth in the Global Economic Crisis*. Bristol: Policy Press.

Freeland, S. (2015) *Addressing the Intentional Destruction of the Environment During Warfare under the Rome Statute of the International Criminal Court*, Doctoral dissertation, Maastricht University.

French, H. (2000) *Vanishing Borders: Protecting the Planet in the Age of Globalization*. New York: WW Norton and Company.

Gamble, J. and Hess, J. (2012) 'Temperature and violent crime in Dallas, Texas: Relationships and implications of climate change', *Western Journal of Emergency Medicine*, 13(3): 239–246.

Gedicks, A. (2005) 'Resource wars against native peoples', in R. Bullard (ed) *The Quest for Environmental Justice: Human Rights and the Politics of Pollution*. San Francisco, CA: Sierra Club Books, pp 168–187.

Gibbs, C., Cassidy, M. and Rivers, III, L. (2013) 'A routine activities analysis of white-collar crime in carbon markets', *Law and Policy*, 35(4): 341–374.

Gillham, P. and Marx, G. (2000) 'Complexity and irony in policing and protesting: The world trade organization in Seattle', *Social Justice*, 27(2): 212–237.

Glasbeek, H. (2003) 'The invisible friend: Investors are irresponsible. Corporations are amoral', *New Internationalist*, July, 358.

Glasbeek, H. (2004) *Wealth by Stealth: Corporate Crime, Corporate Law, and the Perversion of Democracy*. Toronto: Between the Lines.

Gleick, P. (2014) 'Water, Drought, Climate Change, and Conflict in Syria', Weather, Climate, and Society, 6: 331–340.

Global Campaign to Demand Climate Justice (2018) 'Fight for climate justice!', www.demandclimatejustice.org.

Global Initiative (2014) 'Water, water everywhere: charting the growth of organized water theft', http://globalinitiative.net/water-smuggling/.

Goldenberg, S. (2016) 'Plans for coal-fired power in Asia are "disaster for planet" warns World Bank', *Guardian*, 6 May, www.theguardian.com/environment/2016/may/05/climate-change-coal-power-asia-world-bank-disaster.

Graham, M. (2008) 'Some thoughts about the philosophical underpinnings of Aboriginal worldviews', *Australian Humanities Review*, 45: 181.

Graham, H. and White, R. (2015) *Innovative Justice*. London: Routledge.

Gray, M. (1996) 'The international crime of ecocide', *California Western International Law Journal*, 26: 215–271.

Green, P. (2005) 'Disaster by design: Corruption, construction and catastrophe', *British Journal of Criminology*, 45(4), 528–546.

Green, P. and Ward, T. (2000) 'State crime, human rights, and the limits of criminology', *Social Justice*, 27(1): 101–115.

Greig, A. and van der Velden, J. (2015) 'Earth hour approaches', *Overland*, 25 March, https://overland.org.au/2015/03/earth-hour-approaches/.

Hagedorn, J. (2008) *A World of Gangs: Armed Young Men and Gangsta Culture*. Minneapolis: University of Minnesota Press.

Haggerty, J. and Campbell, H. (2012) 'Farming and the environment – biodiversity and greenhouse gas changes', *Te Ara: The Encyclopaedia of New Zealand*, www.teara.govt.nz/en/cartoon/17915/the-fart-tax.

Haines, F. and Parker, C. (2017) 'Moving towards ecological regulation: The role of criminalisation', in C. Holley and C. Shearing (eds) *Criminology and the Anthropocene*. London: Routledge.

Haines, F. and Reichman, N. (2008) 'The problem that is global warming: An introduction', *Law and Policy*, 30(4): 385–393.

Hall, M. (2013) *Victims of Environmental Harm: Rights, Recognition and Redress Under National and International Law*. London: Routledge.

Hall, M. and Farrall, S. (2013) 'The criminogenic consequences of climate change: Blurring the boundaries between offenders and victims', in N. South and A. Brisman (eds) *Routledge International Handbook of Green Criminology*. London: Routledge.

Hamilton, M. (2008) 'Restorative justice intervention in an environmental law context: Garrett v Williams, Prosecutions under the Resource Management Act 1991 (NZ), and beyond', *Environmental Planning and Law Journal*, 25: 263.

Hamilton, M. (2014) 'Restorative justice intervention in an aboriginal cultural heritage protection context: Conspicuous absences?', *Environmental Planning and Law Journal*, 31: 352.

Hamilton-Smith, L. (2017) 'Heatwaves to be hotter, longer and more frequent, climate change report says', *Australian Broadcasting Corporation (ABC) News*, 8 February, www.abc.net.au/news/2017-02-08/heatwaves-to-be-hotter-longer-and-more-often-report-says/8248304.

Hansen, J. (2009) *Storms of My Grandchildren: The Truth About the Coming Climate Catastrophe and Our Last Chance to Save Humanity*. New York: Bloomsbury USA.

Harper, D. and Frailing, K. (2012) *Crime and Criminal Justice in Disaster*. Durham, NC: Carolina Academic Press.

Harvey, D. (2005) *A Brief History of Neoliberalism*. Oxford: Oxford University Press.

Heckenberg, D. and Johnston, I. (2012) 'Climate change, gender and natural disasters: Social differences and environment-related victimisation', in R. White (ed) *Climate Change from a Criminological Perspective*. New York: Springer.

Heede, R. (2014) 'Tracing anthropogenic carbon dioxide and methane emissions to fossil fuel and cement producers, 1854–2010', *Climate Change*, 122: 229–241.

Hellman J (2014) 'The fifth crime under international criminal law: Ecocide?', in D. Brodowski, M. Espinoza de los Monteros de la Parra, K. Tiedman and J. Vogel (eds) *Regulating Corporate Criminal Liability*. New York: Springer.

Hertsgaard, M. (2011) *Hot: Living Through the Next Fifty Years on Earth*. Boston, MA: Houghton Mifflin.

Higgins, D. and White, R. (2016) 'Collaboration at the front line: INTERPOL and NGOs in the same nest', in G. Pink and R. White (eds) *Environmental Crime and Collaborative State Intervention*. Basingstoke: Palgrave Macmillan.

Higgins, P. (2010) *Eradicating Ecocide: Laws and Governance to Prevent the Destruction of our Planet*. London: Shepheard-Walwyn Publishers Ltd.

Higgins, P. (2012) *Earth is our Business: Changing the Rules of the Game*. London: Shepheard-Walwyn Publishers Ltd.

Higgins, P., Short, D. and South, N. (2013) Protecting the planet: A proposal for a law of ecocide, *Crime Law and Social Change*, 59(3), 251–266.

Hillyard, P. and Tombs, S. (2007) 'From "crime" to social harm?', *Crime, Law and Social Change,* 48(1): 9–25.

Hillyard, P., Pantazis, C., Tombs, S. and Gordon, D. (eds) (2004) *Beyond Criminology? Taking Harm Seriously*. London: Pluto Press.

Hillyard, P., Pantazis, C., Tombs, S., Gordon, D. and Dorling, D. (2005) *Criminal Obsessions: Why Harm Matters More than Crime*. London: Crime and Society Foundation.

Holley, C. and Shearing, C. (eds) (2017) *Criminology and the Anthropocene*. London: Routledge.

Homer-Dixon, T. (1999) *Environment, Scarcity, and Violence*. Princeton, NJ: Princeton University Press.

Howard, E. (2016) 'Philippines investigates Shell and Exxon over climate change', *Guardian*, 7 May, www.theguardian.com/sustainable-business/2016/may/07/climate-change-shell-exxon-philippines-fossil-fuel-companies-liability-extreme-weather.

Hu, X., Wu, J., Chen, P., Sun, T. and Li, D. (2017) 'Impact of climate variability and change on crime rates in Tangshan, China', *Science and Total Environment*, 609: 1041–1048.

Hulme, K. and Short, D. (2014) 'Ecocide and the "polluter pays' principle: The case of fracking', *Environmental Scientist*, April, pp 7–10.

Hulme, M. (2014) *Can Science Fix Climate Change? A Case against Climate Engineering*. Cambridge: Polity Press.

IPCC (Intergovernmental Panel on Climate Change) (2013) *Working Group I: Contribution to the IPCC Fifth Assessment Report Climate Change 2013. The Physical Science Basis: Summary for Policymakers*, www.ipcc.ch/pdf/assessment-report/ar5/wg1/WG1AR5_SPM_FINAL.pdf.

IPCC (Intergovernmental Panel on Climate Change) (2014) *Climate Change 2014 Synthesis Report, Approved Summary for Policymakers*, www.ipcc.ch/pdf/assessment-report/ar5/syr/AR5_SYR_FINAL_SPM.pdf.

Iyer, L. and Topalova, P. (2014) 'Poverty and crime: Evidence from rainfall and Trade shocks in India', *Working Paper* 14-067, Harvard Business School, 2 September.

Jarrell, M. and Ozymy, J. (2012) 'Real crime, real victims: environmental crime victims and the Crime Victims' Rights Act (CVRA)', *Crime, law and social change*, 58(4): 373–389.

Jayne, T., Chamberlin, J. and Headley, D. (2014) 'Land pressures, the evolution of farming systems, and development strategies in Africa: A synthesis', *Food Policy*, 48: 1–17.

Jeffrey, C. (2010) *Timepass: Youth, Class, and the Politics of Waiting in India.* Stanford: Stanford University Press.

Johnston, H., South, N. and Walters, R. (2016) 'The commodification and exploitation of fresh water: Property, human rights and green criminology', *International Journal of Law, Crime and Justice* 44: 146–162.

Kavitha, A., Somashekar, R. and Nagaraja, B. (2015) 'Urban expansion and loss of Agricultural land: A case of Bengaluru city', *International Journal of Geomatics and Geosciences*, 5(3): 492–498.

Kenya Water for Health Organisation (2009) *Enhancing Water and Sanitation Governance in Kenya: Human Rights Based Approach for Reforms in the Kenya Water Sector*. Nairobi, Kenya: KWAHO.

Khagram, S. (2004) *Dams and Development: Transnational Struggles for Water and Power*. Ithaca, NY: Cornell University Press.

Kim, B., Neff, R., Santo, R. and Vigorito, J. (2015) 'The importance of reducing animal product consumption and wasted food in mitigating catastrophic climate change', *John Hopkins Center for a Livable Future*, doi: 10.13140/RG.2.1.3385.7362.

Klare, M. (2001) *Resource Wars: The New Landscape of Global Conflict*. New York: Owl Books, Henry Holt and Company.

Klare, M. (2012) *The Race for What's Left: The Global Scramble for the World's Last Resources*. New York: Metropolitan Books, Henry Holt and Company.

Klein, N. (2014) *This Changes Everything: Capitalism Versus the Climate*. New York: Simon and Schuster.

Kos, A. (2016a) Indigenous challenge to Adani Carmichael coal mine dismissed by Federal Court, *Australian Broadcasting Corporation (ABC) News*, 19 August, www.abc.net.au/news/2016-08-19/indigenous-challenge-to-adani...coal.../7765466.

Kos, A. (2016b) '"Global warming" challenge against Rinehart coal mine dismissed by Queensland Court of Appeal', *Australian Broadcasting Corporation (ABC) Environment News*, 27 September, www.abc.net.au/news/2016-09-27/global-warming-challenge-against-Rinehart.../7880358.

Kramer, R. (2013a) 'Carbon in the atmosphere and power in America: Climate change as state-corporate crime', *Journal of Crime and Justice*, 36(2), 153–170.

Kramer, R. (2013b) 'Public criminology and the responsibility to speak in the prophetic voice concerning global warming', in E. Stanley and J. McCulloch (eds) *State Crime and Resistance*. London: Routledge, pp 41–53.

Kramer, R. and Michalowski, R. (2012) 'Is global warming a state–corporate crime?', in R. White (ed) Climate Change from a Criminological Perspective. New York: Springer, pp 71–88.

Lambrecht, J. and Ituarte-Lima, C. (2016) 'Legal innovation in national courts for planetary challenges: Urgenda v state of the Netherlands', *Environmental Law Review*, 18(1): 57–64.

Larkins, M., Gibbs, C. and Rivers III, L. (2013) 'Toward advancing research on the social and environmental impacts of confined animal feeding operations', *CRIMSOC: Journal of Social Criminology*, 4: 10–63.

Lawrence, K. (2009) 'The thermodynamics of unequal exchange: Energy use, CO_2 emissions, and GDP in the world-system, 1975–2005', *International Journal of Comparative Sociology*, 50(3–4): 335–359.

Lawrence, P. (2014) *Justice for Future Generations: Climate Change and International Law*. Cheltenham: Edward Elgar.

Le Billon, P. (2012) *Wars of Plunder: Conflicts, Profits and the Politics of Resources*. New York: Columbia University Press.

Levene, M. and Conversi, D. (2014) 'Subsistence societies, globalisation, climate change and genocide: Discourses of vulnerability and resistance', *The International Journal of Human Rights*, 18(3): 281–297.

Lever-Tracy, C. (2011) *Confronting Climate Change*. London: Routledge.

Lin, A. (2006) 'The unifying role of harm in environmental law', *Wisconsin Law Review*, 3: 898–985.

Loader, I. and Sparks, R. (2011) *Public Criminology?* London: Routledge.

Los Angeles Times (2016) 'US court rules for Chevron in Ecuador rainforest-damage case', *Los Angeles Times*, 8 August, www.latimes.com/business/la-fi-chevron-ecuador-20160808-snap-story.html.

Lynch, M. and Stretesky, P. (2010) 'Global warming, global crime: A green criminological perspective', in R. White (ed) *Global Environmental Harm: Criminological Perspectives*. Cullompton: Willan.

Lynch, M. and Stretesky, P. (2012) 'A proposal for a new vehicle-based carbon tax (V-CART): Vehicle-based global warming policy and green criminology', in R. White (ed) *Climate Change from a Criminological Perspective*. New York: Springer.

Lynch, M. and Stretesky, P. (2014) *Exploring Green Criminology: Toward a Green Criminological Revolution*. Farnham: Ashgate.

Lynch, M., Burns, R. and Stretesky, P. (2010) 'Global warming and state–corporate crime: The politicalization of global warming under the Bush administration', *Crime, Law and Social Change*, 54: 213–239.

Macaulay, C. (2016) 'Species on the move worldwide', *The Mercury*, Hobart, pp 14–15.

Maloney, M. and Burdon, P. (eds) (2014) *Wild Law: In Practice*. Abingdon: Routledge.

Mandel, E. (1968) *Marxist Economic Theory*. London: Merlin Press.

Mandel, E. (1975) *Late Capitalism*. London: Verso.

Marciniak, C. (2016) 'Impact of climate change on Indigenous communities', *Australian Broadcasting Corporation (ABC) News*, 14 April, www.abc.net.au/news/2016-04-14/impact-of-climate-change-on-indigenous-communities/7289604.

Mares, D. (2010) 'Criminalizing ecological harm: Crimes against carrying capacity and the criminalization of eco-sinners', *Critical Criminology*, 18: 279–293.

Mares, D. (2013) 'Climate change and crime: Monthly temperature and precipitation anomalies and crime rates in St. Louis, MO 1990–2009', *Crime, Law and Social Change*, doi: 10.1007/s10611-013-9411-8.

Martin, P. and Walters, R. (2013) 'Fraud risk and the visibility of carbon', *International Journal for Crime, Justice and Social Democracy*, 2(2): 27–42.

Marx, K. (1954) *Capital, Volume 1*. Moscow: Progress Publishers.

Mascher S (2016) 'Climate change justice and corporate responsibility: Commentary on the International Bar Association recommendations', *Journal of Energy and Natural Resources Law*, 34(1): 57–69.

Massachusetts v. Environmental Protection Agency, 549 U.S. 497, 127 S. Ct. 1438, 167 L. Ed. 2nd 248

Massola, J., Ker, P. and Cox, L. (2014) 'Coal is "good for humanity", say Tony Abbott at mine opening', *Sydney Morning Herald* [online], www.smh.com.au/politics/federal/coal-is-good-for-humanity-says-tony-abbott-at-mine-opening-10441013-115bgs.

McAdam, J. and Saul, B. (2008) 'An insecure climate for human security? Climate-induced displacement and international law', in A. Edwards and C. Fertsman (eds) *Human Security and Non-Citizens: Law, Policy and International Affairs*. Cambridge: Cambridge University Press.

McCarthy, M. (2008) 'Cleared! Jury decides that threat of global warming justifies breaking the law', *The Independent*, 11 September, www.commondreams.org/news/2008/09/11/cleared-jury-decides-threat-global-warming-justifies-breaking-law.

McGarrell, E. and Gibbs, C. (2014) 'Conservation criminology, environmental crime, and risk: An application to climate change', *Oxford Handbooks Online (Subject: Criminology and Criminal Justice, Criminological Theories)*, doi: 10.1093/oxfordhb/9780199935383.54.

McKie, R., Stretesky, P. and Long, M. (2015) 'Carbon crime in the voluntary market: An exploration of modernization themes among a sample of criminal and non-criminal organizations', *Critical Criminology*, 23: 473–486.

McLaughlin, E. (2010) 'Critical criminology', in E. McLaughlin and T. Newburn (eds) *The SAGE Handbook of Criminological Theory*. London: Sage.

McPherson, C.B. (1977) *The Life and Times of Liberal Democracy*. Toronto: Oxford University Press.

Mehta, M.C. (2009) *In the Public Interest: Landmark Judgements and Orders of the Supreme Court of India on Environment and Human Rights (Volume 1)*. New Delhi: Prakriti Publications.

Merchant, C. (2005) *Radical Ecology: The Search for a Livable World*. New York: Routledge.

Meyer, L. and Roser, D. (2010) 'Climate justice and historical emissions', *Critical Review of International Social and Political Philosophy*, 13(1): 229–253.

Mgbeoji, I. (2006) *Global Biopiracy: Patents, Plants, and Indigenous Knowledge*. Vancouver: University of British Columbia Press.

Michalowski, R. and Kramer, R. (2006) *State–Corporate Crime: Wrongdoing at the Intersection of Business and Government*. New Brunswick, NJ: Rutgers University Press.

Michel, S., Wang, H., Selvarajah, S., Canner, J. et al (2016) 'Investigating the relationship between weather and violence in Baltimore, Maryland, USA', *Injury*, 47(1): 272–276.

Minors Oposa v Secretary of State for the Department of Environment and Natural Resources, Philippines Supreme Court.

Mitchell, D. (2008) 'A note on rising food prices', Draft World Bank paper, circulated on-line by the *Guardian*, website, guardian.co.uk/environment.

Mol, H. (2013) '"A gift from the tropics to the world": Power, harm, and palm oil', in R. Walters, D. Westerhuis and T. Wyatt (eds) *Emerging Issues in Green Criminology*, Basingstoke: Palgrave Macmillan, pp 242–260.

Morris, J. and Ruru, J. (2010) 'Giving voice to rivers: Legal personality as a vehicle for recognising indigenous peoples' relationships to water?', *Australian Indigenous Law Review*, 14(2): 49.

Munro, M. (2007) 'Biofuels come up short as way to reduce carbon load, study finds', *The Vancouver Sun*, 17 August: A3.

O'Brien, M. (2008) 'Criminal degradations of consumer culture', in R. Sollund (ed) *Global Harms: Ecological Crime and Speciesism*. New York: Nova Science Publishers.

O'Connor, J. (1994) 'Is sustainable capitalism possible?', in M. O'Connor (ed) *Is Capitalism Sustainable?: Political Economy and the Politics of Ecology*. New York: The Guilford Press.

Onimode, B. (1985) *An Introduction to Marxist Political Economy*. London: Zed Books.

Oxfam (2018) *Reward Work, Not Wealth*. Nairobi: Oxfam.

Oxford Geoengineering Programme (2017) 'The principles'. *Oxford Principles*, www.geoengineering.ox.ac.uk/oxford-principles/principles/.

Page, E. (2008) 'Distributing the burdens of climate change', *Environmental Politics*, 17(4): 556–575.

Panjabi, R.K.L. (2014) 'Not a drop to spare: The global water crisis of the twenty-first century', *Georgia Journal of International and Comparative Law*, 42(2): 277–424.

Pearse, G. (2012) *Greenwash: Big Brands and Carbon Scans*. Collingwood, Victoria: Black Inc.

Pease, K. and Farrell, G. (2011) 'Climate change and crime', *European Journal of Criminological Policy and Research*, 17: 149–162.

Peeters, P. and Dubois, G. (2010) 'Tourism travel under climate change mitigation constraints', *Journal of Transport Geography*, 18(3): 447–457.

Pelizzon, A. and Ricketts, A. (2015) 'Beyond anthropocentrism and back again: From ontological to normative anthropocentrism', *The Australasian Journal of Natural Resources Law and Policy*, 18(2): 105.

Pemberton, S. (2016) *Harmful Societies: Understanding Social Harm*. Bristol: Policy Press.

Peng, C., Xueming, S., Hongyong, Y. and Dengsheng, L. (2011) 'Assessing temporary and weather influences on property crime in Beijing, China', *Crime, Law and Social Change*, 55: 1–13.

Pepper, D. (1993) *Eco-Socialism: From Deep Ecology to Social Justice*. New York: Routledge.

Pickering, S. (2005) *Refugees and State Crime*. Sydney: Federation Press.

Picou, J., Formichella, C., Marshall, B. and Arata, C. (2009) 'Chapter 9: Community impacts of the Exxon Valdez oil spill: A synthesis and elaboration of social science research', in S. Braund and J. Kruse (eds) *Synthesis: Three Decades of Research on Socioeconomic Effects related to Offshore Petroleum Development in Coastal Alaska*. Anchorage, AK: United States Department of the Interior.

Piketty, T. (2014) *Capital in the Twenty-First Century*. Cambridge, MA: The Belnap Press of Harvard University Press.

Pimental, D., Marklein, A., Toth, M., Karpoff, M. et al (2009) 'Food versus biofuels: Environmental and economic costs', *Human Ecology*, 37(1): 1–12.

Pink, G. and White, R. (eds) (2016) *Environmental Crime and Collaborative State Intervention*. Basingstoke: Palgrave Macmillan.

Poff, N. and Zimmerman, J. (2010) 'Ecological responses to altered flow regimes: A literature review to inform the science and management of environmental flows', *Freshwater Biology*, 55: 194–205.

Preston, B. (2007) 'Principled sentencing for environmental offences. Part 1: Purposes of sentencing', *Criminal Law Journal*, 31 (3): 142–164.

Preston, B. (2011) 'The use of restorative justice for environmental crime', *Criminal Law Journal*, 35: 136–145.

Ranson M (2014) 'Crime, weather and climate change', *Journal of Environmental Economics and Management*, 67: 274–302.

Readfearn, G. (2017) 'Tony Abbot dares us to reject evidence on climate, but reveals a coward', *Guardian*, 11 October, www.theguardian.com/environment/planet-oz/2017/oct/11/tony-abbott-dares-us-to-reject-evidence-on-climate-but-reveals-a-coward.

Redgwell, C. (2012) 'International legal responses to the challenges of a lower carbon future: Energy law for the twenty-first century', in S. Farrall, T. Ahmed and D. French (eds) *Criminological and Legal Consequences of Climate Change*. Oxford and Portland, OR: Hart Publishing, pp 27–46.

Refugee Studies Centre (2008) *Forced Migration Review: Climate Change and Displacement*, Issue 31. University of Oxford: Refugee Studies Centre.

Reicher, S., Stott, C., Cronin, P. and Adang, O. (2004) 'An integrated approach to crowd psychology and public order policing', *Policing: An International Journal of Police Strategies and Management*, 27(4): 558–572.

Reuveny, R. (2007) 'Climate change-induced migration and violent conflict', *Political Geography*, 26: 656–673.

Rio Declaration, United Nations Doc.A/CONF.151/26 (vol.1); 31 ILM 874 (1992) (Rio Declaration).

Rist, L., Ser Huay Lee, J. and Pin Koh, L. (2009) 'Biofuels: Social benefits', Letters, *Science*, 326: 1344.

Roberts, G. (2008) 'The bad oil on ethanol: Biofuels are losing favour but some governments are still backing them', *The Weekend Australian*, Inquirer, 31 May–1 June, 20.

Robin, M.-M. (2010) *The World According to Monsanto: Pollution, Corruption and the Control of Our Food Supply*. New York: The New Press.

Robinson, M. (2015) 'Mary Robinson: Climate change "very likely" to increase radicalisation', *The Conversation*, 7 December, http://theconversation.com/mary-robinson-climate-change-very-likely-to-increase-radicalisation-51508.

Robyn, L. (2002) 'Indigenous knowledge and technology', *American Indian Quarterly*, 26(2): 198–220.

Rodriquez, H., Quarantelli, E. and Dynes, R. (eds) (2007) *Handbook of Disaster Research*. New York: Springer.

Rogers, N. (2012) 'Climate change litigation and the awfulness of lawfulness', *Alternative Law Journal*, 37(3): 20.

Roth, J. (1994) 'Understanding and preventing violence. Research in brief', Washington, DC: National Institute of Justice, US Department of Justice.

Rothe, D. and Friedrichs, D. (2015) *Crimes of Globalization: New Directions in Critical Criminology*. London: Routledge.

Rothe, D. and Kauzlarich, D. (2016) *Crimes of the Powerful: An Introduction*. London: Routledge.

Rotton, J. and Cohn, E. (2003) 'Global warming and US crime rates: An application of routine activity theory', *Environment and Behavior*, 35(6): 802–825.

Ruggiero, V. and South, N. (2013) 'Toxic state–corporate crimes, neo-liberalism and green criminology: The hazards and legacies of the oil, chemical and mineral industries', *International Journal for Crime, Justice and Social Democracy*, 2(2): 12–26.

Russell, S. (2002) 'The continuing relevance of Marxism to critical criminology', *Critical Criminology*, 11(2): 113–135.

Sankoff, P. and White, S. (eds) (2009) *Animal Law in Australasia: A New Dialogue*. Sydney: The Federation Press.

SCBD (Secretariat of the Convention on Biological Diversity) (1992) *Convention on biological diversity (with annexes)*, concluded at Rio de Janeiro on 5 June, registered ex officio on 29 December 1993.

SCBD (Secretariat of the Convention on Biological Diversity) (2010) *Global Biodiversity Outlook* 3, Montreal: SCBD.

Schapiro, M. (2014) *Carbon shock: A Tale of Risk and Calculus on the Front Lines of the Disrupted Global Economy*. White River Junction, VT: Chelsea Green Publishing.

Schinasi, L. and Hamra, G. (2017) 'A time series analysis of associations between daily temperature and crime events in Philadelphia, Pennsylvania', *Journal of Urban Health*, doi: 10.1007/s11524-017-0181-y.

Schlosberg, D. (2007) *Defining Environmental Justice: Theories, Movements, and Nature*. Oxford: Oxford University Press.

Schmidt, C. (2004) 'Environmental crimes: Profiting at the Earth's expense', *Environmental Health Perspectives*, 112(2): A96–A103.

Schneeberger, K. (2011) 'Intergenerational equity: Implementing the principle in mainstream decision-making', *Environmental Law and Management*, 23(1): 20–29.

Scott, D. (2005). 'When precaution points two ways: Confronting "West Nile Fever"', *Canadian Journal of Law and Society*, 20(2): 27–65.

SEI (Stockholm Environment Institute) (2018) *Climate Equity Reference Calculator*, 'tools', SEI, www.sei.org/projects-and-tools/tools/climate-equity-reference-calculator/.

Shearing, C. (2015) 'Criminology and the Anthropocene', *Criminology and Criminal Justice*, 15(3): 255–269.

Sheptycki, J. (2005) 'Policing political protest when politics go global: Comparing public order policing in Canada and Bolivia', *Policing and Society*, 15(3): 327–352.

Shiva, V. (2008) *Soil Not Oil: Environmental Justice in an Age of Climate Crisis*. Brooklyn, NY: South End Press.

Short, D. (2016) *Redefining Genocide: Settler Colonialism, Social Death and Ecocide*. London: Zed Books

Singh, M. (1996) 'Environmental security and displaced people in Southern Africa', *Social Justice*, 23(4): 125–133.

Skinnider, E. (2011) *Victims of Environmental Crime: Mapping the Issues*. Vancouver: The International Centre for Criminal Law Reform and Justice Policy.

Skudder, H., Druckman, A., Cole, J., McInnes, A., Bruton-Smith, I. and Ansaloni, G. (2016) 'Addressing the carbon-crime blind spot', *Journal of Industrial Ecology,* 21(4): 829–843.

Smail, S. (2016) 'Alpha coal mine legal case could set "important precedent" with global warming argument', *Australian Broadcasting Corporation (ABC) News*, 7 June, www.abc.net.au/news/2016-06-07/alpha-coal-mine-legal-case-could-set.../7484922.

Smandych, R. and Kueneman, R. (2010) 'The Canadian-Alberta tar sands: A case study of state–corporate environmental crime', in R. White (ed) *Global Environmental Harm: Criminological Perspectives.* Cullompton: Willan, pp 87–109.

Smith, O. and Raymen, T. (2016) 'Deviant leisure: A criminological perspective', *Theoretical Criminology*, 22(1): 63–82.

Smith, D. and Vivekananda, J. (2007) *A Climate of Conflict: The Links Between Climate Change, Peace and War.* London: International Alert.

Smith, M. (1998) *Ecologism: Towards Ecological Citizenship.* Minneapolis, MN: University of Minnesota Press.

Solano, J. and Ferrero-Waldner, B. (2008) 'Climate change and international security', *Paper from the High Representative and the European Commission to the European Council.* Brussels: European Union.

Sollund, R. (2012) 'Oil production, climate change and species decline: The case of Norway', in R. White (ed) *Climate Change from a Criminological Perspective.* New York: Springer.

South, N. (2010) The ecocidal tendencies of late modernity: Transnational crime, social exclusions, victims and rights', in R. White (ed) *Global Environmental Harm: Criminological Perspectives.* Cullompton: Willan, pp 228–247.

South, N. (2012) 'Climate change, environmental (in)security, conflict and crime', in S. Farrell, T. Ahmed and D. French (eds) *Criminological and Legal Consequences of Climate Change.* Oxford: Hart Publishing.

South, N. and Brisman, A. (eds) (2013) *The Routledge International Handbook of Green Criminology.* New York: Routledge.

Southalan, J. (2013) 'Book review, *Criminological and Legal Consequences of Climate Change* (eds S Farrell, T Ahmed, D French)', *Oil, Gas and Energy Law Intelligence 5*, www.ogel.org/journal-advance-publication-article.asp?key=375.

Spapens, T. (2018) 'The "Dieslegate" scandal: A criminological perspective', in T. Spapens, W. Huisman, R. White and D. van Ulm (eds) *Environmental Crime and Dirty Money.* London: Routledge.

Steffen, W. (2018) 'Why it's sweltering in Penrith while Florida is in deep freeze', *The Sydney Morning Herald*, 9 January, p 21.

Stephens, S. (1996) 'Reflections on environmental justice: Children as victims and actors', *Social Justice*, 23(4): 62–86.

Stephenson, W. (2014) 'Fuck Earth Day: Let this year's be the last', *The Nation*, 22 April, www.commondreams.org/view/2014/04/22-4.

Stilwell, M. (2018) 'Climate justice: International civil society perspectives', Presentation at the *Imagining a Different Future, Climate Justice Conference*, Hobart, Tasmania, 9 February.

Stone, C. (1972) 'Should trees have standing? Toward legal rights for natural objects', *Southern California Law Review*, 45: 450.

Stott, C., Adang, O., Livingstone, A.G. and Schreiber, M. (2007) 'Variability in the collective behaviour of England fans at Euro2004: "Hooliganism", public order policing and social change', *European Journal of Social Psychology*, 37: 75–100.

Stretesky, P. and Lynch, M. (2009) 'A cross-national study of the association between per capita carbon dioxide emissions and exports to the United States', *Social Science Research*, 38, 239–250.

Stretesky, P., Long, M. and Lynch, M. (2014) *The Treadmill of Crime: Political Economy and Green Criminology*. London: Routledge.

Stubbs, J. and Tomsen, S. (eds) (2016) *Australian Violence: Crime, Criminal Justice and Beyond*. Sydney: The Federation Press.

Sundström, J.F., Albihn, A., Boqvist, S., Ljungvall, K. et al (2014) 'Future threats to agricultural food production posed by environmental degradation, climate change, and animal and plant diseases – a risk analysis in three economic and climate settings', *Food Security*, 6: 201–215.

Sutherland, W.J. and Woodroof, H.J. (2009) 'The need for environmental horizon scanning', *Trends in Ecology and Evolution*, 24(10): 523–527.

Sutherland, W.J., Clout, M., Cote, I., Daszak, P. et al (2009) 'A horizon scan of global conservation issues for 2010', *Trends in Ecology and Evolution*, 25(1): 1–7.

Suzuki, D. (2010) *The Legacy: An Elder's Vision for our Sustainable Future. Vancouver.* Greystone Books, an Imprint of D & M Publishers.

Sydney Morning Herald (2017) 'Comment: We can no longer tolerate climate change denial', *Sydney Morning Herald*, Wednesday 30 August, p 18.

Sykes, G. and Matza, D. (1957) 'Techniques of neutralization: A theory of delinquency', *American Sociological Review*, 22(6): 664–670.

Szerszynski, B., Kearnes, M, Macnaghten, P., Owen, R. and Stilgoe, J. (2013) 'Why solar radiation management geoengineering and democracy don't mix', *Environment and Planning A*, 45(12): 2809–2816.

Te Awa Tupua Act 2016 (NZ)

Te Urewera Act 2014 (NZ)

Teclaf, M. (1994) 'Beyond restoration: The case of ecocide', *Natural Resources Journal*, 34(4), 933–956.

Tekayak, D. (2016a) 'From "polluter pays" to "polluter does not pollute"', *Geoforum*, 71: 62–65.

Tekayak, D. (2016b) 'Protecting earth rights and the rights of indigenous peoples: Towards an international crime of ecocide', *Fourth World Journal*, 14(2): 5–11.

Thornton, W.E. and Voigt, L. (2007) 'Disaster rape: Vulnerability of women to sexual assaults during Hurricane Katrina', *Journal of Public Management and Social Policy*, 13(2): 23–49.

Tilman, D., Socolow, R., Foley, J., Hill, J. et al (2009) 'Beneficial biofuels: The food, energy, and environment trilemma', *Science*, 325: 270–271.

Timilsina, G., Mevel, S. and Shrestha, A. (2011) 'Oil prices, biofuels and food supply', *Energy Policy*, 39: 8098–8105.

Tombs, S. and Whyte, D. (2015) *The Corporate Criminal: Why Corporations Must be Abolished*. London: Routledge.

Tucker, W. (2012) 'Deceitful tongues: Is climate change denial a crime?', *Ecology Law Quarterly*, 39: 831–894.

UN Economic and Social Council (2010) 'Study on the need to recognize and respect the rights of Mother Earth', Permanent Forum on Indigenous Issues, Ninth session. New York: UN.

UNDP (United Nations Development Programme) (2010a) 'Gender, climate change and food security', *Gender and Climate Change Africa: Policy Brief* 4. New York: UNDP.

UNDP (United Nations Development Programme) (2010b) *Biodiversity Conservation and Sustainable Land Management*. Website information, UNDP.

UNDP (United Nations Development Programme) (2013) 'Overview of linkages between gender and climate change', *Gender and Climate Change: Asia and the Pacific, Policy Brief* 1. New York: UNDP.

UNEP (United Nations Environment Programme) (2006) *Call for Global Action on E-waste*. New York: UNEP.

UNEP (United Nations Environment Programme) (2007) *Global Environment Outlook*. New York: UNEP.

UNEP (United Nations Environment Programme) (2010a) *Disasters and Conflicts. UNEP Year Book 2010*, pp 43–54.

UNEP (United Nations Environment Programme) (2010b) 'Fact sheet: Disasters and conflicts', United Nations Environment Programme, http://apps.unep.org/repository/publication-type/factsheets.

UNEP (United Nations Environment Programme) (2017) *The Status of Climate Change Litigation: A Global Review*. Nairobi: UNEP.

UNISDR (United Nations Office for Disaster Risk Reduction) (2018) *Official Terminology Guide*. New York: UN.

United Nations (2015) *Framework Convention on Climate Change*, Conference of the Parties, Twenty-first session, Paris, 30 November to 11 December 2015, Adoption of the Paris Agreement (includes Annex: Paris Agreement)

United Nations Women Watch (2009) 'Fact sheet: Women, gender equality and climate change', www.un.org/womenwatch.

Urgenda Foundation v. The State of The Netherlands, ENLI: NL: RBDHA: 2015: 7196, C/09/456689/HA ZA 13-1396 (English translation).

USEPA (United States Environmental Protection Agency) (2009) 'Endangerment and cause or contribute findings for greenhouse gases under Section 202(a) of the Clean Air Act', *Federal Register, Part III, Environmental Protection Agency*, www.epa.gov/ghgemissions/.

Varkkey, H. (2013) 'Oil palm plantations and transboundary haze: Patronage networks and land licensing in Indonesia's peatlands', *Wetland*, 33: 679–690.

Victorian Government (2009) *Securing Our Natural Future: A White Paper for Land and Biodiversity at a Time of Climate Change*. Melbourne: Victoria.

Vorosmarty, C., McIntyre, P., Gessner, M., Dudgeon, D. et al (2010) 'Global threats to human water security and river biodiversity', *Nature*, 467: 555–561.

Wachholz, S. (2007) '"At risk": Climate change and its bearing on women's vulnerability to male violence', in P. Beirne and N. South (eds) *Issues in Green Criminology: Confronting Harms Against Environments, Humanity and Other Animals*. London: Routledge, pp 161–185.

Walklate, S. and Mythen, G. (2015) *Contradictions of Terrorism: Security, Risk and Resilience*. London: Routledge.

Wallace-Wells, D. (2017) 'The uninhabitable earth', *New York Magazine*, 10 July, http://nymag.com/daily/intelligencer/2017/07/climate-change-earth-too-hot-for-humans.html.

Walters, B. (2011) 'Enlarging our vision of rights: The most significant human rights event in recent times?', *Alternative Law Journal*, 36(4): 263–268.

Walters, R. (2011) *Eco Crime and Genetically Modified Food*. New York: Routledge.

Walters, R. (2013) 'Air crimes and atmospheric justice', in N. South and A. Brisman (eds) *The Routledge International Handbook of Green Criminology*. London: Routledge.

Walters, R. and Martin, P. (2013) 'Crime and the commodification of carbon', in R. Walters, D. Westerhuis and T. Wyatt (eds) *Emerging Issues in Green Criminology*. Basingstoke: Palgrave Macmillan.

Walters, R. and Westerhuis, D.S. (2013) 'Green crime and the role of environmental courts', *Crime Law and Social Change*, 59: 279–290.

Ward, T. and Green, P. (2000) 'Legitimacy, civil society and state crime', *Social Justice*, 27, 76–93.

Watts, N., Adger, W.N., Ayeb-Karlsson, S., Bai, Y. et al (2017) 'The Lancet countdown: tracking progress on health and climate change', *The Lancet*, 389: 1151–1164.

White, R. (2008) *Crimes Against Nature: Environmental Criminology and Ecological Justice*. Cullompton: Willan.

White, R. (2011) *Transnational Environmental Crime: Toward an Eco-Global Criminology*. London: Routledge.

White, R. (2012a) 'The criminology of climate change', in R. White (ed) *The Criminology of Climate Change: Climate Change from a Criminological Perspective*. New York: Springer.

White, R. (2012b) 'Climate change and paradoxical harm', in S. Farrall, T. Ahmed and D. French (eds) *Criminological and Legal Consequences of Climate Change*. Oxford and Portland, OR: Hart Publishing, pp 63–77.

White, R. (2012c) 'NGO engagement in environmental law enforcement: Critical reflections', *Australasian Policing: A Journal of Professional Practice and Research*, 4(1): 7–12.

White, R. (2013a) *Environmental Harm: An Eco-Justice Perspective*. Bristol: Policy Press.

White, R. (2013b) *Youth Gangs, Violence and Social Respect: Exploring the Dynamics of Provocations and Punch-Ups*. London: Palgrave Macmillan.

White, R. (2013c) 'Environmental activism and resistance to state–corporate crime', in E. Stanley and J. McCulloch (eds) *State Crime and Resistance*. London: Routledge, pp 128–140.

White, R. (2014) 'Environmental insecurity and fortress mentality', *International Affairs*, 90(4): 835–851.

White, R. (2015a) 'Environmental victimology and ecological justice', in D. Wilson and S. Ross (eds) *Crime, Victims and Policy: International Contexts, Local Experiences*. Basingstoke: Palgrave Macmillan.

White, R. (2015b) 'Imagining the unthinkable: Climate change, ecocide and children', in J. Frauley (ed) *C. Wright Mills and the Criminological Imagination: Prospects for Creative Inquiry*. Farnham: Ashgate.

White, R. (2015c) 'Climate change, ecocide and crimes of the powerful', in G. Barak (ed) *The Routledge International Handbook of the Crimes of the Powerful*. London: Routledge.

White, R. (2016) 'Inter-species violence: Humans and the harming of animals', in J. Stubbs and S. Tomsen (eds) *Australian Violence: Crime, Criminal Justice and Beyond*. Sydney: The Federation Press.

White, R. (2017a) 'Carbon economics and transnational resistance to ecocide', in M. Hall, T. Wyatt, N. South, A. Nurse, G. Potter and J. Maher (eds) *Greening Criminology in the 21st Century*. Farnham: Ashgate.

White, R. (2017b) 'Carbon criminals, climate change and ecocide', in C. Holley and C. Shearing (eds) *Criminology and the Anthropocene*. London: Routledge.

White, R. (2017c) 'Criminological perspectives on climate change, violence and ecocide', *Current Climate Change Reports*, doi: 10.1007/s40641-017-0075-9.

White, R. (2018) 'Green criminology and the non-human victim', *International Review of Victimology*, 24(2): 239–255.

White, R. and Graham, H. (2015) 'Greening justice: Examining the interfaces of criminal, social and ecological justice', *British Journal of Criminology*, 55(5): 845–865.

White, R. and Heckenberg, D. (2011) 'Environmental horizon scanning and criminological research and practice', *European Journal of Criminal Policy and Research*, 17(2), 87–100.

White, R. and Heckenberg, D. (2014) *Green Criminology: An Introduction to the Study of Environmental Harm*. London: Routledge, p 40.

White, R. and Kramer, R. (2015) 'Critical criminology and the struggle against climate change ecocide', *Critical Criminology*, 23: 383–399.

White, R. and Perrone, S. (2015) *Crime, Criminality and Criminal Justice*. Melbourne: Oxford University Press.

White, R., Haines, F. and Asquith, N. (2017a) *Crime and Criminology*. Melbourne: Oxford University Press.

White, R., Wyn, J. and Robards, B. (2017b) *Youth and Society*. Melbourne: Oxford University Press.

WHO (World Health Organization) (2009) *Protecting Health from Climate Change: Connecting Science, Policy and People*. Geneva: WHO Press.

Williams, C. (1996) 'An environmental victimology', *Social Justice*, 23(4): 16.

Williams, C. (2013) 'Wild law in Australia: Practice and possibilities', *Environmental Planning and Law Journal*, 30: 259.

Wood, M.C. (2014) *Nature's Trust: Environmental Law for a New Ecological Age*. New York: Cambridge University Press.

Index

350.org campaign 153

A

Aarhus Convention 119
Abbott, Tony 36, 108, 145
abiotic sphere 13, 16, 81, 144, 146
accountability 14, 39, 97, 99, 119, 122, 130–4, 140
action plan 135–6, 137
activism 21, 37–8, 93, 121–2, 126, 134, 137, 144–7, 148–54
adaptation
  and ecocide as a crime 40
  farming 28
  interconnectedness 14
  key theme of climate change criminology 14–15
  legal action 121
  limits 6
  as means to deal with climate change 8, 10
  nation-states 134
  paying for 65, 132–3
  policing 127
  recognition of victimisation 117
  state-corporate crime 26
adjudication 125, 135, 137, 151
aesthetic values 24
Africa 30, 43, 61, 69, 71, 74, 90, 102
agency 20, 56, 104, 112, 119
Agnew, R. 23, 24, 44, 51, 52, 53, 74, 114, 115
agriculture
  and biodiversity loss 102
  carbon emissions crime 53
  and climate-induced migration 71
  flex crops 29–30, 34
  intensive farming 29, 82
  monocultures 29, 31, 34, 70, 82
  risks for food production 68–70
  slow disasters 61, 62
  species migration 72
  and state-corporate crime 27, 28–31, 34, 36
  victims of climate change 82, 92
agro-industrial food systems/agribusiness 29, 70, 103
aid funds, misappropriation of 65
air
  commodification 101, 105
  democratic control 130, 149, 152
  pollution 30, 54, 75
air travel 32
albedo effect 43
Alberta Tar Sands 26, 27–8, 92, 107
Alpha coal mine, Queensland 120
Alston, M. 53, 62
alternative energy sources 35, 69, 75, 109, 118
Amazon basin 83, 92
Anderson, C. 49
Andresen, M. 50
animals *see* non-human environmental entities
Antarctic 5, 43
anthropocene 7–9, 15, 19, 21, 42
anthropocentrism 24
anti-globalisation protests 126–7
appropriation 69
Arctic
  boundary rights 74
  Indigenous people 92
  warming 4, 5, 42, 43
Argentina 30
armed conflict 43, 68
Arora-Jonsson, S. 53, 66
Asia 30, 83, 90, 102, 111
  see also specific countries
asylum seeking 32, 46, 63, 124
Athanasiou, T. 37
Australia
  bush fires 43
  'climate change is good' propositions 36, 39
  climate change not a main topic 140
  climate-induced migration 71
  flooding 8
  food production 69
  Great Barrier Reef 4, 32, 120
  legal action 120–1
  non-native species 20, 72
  resource-dependent economy 107
  selling air 105
  state support for risky businesses 27, 75, 111
Australian Academy of Science 42, 43

B

Baatz, C. 132, 133
Baer, H. 76, 108
Bakan, J. 98, 99
Baker, D. 126
Bancroft-Hinchey, T. 130
Bangladesh 65, 76
Bann, Getano 90
Barnett, J. 71
Barrett, Oliver Leighton 71
Bates, G. 80

Beck, U. 83
Beder, S. 37, 106
Bell, S. 11
Bell-James, J. 121
Bello, W. 70
Bennett, K. 121
Bergin, A. 45
Berry, T. 22
bias 136
biocentrism 94
biodiversity 29, 31, 35, 36, 80, 82, 100, 102
biofuels 27, 30, 34–5, 36, 70, 75, 84, 109
bio-piracy 70
bio-prospecting 69
biosphere 13, 15, 81, 99, 127, 146, 154
bio-technologies 36, 100
blackmarketeering 44
Bocock, R. 104
Boekhout van Solinge, T. 27, 92
Bolivia 126
borders 60, 74
Borras Jr., S. 29, 30
boundary rights 63
Boyanowsky, E. 48, 49
Boyer, P. 3–4, 39, 132
BP 98
Brazil 8, 27, 34, 71, 83, 92
breastfeeding 93
Brecher, J. 135
bribery 55, 122
Briggs, C. 120
Brisman, A. 2, 36, 37, 39, 44, 53, 67, 75, 89, 104, 109, 139
Brook, D. 22
Brown Weiss, E. 85, 121
Brunei 30
Bulkeley, H. 34, 55, 84, 107
Burke, M. 43, 49
business as usual 27, 110–11, 115, 141

C

Caisley, O. 105
Cambodia 30
Canada 27–8, 50, 74, 92, 107, 108, 111, 126
Caneppele, S. 44, 114
capabilities 44
capitalism
  ability and responsibility to pay 133
  business as usual 27, 110–11, 115, 141
  commodification 24–5, 54, 55, 56, 70, 100–6, 110, 112
  green capitalism 110–11
  growth models (economic) 8, 17, 23, 98–9, 106
  market forces 39, 56, 100–6, 107, 110, 121
  and power 79, 97, 98–9
  profit motives 17, 23, 25, 29, 34, 55, 98–9, 100, 101, 103, 106, 112
  and resource exploitation 7, 25, 79, 98–9, 100–6, 107, 140
  responses to climate change 106–11
  and slow crisis scenarios 64
  and social conflict 69
  state-corporate nexus 25–8, 38–9, 40, 141
  versus trusteeship paradigms 22
carbon capture and storage (CCS) 109–10
carbon colonialism 55
carbon dioxide emissions
  agreements on 27, 54, 107
  Arctic warming 42
  aviation 32
  calculating 131
  carbon criminals 97–116
  carbon dioxide removal 109
  carbon emissions crime 54–6, 113–15
  and deforestation 27
  energy inequality 33
  fake carbon credits 55
  farming 29–30
  fires 30
  fraud 44, 54, 55
  and global warming 6, 34
  and intergenerational equity 94
  lack of action to address 21
  legal action 120
  palm oil 34
  per capita inequalities 33–4
  and the profit motive 34
  state-corporate nexus 28
  theft of carbon credits 54, 114
carbon footprints 111
carbon neutrality 32, 35
carbon offsetting 30, 32, 54, 55
carbon sequestration projects 55, 142
carbon sinks 55
carbon taxes 27
carbon trading 54, 110
Carmichael Mine, Queensland 120
Carrington, K. 13
carrying capacity 121
cash crops 27
Castles, S. 71
catastrophes 59–77
cattle farming 30, 90, 92
causes and consequences 8, 14–15, 143, 147
Chevron 122
child soldiers 46
China 49, 50, 68, 74, 105, 111, 131, 142
Chippewa people 91
choice, human 24–5
civil law 118, 120
Clark, B. 91
class-related processes 44, 79, 114, 133, 141, 148
Clean Air Act (1963) 120

climate apartheid 53
climate change
  climate change-crime nexus 143–4
  defined 2–10
  denial of 2, 3, 9, 36–40, 107, 140
  as global phenomenon 12
  key risks 5–6
climate change criminology, key themes 10–17, 142–7
'climate change is good' propositions 36, 37
climate disruption 2
climate justice 16, 26, 55, 92, 118–30, 144–7, 150
Climate Justice Network 152–3
climate modelling 94
climate system interventions 109, 141, 150
coal 108, 111, 118, 120
  see also 'dirty industries'
coercion 3, 46, 74, 122, 126, 127
Cohen, L. 50
Cohen, S. 36
Cohn, E. 48
Colangelo, A. 6
cold weather 50
Coleman, R. 97
collective ownership of resources 103
collective security 43, 44
collusion 27–8, 34, 36, 38–9, 139
Colombia 83, 92
colonialism 7, 55, 68, 90, 92, 102
co-management regimes 130
Commission on Human Rights of the Philippines 119
commodification 24–5, 54, 55, 56, 70, 100–6, 110, 112
commodity markets 105
common good arguments 115
communal ownership 103, 104, 130, 149
communes 112
community corrections 125
company law 119
compensation 117, 120, 122, 133
computer crimes 54
condemnation of the condemners 37
conflict over resources 67–73
conflict resolution methods 15
Connelll, R. 91
consequences of climate change
  catastrophes 59–77
  criminological responses to 14–15, 141, 143, 147
  heat-related 41–57
  victims of climate change 79–95
consequences of consequences 60–1
construction standards 65
consumerism 24, 25, 33, 98, 100–6, 112, 115, 139
contrarianism 19, 27, 36–40, 142, 143
cooperatives 103, 105, 112
coral reefs 4, 6, 32, 72, 120
corn (maize) 30, 34, 70, 82
corporations
  apportioning responsibility 130–4
  avoiding legal accountability 122
  carbon dioxide emissions 133–4
  corporate crimes 65, 113
  and food production 68–70
  intrinsic criminogenicity of 98
  legal action against 119
  power of 107
  state-corporate crime 26, 97, 113
  state-corporate nexus 19, 25–8, 36–40, 74, 84, 106, 107, 135, 141, 148
  see also capitalism; transnational corporations
corruption 30, 55, 114, 122
cost-benefit balances 11, 107
Council of Europe 21, 119–20, 128
courts 125, 137, 151
Crank, J. 5, 9, 45, 53
crime, wider definitions of 11
crime control 15–17
crime prevention 44
crime typologies 43–6
crimes against humanity 20, 148, 150
crimes against nature 38
crimes against peace 21, 131
Criminal Damage Act 1973 122
criminal justice system 97, 114, 117–36
criminal offences typology 45
criminality, concepts of 11
criminogenic mechanisms 52
critical criminology 1, 17, 40, 56, 81, 97
Croall, H. 102
Crook, M. 92, 106, 107, 111
crop failure 71, 82
crop substitutions 69, 90
crop yields 5, 6, 31
Cullinan, C. 13, 80
cultural values 24
Cunneen, C. 93, 94
cyclones 8, 60, 65

D

dairy production 29
dams 38, 62, 92
Davies, P. 81
De Lucia, V. 24
death
  crimes of 22
  disaster-related 84
  heat-related human mortality 5, 6, 43, 83
decarbonization 108
decentralised systems 153
deep earth repositories 140
deep-drill oil exploration 27, 107, 111
defoliants 20
deforestation 6, 23, 27, 34, 38, 68, 83, 89, 90, 102, 121
Della Porta, D. 126

democracy 13, 25, 106, 124, 130, 133, 142, 147, 149, 150
denial of climate change 2, 3, 9, 36–40, 107, 140
de-regulation 106
desertification 43, 69, 75
Dieselgate (Volkswagen) 54–5
differential risks 87–8
differential victimisation 82–5
director duties/liabilities 119
'dirty industries' 7, 8, 21, 27, 35, 38, 98, 107, 111, 117
disabled people 3
disasters 59–67, 84
disclosure requirements 119
disconnection 34, 104
disease 5, 6, 31, 66, 88
displacement 7, 13, 34, 52, 62–3, 70–3, 84, 93, 135, 142
dispossession 7, 13, 55, 92
double-edged diplomacy 107
drought 4, 30, 43, 53, 59, 60, 62, 63
due diligence 119
Duffy, R. 84
duties to nature 22
duty of care 120

E

Earth Day 38
Earth stewardship 22
Earth-people connection 91–2, 130
ecocentrism 22, 81, 94
ecocide
  and capitalism 99
  carrying capacity 121
  as crime 19–23, 111–15
  as a crime against humanity 150
  defined 16, 20
  five pillars of climate change criminology 147
  global warming as 19–40, 87
  as international crime 119, 129, 150
  legislation 118
  and social change 135
  as 'strict liability' offence 131
eco-justice
  action plan 137
  and capitalism 99, 113–14
  and concept of harm 80, 81, 94
  defined 13–14, 15
  and ecocide 23
  social action 146, 151
ecological citizenship 94–5, 124, 135
ecological debt 65
ecological justice 1, 15, 23, 80, 114, 124
ecological wellbeing 44
ecology, defined 12
economic efficiency 100
economics, and ecocide 23–36
  see also capitalism; neoliberalism
eco-prisons 124
eco-security 135
ecosystem damage 5–6, 19–23, 72, 79, 80–1
  see also biodiversity
eco-terrorism 45, 139
Ecuador 122, 130
education 64
Edwards, M. 42
elderly people 3, 65–6
electoral law 38
electric vehicles 24, 140
elites 53, 84, 122, 141–2
  see also power
ends-in-themselves, humans as 24
energy
  alternative energy sources 35, 69, 75, 109, 118
  commodification 101–2
  concentrated ownership of 107
  democratic control 130, 149, 152
  and global warming 33–5
  mitigation 109
  paradoxical harm 36
  pressures on basic resources of 75
  unequal energy flows 33
  see also resource exploitation
enteric fermentation 29
environmental impact assessments 74
environmental justice 3, 15, 23, 80, 113–14
environmental law 137
environmental PR 38
environmental refugees 71
environmental rights 128
environmental security 74
environmental victimology 79–85
Etchart, E. 93
ethnicity 79
European Convention on Human Rights 119–20
European Social Charter 120
European Union 35, 54, 68, 71
everyday practices 23–4, 25, 114
excusable ignorance 131
externalisation of harm 39
extinction risks 73
extreme energy industries 111
extreme weather events 5, 6, 42–3, 48–9, 53, 65, 76, 85

F

failure to act 17, 26, 65, 97, 113, 118
farming 28–31
Farrell, S. 63
Fattah, E. 81, 128
feed crops 29
feedback loops 10, 43, 140, 145
fertiliser 70, 82
Field, R. 88
fires 30, 33, 43

Fisher, D. 22
fishing 5, 31, 44
flex crops 29–30, 34
flooding 4, 5, 6, 8, 60, 65, 76, 77
Flynn, M. 80, 81, 130
food
  and biodiversity 31
  commodification 103, 105
  concentrated ownership of 107
  crimes associated with 44
  and ecological sustainability 43–4
  food riots 44, 69, 70, 126
  food security 6, 73–6
  global food crisis 3, 4
  meat consumption 23, 24, 29
  paradoxical harm 35–6
  poor people at greater risk of food shortages 84
  and resource conflicts 68–70
  risks for food production 28–31, 68–70
  species migration 72
  theft of 44, 71
  and tourism 32
foreknowledge 113, 121, 131, 133
foreseeability of harm 17, 22, 35, 47, 113, 118, 119, 142, 150
fortress mentality 64, 71, 135
fossil fuels 7, 8, 24, 111, 119
  see also 'dirty industries'
Foster, J. 25, 40, 99, 101, 106
fracking 27, 69, 75, 107, 111
fraud 44, 54, 114, 122
free market principles 107
free trade 27, 70, 106, 111
freedom of information 38
Freeland, S. 20
French, H. 31, 34, 69, 82
funding 38

G

Gamble, J. 50
gangs 45, 46, 53, 65
Gedicks, A. 7, 90
gender 51, 53, 61, 65–6, 79
General Affective Aggression Model (GAMM) 49
general strain theory (GST) 51–2
genetically modified organisms (GMOs) 29, 31, 82, 102
genocide 22, 47, 92, 93, 111
geocide 22
geo-engineering solutions 109–10, 150–1
geopolitics 53
Gibbs, C. 6, 54
glaciers 43, 75
Glasbeek, H. 98
Gleick, P. 62, 63
Global Campaign to Demand Climate Justice 152–3
global commons 124
global economic crisis (2008) 25, 101
Global Initiative 30, 44
Global North 3, 13, 74
Global South 3, 13, 54, 65, 74, 141
global warming
  acceleration of 43, 145
  agreed limits on 41–2, 77
  anthropogenic causes of 4
  and biodiversity 31
  defined 2
  disagreements over speed of 3–4
  as ecocide 19–40
  farming 29
  fires 43
  key drivers of 6
  in last decades 42
  paradoxical harm 36
  scientific evidence for 4–5
  state-corporate nexus 28
globalisation 14
goods and services, environmental 67
Graham, H. 124, 125
Graham, M. 91
grain trade 69–70
grass 31, 82
Gray, M. 20
Great Barrier Reef 4, 32, 120
Green, P. 65
green capitalism 110–11
green criminology framework 1
green victimology 79–85
greenhouse gas emissions
  and biofuels 35
  and coal 108
  direct versus indirect emissions 133–4
  fires 30
  and global warming 42, 68
  legal action 120
  and the military 76
  ruminant animal farts 29
  see also carbon dioxide emissions
greening justice initiatives 123
Greenland 4, 5, 43
Greenpeace activists 122
greenwashing 37–8
Greig, A. 7
growth models (economic) 8, 17, 23, 98–9, 106
guardianship 54
Gulf of Mexico oil spill 98
Gulf War 20, 101

H

habitat loss 6, 44
hacking 54
Hagedorn, J. 48
Haines, F. 21, 40, 119
Hall, M. 72, 80, 81, 89, 129
Hamilton-Smith, L. 42
Hanna, Liz 83

Hansen, J. 7, 54, 110
harm
  defined in capitalism-friendly ways 141
  differential risks 87–8
  ecocide as a crime 19–23
  environmental harm and concepts of crime 11
  externalisation of 39
  five pillars of climate change criminology 146
  foreknowledge 113, 121, 131, 133
  foreseeability 17, 22, 35, 47, 113, 118, 119, 142, 150
  interventions to prevent 134–6
  key theme of climate change criminology 11–12
  malum in se 12, 146
  new concepts of 122–3
  paradoxical harm 19, 35–6
  as a by-product 17
  setting thresholds of 131–2
  social definitions of climate injustice 142
  victims of climate change 14, 79–95
harmony 7, 92
Harvey, D. 99, 106
health and wellbeing 6, 21, 29, 44, 62, 75, 90
heat stress 31, 81–2
heat waves 43, 65, 83
heat-related human mortality 5, 6, 43, 83
Heckenberg, D. 5, 37, 44, 45, 63, 65, 66, 81
Heede, R. 7
Hellman, J. 114, 150
Higgins, D. 151
Higgins, P. 16, 20, 21, 114, 131, 136
Hillyard, P. 17
historical perspectives 131
holistic approaches 144
Holley, C. 9, 42
Holocene 42
Homer-Dixon, T. 67, 68
homicide 22
horizon scanning 63
Howard, E. 119
Hu, X. 49
Hulme, M. 109
human rights 21, 64, 71, 72, 119, 124, 128, 142
human trafficking 44, 53
humanitarian issues 72
humidity, and crime 49
Hunt, Greg 39
Hurricane Harvey 8, 60, 76
Hurricane Maria 67
hybrid cars 109
hydro-power 62, 92

I

ice loss 4, 5, 42–3, 75
illegal trade 44
impact distribution 6
imperialism 7, 68, 90, 102
incentives 34–5
India 51, 68, 76, 88–9, 105, 111, 129–30, 131
Indigenous people 34, 55, 69, 79, 84, 90–4, 130
individual factors in criminology 47
individualism 99, 140
Indonesia 27, 30, 34, 83, 111
industrialisation 7, 42, 132–3
inequality
  and capitalism 102, 106
  and carbon emissions crimes 114
  and crime 53
  and disasters 62, 64, 65, 66–7
  eco-justice 13
  marginalisation 48, 66, 141
  risk factors for social conflict 83–4
  securitisation of resources 74, 77
  social inequality 3, 64
  unequal trading relations 33
  in US 112
  vested interests in maintaining 110
  and young people 85
information strategies 126
instrumental values 22, 81
insurance fraud 65
insurgency crime 113
intellectual property 69
intensive farming 29, 82
intentional harm 108, 113
interconnectedness 12–14, 91–2, 146
interest groups 15–17
intergenerational distributions of wealth 64, 84
intergenerational environmental suffering 60
intergenerational equity 85–7, 89, 94–5, 118, 121, 129, 135
intermediaries, payments to 55
International Bar Association 119
international crimes 119
International Criminal Court 21, 89
International Environmental Court 127, 137, 151
international financial institutions crime 113
international law 21, 119
international law of ecocide 114
International Monetary Fund 34, 70, 113
INTERPOL 'National Environmental Security Taskforce' (NEST) model 151
intrinsic value 13, 22, 130
invasive species 20
investment 55, 98
iodine deficiency 60
IPCC (Intergovernmental Panel on Climate Change) 3, 4, 5, 6, 7, 19, 28, 43, 52, 73, 82, 108, 145

irritability in hot weather 49
island communities 33, 69, 71, 93, 94
Iyer, L. 51

J

Jacoby, L. 5, 9, 45, 53
Japan 74
Jarrell, M. 89
Jayne, T. 29
Jeffrey, C. 64
Jim Yong Kim 111
Johnston, H. 44
Johnston, I. 65, 66

K

Kaplan, Judge Lewis A 122
Kauzlarich, D. 98, 113
Kenya Water for Health Organisation 30
Kim, Jim Yong 111
Kingsnorth 122
Kiribati 3, 94
Klare, M. 7, 28, 68, 108
Kos, A. 120
Kramer, R. 2, 9, 26, 37, 38, 39, 135, 136, 137, 141, 144, 150
Kueneman, R. 27, 28

L

labour, exploitation of 100, 102, 103
Lambrecht, J. 120
Lancet Countdown 6
land
  acquisitions 69, 84
  changes in land use 27, 29
  clearances 92
  commodification 101
  concentrated ownership of 107
  democratic control 130, 149, 152
  Indigenous people 90–4
  intrinsic rights 130
  ownership 61, 62, 69, 90, 91, 140
  securitisation of resources 74, 75
landscape 81, 130
Larkins, M. 29
law 11, 25, 35, 89, 118–30, 134, 137
law enforcement 10, 38, 45, 127, 134–5, 137, 148, 151
  see also policing
Lawrence, P. 33, 121
lawsuits, strategic 37, 38
Le Billon, P. 7, 68
legal reform 137, 150
Levene, M. 111
Lever-Tracy, C. 2, 3
liability 118, 119, 120, 130–4
libel suits 38
Lin, A. 24
lionfish 72
litigation 118–23
livestock production 23, 29
Lloyd's of London 120
Loader, I. 144
lobbying groups 11, 27, 34, 107, 110, 115, 148
local exchange trading systems (LETS) 105
logging 127
looting 44, 65
Lynch, M. 9, 33, 37, 38, 40, 112

M

Macaulay, C. 31, 72
Mafia 113
maize (corn) 30, 34, 70, 82
Malaysia 30, 83
Maldives 3, 33, 94
malum in se 12, 146
malum prohibitum 11, 146
Mandel, E. 100, 104
Manual on Human Rights and the Environment (Council of Europe, 2012) 21
manure 29
Maori people 91
Mares, D. 51, 71, 121
marginalisation 48, 66, 141
market forces 39, 55, 56, 100–6, 107, 110, 121
Marshall Islands 94
Martin, P. 54, 55, 56, 110
Mary Robinson Foundation - Climate Justice 64
Mascher, C. 119, 134
Massachusetts v EPA 120
McAdam, J. 71
McCarthy, M. 122
McGarrell, E. 6
McKie, R. 55
McLaughlin, E. 97
McPherson, C.B. 99
meat consumption 23, 24, 29
media 25, 37, 151–2
megacities 53
mega-mines 27, 69, 107, 111
Mehta, M.C. 85, 88–9
men 53, 66
Merchant, C. 12, 81
meta-analyses 49
metabolic rift 106
methane 42
methodologies for the study of crime 47
Meyer, L. 133
Mgbeoji, I. 70
Michalowski, R. 26, 37, 38, 39
Michel, S. 49, 50
Middle East 43, 101–2
migration
  climate-induced 3, 44, 70–3
  and crime rates 52–3
  criminalisation of 72, 85

and disasters 65
greening justice initiatives 124
inequality and radicalisation 64
non-human 31, 72
rural to urban 62, 63
social conflict 69
and tourism 32
militant action 152
militarism 7
military, and resource conflicts 76
military crimes 20
militia crime 113
mining 27, 39, 69, 90, 91, 92, 107, 118
Minors Oposa v Secretary of State for the Department of Environment and Natural Resources 89
mitigation
capitalist responses to climate change 109–11
criminalisation of carbon emissions 117
defined 14
and ecocide as a crime 40
farming 28
interconnectedness 14
key theme of climate change criminology 14–15
legal action 121
legislation 118
as means to deal with climate change 8
nation-states 134
paying for 65, 132–3
policing 127
state-corporate crime 26
monocultures 29, 31, 34, 70, 82
moral behaviour 24
moral condemnation 40
moral goods 64
Morris, J. 91
mountains 80, 111
multi-disciplinary approaches 143–4, 145
multiple sites of intervention 147, 148–9
Myanmar 83

N

nation states
apportioning responsibility 130–4
and capitalism 141–2
carbon emissions crime 115
governments as main target for legal action 119
national security 9
as perpetrators of crime 25–8
policing 127
resistance 148
and solutions to climate change 151
sovereignty 102
state crime 46
see also state-corporate nexus
national interest arguments 25, 27, 111, 115, 141
Native Titles 120
natural disasters 59, 60, 65, 85
natural objects 80
neoliberalism 38–9, 62, 99, 101, 105–6, 111
Nepal 76
Netherlands 120
neutralisation techniques 19, 36–40, 142, 143
New Zealand 69, 130
Newell, P. 34, 55, 84, 107
NGOs (non-governmental organisations) 107, 120, 134, 151
non-capitalist production models 105
non-human biota 81
see also abiotic sphere
non-human environmental entities
and climate change criminology 13, 15, 16, 146
and climate justice 144
ecocide 19, 21
and eco-justice 23
ecological citizenship 95
exploitation of by global capitalism 79
extinction risks 73
extreme weather events 76
harm 21, 82
legal system 129–30
as means to attain human goals 24
migration 72
rights 13, 22, 80, 81, 129–30
victims of climate change 79–85, 129–30
non-native species 72
non-renewable resources 67
see also 'dirty industries'
Norway 74
nuclear energy 109

O

obligation 95, 114, 119
O'Brien, M. 104
oceans
acidification 5, 73
algae blooms 141
heat energy in 4, 5, 43
international spaces 127
iron fertilisation 109
marine species loss 73
rising sea levels 3, 5, 43, 65, 73, 84, 93
O'Connor, J. 25, 102
oil palm 30, 34
oil resources 20, 27, 34, 67, 75, 76, 84, 92
see also 'dirty industries'
omission to act 17, 26, 65, 97, 113, 118
Onimode, B. 100
open-cut mining 27, 107
ordinary harms 24
organised crime 44, 46, 113, 114
Oxford Principles 150–1

P

Page, E. 131, 133
Pakistan 65
palm oil 30, 34
Panjabi, R.K.L. 30, 44
paradoxical harm 19, 35–6
Paris Agreement 41–2, 77, 111, 134
Parker, C. 21, 40, 119
patent processes 69, 70
payouts 120
Pearse, G. 38
Pease, K. 114
peatlands 30
Peeters, P. 32
Pelizzon, A. 24
Pemberton, S. 17
Peng, C. 50
Pentagon 76
Pepper, D. 100, 104
permafrost 42, 43
perpetrators 14, 45–6, 99, 112–15, 147
Perrone, S. 47
personal security 9, 64
pests 31, 82, 87
Philippines 30, 69–70, 74, 89, 119, 142
phishing 54
Picou, J. 60
Piketty, Thomas 106
Pink, G. 136
place-based activities 50–1, 143
planetary police 127
plankton 109
planning rules 74
plants 73, 80
  see also non-human environmental entities
poaching 44, 71
polar bears 142
policing 54, 124–7, 137, 151
political correctness 38
pollution
  air pollution 30, 54, 75
  allowable 11
  Arctic 92–3
  bio-technologies 36
  and capitalism 8, 99, 105
  carbon emission trading 110
  constructing risk 88
  corporate responses to 108
  cross-border nature of 60
  legal action against 120
  'polluter pays' principle 131
  securitisation of resources 75
  setting thresholds of 132
  war 20
population density 29
population growth 30, 62, 86
Portugal 43
poverty 48, 52, 60–1, 64, 84
power
  ability and responsibility to pay 133
  and the bifurcation of crime 46
  and capitalism 79, 115–16
  contesting the future 148–54
  contrarianism 37
  crimes of the powerful 46, 113
  and critical criminology 97
  and differential victimisation 84
  and harm 141–2
  inequality 53
  key theme of climate change criminology 15–17, 147
  and neoliberalism 105–6
  powerful interests and the definition of crime 11
  and securitisation of resources 74
  victims of climate change 60
  and women 66
precautionary principle 22, 132
Preston, B. 80, 81, 85
price controls 70
price fixing 30
prisons 123–4, 125
private security 46, 74
privatisation 63, 106
privilege 13, 32, 85
profit motives 17, 23, 25, 29, 34, 55, 98–9, 100, 101, 103, 106, 112
prohibitions 114
propaganda campaigns 38
property ownership 22, 30, 69, 74, 105, 140, 149, 152
proportional payments 133
protective factors 83
protest control 126
Pruitt, Scott 77
psychology 67, 71
public benefits 74
public criminology 135, 144
public interests 85, 101, 108, 118, 122, 140
public order 65, 126
public trust 85, 118, 150
Puerto Rico 67
punishment 131

Q

quick disasters 65–7, 76

R

race 79
radical politics 62, 64
radioactive waste 109
Ranson, M. 49
rape 12, 44, 51, 65
Raymen, T. 33
'real' crimes and carbon emissions 114
reasons for concern (RFCs) 6
Redgwell, C. 35, 109
refugee camps 124
Refugee Studies Centre 71

regulation 11–12, 25, 99, 119, 120, 133, 134, 148
regulatory offences 45, 54
Reicher, S. 126
remediation 22
renewable resources 67, 109
reparations 117
research into climate change criminology 9–10
resilience 29, 31, 44, 53, 61, 70, 82, 118, 154
resistance 27, 93, 148
resource allocation 13, 25, 45
resource conflicts 67–73
resource exploitation
  and capitalism 7, 25, 79, 98–9, 100–6, 107, 140
  carbon emissions crime 115
  and climate justice 16
  commodification 100–1
  conflict over resources 67–73
  crimes of the powerful 46
  and ecocide as a crime 23, 150
  and Indigenous people 91
resource extraction 39, 67, 114, 118, 119, 133
  see also 'dirty industries'; mining
responsibility 65, 97, 99, 111, 112, 130–4
restorative justice 15
Reuveny, R. 71
Ridley's paradox 36
rights
  of children 89
  extinction of 84
  intergenerational equity 85–7, 89, 94–5, 118, 121, 129, 135
  land rights 93
  of Mother Earth 92
  of nature 22
  non-human environmental entities 13, 22, 81, 129–30
risk factors 48, 83
rivers 80, 91, 130
Robin, M.-M. 29
Robinson, Mary 64
Rodriquez, H. 65
Rome Statues 21
Roome, John 111
Roth, J. 48
Rothe, D. 98, 113
Rotton, J. 48
routine activities theory (RAT) 50
Ruggiero, V. 39
Ruru, J. 91
Russell, S. 97
Russia 68, 74, 83, 92, 102, 142

S

sanctions 24, 131
sanctuary 72
Sankoff, P. 80
Saudi Arabia 74
scarcity 68, 102, 104
SCBD (Secretariat of the Convention on Biological Diversity) 31, 72, 80–1, 82
scepticism 36
  see also denial of climate change
Schapiro, M. 120
Schinasi, L. 50
Schlosberg, D. 22
Schmidt, C. 60
Schneeberger, K. 86, 89, 94, 149
Science 3
science of climate change, challenging 107
  see also denial of climate change
Scott, D. 88
sea level rises 3, 5, 33, 43, 65, 73, 84, 93
securities law 119
securitisation of resources 30, 73–6
security 43, 64, 71, 72, 135
SEI (Secretariat of the Convention on Biological Diversity) 133, 134
self-determination 93
self-help environmental groups 104
self-interest 99, 104
self-sufficiency 33, 69, 70, 103
sexual abuse 66
shareholder interests 98–9, 105
sharing economy 112
Shearing, C. 7, 9, 42
Sheptycki, J. 127
Shiva, V. 7, 82, 84, 110
Short, D. 90, 92, 106, 107, 111
side effects 87–8
Singapore 30
Singer, M. 76, 108
situational factors in criminology 47, 48, 50–1
Skinnider, E. 81, 89
Skudder, H. 114
'slow crisis' 7–8
slow disasters 60–4, 76
Smail, S. 120
Smandych, R. 27, 28
Smith, D. 61
Smith, M. 13, 95
Smith, O. 33
smoke haze 30
snow 50
social action 134–6, 144–7
social change 134–6, 149
social conflict 9–10, 26, 36, 43, 46–53, 67–73, 83, 124
social construction of environmental issues 25
social construction of violence 47
social exclusion 64
social inequality 64
social infrastructure 25, 51–3
social justice 13, 16, 85, 124
social strains 52–3, 143

societal peace 44
socio-historical construction of crime and crime control 15–17
soft law 129
soil health 75, 82
Solano, J. 72
solar power 153
solar radiation management 109, 141, 150
Sollund, R. 45
Somalia 71
South, N. 39, 44, 67, 104, 136, 139
South America 71
South Korea 74
South Pacific 69, 71
Southalan, J. 63
South-East Asia 83
southern criminology 13
sovereignty 102
soya 30, 34, 70
Spapens, T. 55
species justice 15, 23, 80, 114
species loss 5, 73, 75
species migration 20
spiritual connections with land 91–2, 93
Sri Lanka 8
state crime 46
state-corporate crime 26, 97, 113
state-corporate nexus 19, 25–8, 36–40, 74, 84, 106, 107, 135, 141, 148
Steffen, W. 2
Stephens, S. 87
Stephenson, W. 148
stewardship paradigms 22, 24, 130, 148
Stilwell, M. 135
Stockholm Declaration 128
Stone, C. 80
Stott, C. 126
strain theory 51–2, 143
street crimes 9, 43, 50, 97, 114, 127
Stretesky, P. 9, 33, 38, 40, 112, 139
structural adjustments 69–70
structural factors in criminology 47
Stubbs, J. 47, 48
'studying up' 1
subsidies 38, 70
subsistence 67, 71, 91, 103, 114
Sudan 63
sugarcane 30
suicide rates 53
Sundström, J.F. 31, 81
Superstorm Sally 60
Superstorm Sandy 8, 83
surface warming 4
survival of the human species 27, 44, 154
sustainability 7, 86, 105, 148
Sutherland, W.J. 72
Suzuki, D. 91
Sykes, G. 36
Syria 62–3
Szerszynski, B. 150

T

tar sands oil production 27, 92
Tauri, J. 93, 94
tax 25, 35, 39, 54, 134
technology 70, 108–10, 141, 150
Tekayak, D. 93, 113, 150
temperature changes 30–1, 41–57, 60, 71, 81–2, 143
territorial ownership 43, 69
terrorism 72
Thailand 30, 83
theft
 of carbon credits 54, 114
 of food 44, 71
 of Indigenous knowledge 69
 of water 30, 44, 69
Thornton, W.E. 65
Tigris-Euphrates basin 62
time 23, 107, 121–2, 145
Tombs, S. 17, 26, 98, 115
Tomsen, S. 47, 48
topic-based focus 143
tort 119
tourism 31–3
toxins 35, 88, 90, 93, 99, 127
transformative social change 135
transnational activism 134
transnational corporations
 capitalism 97, 98, 111, 141
 carbon emissions crime 115
 and greenhouse gases 130
 resource conflicts 68, 69
 state-corporate nexus 25, 26, 29, 37
 tax payments 134
transnational politics 126
transnational value systems 127
transportation costs 32
trees 74
triple bottom line 98–9
tropical forests 27, 32, 34, 38, 83, 122
Trump, Donald 37, 67, 77, 108, 134, 145, 149, 151
trusteeship paradigms 22
Tuvalu 3, 94

U

Uganda 55
unintended consequences 35, 142
United Arab Emirates 74
United Nations
 common but differentiated responsibility 134
 consumer demand 33–4
 Declaration of Basic Principles of Justice for Victims of Crime and Abuses of Power 128, 129
 disasters 60
 and ecocide 21
 Economic and Social Council 92

UNDP (United Nations Development Programme) 62
UNEP (United Nations Environmental Programme) 60, 65, 70, 92, 118, 119
Women Watch 62
United States
and the Arctic 74, 92
and capitalism 102
carbon footprints 111
cases against fossil fuel sector 119
climate-induced migration 71
conflict over resources 68
contrarianism 37
Environmental Protection Agency 77, 120
fires 43
food production 69
hegemony 106
Indigenous people 91
legal action 122
non-native species 72
and the Paris Agreement 41–2, 77
populism 142
and resource conflicts 76
Super Storm Sandy 8
support for extreme energy businesses 111
violence related to high temperatures 49, 50
universal human interests 27, 99, 135
universal victimisation 82–5
urban concentrations 53
urgency 2, 3, 21, 34, 110, 129, 140, 145
Urgenda v State of the Netherlands 120
US National Academy of Sciences 3
utilitarian values 22, 81

V

Varkkey, H. 30
Venezuela 71
victimless crimes 81
victims of climate change
climate-induced migration 72
consequences of climate change 79–95, 147
criminal justice responses 127–30
defining victimhood 81
denial of 37
environmental casualties 60
slow disasters 60
wider than just humans 14–15 *see also* non-human environmental entities
Vietnam 30, 74, 105, 111
violence 30, 43, 46–53, 61, 75, 126
Vivekananda, J. 61
Volkswagen 54–5
vulnerable groups 13, 14–15, 16, 53, 60–1, 64, 65, 79, 84, 87–8

W

Wachholz, S. 53
Walklate, S. 64
Wallace-Wells, D. 42
Walters, Brian 22
Walters, R. 29, 54, 55, 56, 110, 136
war 20, 63, 75, 76
waste 8, 33, 99, 102, 104, 109
water
altered hydrological systems 5
commodification 101, 104, 105
concentrated ownership of 107
democratic control 130, 149, 152
and ecological sustainability 43–4
health and wellbeing 31
illegal trade in 44
intrinsic rights 130
key risks 5
and non-human entities 82
scarcity 30, 68, 69, 75
securitisation of resources 30, 73–6
in Syria 62
theft of 30, 44, 69
undrinkable 3
Watts, N. 6, 7
weather, defined 2
weather and crime 46–53
weather shocks 51
welfare systems 46, 106, 142
Westerhuis, D. 136
western lifestyles 23
Whanganui River 130
White, R. 5, 7–8, 9, 13, 22, 23, 35, 37, 38, 44, 45, 47, 48, 60, 62, 63, 64, 65, 67, 70, 74, 83, 85, 102, 114, 124, 125, 128, 131, 134, 136, 137, 141, 143, 150
White, S. 80, 81
white-collar crimes 65
Whyte, D. 26, 98, 115
Williams, C. 22, 60
winter, crime in 50
women
crimes against 51, 53
and disasters 65–6
invisible labour of 62
and power 66
vulnerabilities in disaster responses 66
vulnerable to consequences of climate change 3, 61–2
World Bank 70, 111, 113
World Resources Institute 30

Y

Yakuza 113
young people 3, 64, 65–6, 85–90, 128–9